Effective Skippering

Other titles of interest

The Art of Pilotage John Mellor
Comprehensively illustrated and including sample charts and pilotage plans, the book covers planning the pilotage, making the landfall, reading signs in the water, fixing position by eye, dangers encountered inshore, entering harbor, blind pilotage in fog and even piloting without a chart.

Boat Handling under Power John Mellor
Covers all aspects of handling boats, both sailing and motor, in closed quarters and on the open sea. There is nothing more impressive than good boat handling. It is a source of pride to the skipper and envy for those watching him.

The Captain's Guide to Liferaft Survival Michael Cargal
Contains everything a castaway needs to know to survive in a liferaft and get rescued as quickly as possible. The book draws on the latest research in equipment, techniques and emergency medicine. It also tells you what you might find to eat and how to capture it. A must in your raft's package.

Anchoring and Mooring Techniques Illustrated Alain Gree
An attractively presented discourse on the art and science of anchoring. The author covers every situation. The first half of the book looks at the equipment while the second studies techniques.

What Now Skipper? Des Sleightholme, Andrew Bray, Tom Cunliffe & Bill Anderson
Four highly experienced yachtsmen have set each other seamanship and navigational problems based on real life situations. The book investigates over 40 problems ranging from man overboard to the best advice to give a daughter about to cross the Atlantic.

Sell up and Sail 2nd edition Bill and Laurel Cooper
A highly readable account of how a couple opted out of the rat race and took to a life at sea. It is packed with the practicalities and pitfalls of early retirement, financing the boat and deep-sea voyaging.

If you would like further information on any of these books or a complete catalog of Sheridan House titles please contact the Publishers.

Effective Skippering

A comprehensive guide to yacht mastery

JOHN MYATT

Illustrations by Neil Myatt

SHERIDAN HOUSE

Acknowledgements

My grateful thanks go to my son, Neil Myatt, for his painstaking work in producing the illustrations and for his reading of the text.

Published 1992 by
Sheridan House Inc.
145 Palisade Street
Dobbs Ferry, NY 10522

Library of Congress Cataloging-in-Publication Data

Myatt, John
   Effective Skippering: a comprehensive guide to yacht
mastery/John Myatt; illustrations by Neil Myatt.
      p.   cm.
   ISBN 0-924486-32-5: $29.95
   1. Yachts and yachting. 2. Yachts and yachting—Maintenance
and repair, 3. Seamanship. I. Title
GV813.M93   1992
797. 1' 256—dc20   92-6904
                                                            CIP

Printed in Great Britain

ISBN 0-924486-32-5

CONTENTS

INTRODUCTION

Mastery of the sea is never possible. Few would dispute that and I am sure it is true. You only have to see the massive damage that can be inflicted by a single storm to appreciate the huge forces involved.

No one can control the sea, yet one can learn to use its forces to advantage. Mastery of the sea is not possible but mastery of one's vessel is. Safety at sea depends very largely on the skipper's control of events. The purpose of this book is to show how such mastery can be achieved.

The major difference that has taken place over comparatively recent years is one of purpose. Until the early part of this century almost all man's activity on the sea was concerned with work. Fishing, communication and commerce were the driving force. Everyone was a professional; often their skills were handed down from one generation to the next. Now all three of these activities are declining yet more vessels are afloat than ever before. Most of them pleasure craft, skippered by people with no maritime background. Very few have had any formal training in their craft and most have had to find out the hard way or from books; the old continuity of knowledge has gone.

In this book some of the old ideas are examined to see how and why they work. Some of the more recent thinking which has changed a few of these ideas is discussed also. Additionally I introduce you to some practical ways to make your sailing safer, more enjoyable and more comfortable. In the process you will also learn how to protect your vessel, your crew and yourself from damage and from strain.

For convenience in use, the book is divided into several parts. Part 1 deals with the choice of boat and explains how differences affect performance. It is included because I suspect that a number of readers will not yet be boat owners. Still more will have sailed on one type of boat only. Most would like to own a boat and hope to do so.

Part 2 explains how sails actually work and how to use them to best advantage in various situations and conditions. It explains how to check them and how to make them work for you before the practical management aspects of sailing a cruising boat are considered in Part 3.

Parts 4–8 are concerned with skippering – with managing a yacht at sea. This involves planning, organisation, supervision and welfare. It is not so different from other types of management. Those readers who have been managers will find some familiar aspects covered but, since these relate to yachts, slanted somewhat differently. The subject includes such diverse items as safety, cooking, personnel and weather.

The final, and largest section, Parts 9 and 10, covers practical seamanship. It starts with 'When things go wrong' because that is the time when seamanship matters most. Such things as harbour manoeuvres, repairs, damage control and dealing with emergencies are explained. The special considerations relating to sailing with children can be found here. It is a bit of a mixed bag since it contains a number of items that I have found useful over the years but don't have an obvious place in earlier sections.

The book gathers together a number of topics normally found in separate volumes, and it is possible to dip in and browse the areas that take your fancy. On occasion I have repeated information so that the particular section stands on its own.

The book is intended for practical sailors who wish to extend their knowledge in order to master their craft. Some knowledge is assumed. If you are just about to skipper on your own, taking the family sailing, thinking about Yachtmaster Examinations, or are contemplating a long voyage, you should find many tips that will make your sailing less expensive, safer and more rewarding.

John Myatt
Fowey
1991

PART 1
Boats

Yachtmastery begins with a boat. It need not be *your* boat; not at least, until you are well on the way to mastery. Getting the right boat for your needs is a long, often painful, process. If you are very lucky you may succeed first time. More probably you will fall in and out of love several times. Until one day, with a fair degree of luck tempered with some experience, you finally settle down with the boat of your dreams.

The chapters in this section will help you to appreciate the effects that differences in design have on performance to help you make a more informed choice. The rest is up to you. You will have to find the right boat for you. Even if you have a boat now it will be worth studying this section because it may give you a new perspective.

1 THE RIGHT BOAT

To buy or not to buy?

The question students ask most is; 'Which boat should I buy?'. So let's begin here.

First, if you can't answer it yourself, it is too soon to buy, and second there is no real answer I could give you. Boats are far too individual. Different people want different things from their boats. The question should be, how can *you* reduce all the many possibilities to manageable size?

Gaining knowledge

If you are going to find the right boat for you, don't rush; wait until you have gained sufficient experience to decide. Go to a school and do a course. Go sailing with any friends that will have you, to boat shows, on flotilla holidays or charter. Try to sail on as many different boats as you can so that you learn what the differences mean in practice. All the time you are doing this, ask yourself which things you like and which you don't so as to build up a picture of the kind of boat that should suit you best. When you are sure of this, you can go out and try to find it!

Suitability

It is surprising how little things, things that you are not too sure about when you first come across them, can become a thundering nuisance when you have to live with them at sea. These are the things to watch for and note when you are looking at boats.

Getting the feel for what suits you best is important; more important than cost in the early stages. Although price will probably become the most important thing if and when you actually get round to buying, don't worry too much about it at the start. If you do you may rule out some things which later you might be able to have.

Charter

If you are not going to be able to spend more than a couple of weeks, and maybe a few weekends, afloat each year charter will probably be the best thing for you rather than boat ownership.

Chartering has many advantages; no maintenance, no mooring fees, freedom to sail anywhere that takes your fancy. These are just a few of the benefits. Against this is the lack of personal involvement and the problem of not being able to change what you don't like.

Counting the cost

If the idea of owning still persists and you actually get to the stage where you are about to buy, cost now must become important. Reality dictates that it is the main limiting factor. You know what you can afford – or at least think you do. Remember that cost does not stop when you buy the boat. You will have to spend quite a lot on running costs each year even if you never take it out. Things like insurance, moorings, anti-fouling, repairs and replacements can add up to a tidy sum. If you think in terms of between 5 and 10 per cent of the cost of the boat per year you will not be far wrong. The cheaper, smaller or older the boat, the more the costs tend towards the higher percentage.

Fitness for purpose

Having decided you can afford it, the next thing to consider is where you intend to use your dream boat. You must also think about where to keep it when it is not in use. These things will affect your choice. A fin keel boat will not be much use to you if you have to keep it on a mud mooring.

Are you going to spend holidays on it or will you mainly day sail? Are you a purist who must have wood, or will you be happy with GRP? Will you race, cruise with the family or do a bit of both? How important is ease of handling? Does the ability to take the ground when the tide goes out matter more to you than a good windward performance? Questions like these can point you in the right direction.

The best piece of advice I can give you is, don't buy your first boat new! Very few people keep the first boat they buy. It is only by owning that you can ultimately find out what matters most to you. If you buy secondhand, and have chosen wisely in the first place, you should not lose much when you change. You may even make a small profit. If you buy new, you will have to face the fact that the value of your purchase will have dropped by about 20 per cent in the first year. It makes it harder when you want to change.

The trouble is that performance, speed, comfort, safety and price, are all a function of size. Of necessity almost all owners start small, usually smaller than they would wish.

The effects of length

When a boat, however well designed, moves through the water rather than over it, a lot of water must be moved out of the way. This has certain effects. One is that, at the point of impact with the stem, water tends to accumulate in front generating a bow wave. The bow wave generates a crest from which the water tends to move upward and outward away from the boat at approximately 45 degrees to the line of passage. The outward movement continues after the initiating force ceases due to the inertia of the water. A trough is thus created towards the stern of the boat.

After a while, gravity reasserts itself and the outward movement is overlaid with an attempt to revert to the normal level. Inertia then takes over again so that a new, but smaller, stern wave is produced.

From the point of view of an observer on the boat the two crests, separated by a trough, appear to be fixed in relation to the boat although the water producing them is moving. The relative heights of the two crests tend to depend on the speed of movement of the boat.

The difference between these heights causes the bow of the boat to lift so that it seems to be climbing the bow wave. This situation is more noticeable in a small motor boat since it can lift the bow right out of the water. On a yacht the water level seems to rise up the transom. It is the need to climb the bow wave that limits the maximum speed of a displacement hull.

Length at the water line (LWL)

The steepness of the slope, hence the maximum speed the boat can achieve, will depend on the horizontal distance between the bow wave crest and the start of the stern wave. This will depend on the boats length. It is a curious fact that length at the water line (LWL) determines the theoretical maximum hull speed for any craft in a non-displacement mode and that this relationship is nearly constant regardless of hull shape or motive power. In simple terms, a longer boat will go faster than a short one.

Many yachts are so designed that the static LWL, ie when the boat is not moving, is much less than the dynamic LWL in motion. This gives a speed advantage in racing craft. An approximate formula for calculating the maximum hull speed in knots is:

$$1.2 \times \sqrt{\text{LWL}} \text{ in feet}$$

Performance

Wave length: the distance between the crests of two successive wind generated waves, tends to depend on depth of water rather than on wind strength, at least in relatively shallow water. In coastal sailing, wavelength tends to average out at about 6 to 8 metres. This gives an advantage to boats over that length since they will be able to ride the waves better.

If you sail a keelboat of under 6 metres on the open sea you will notice how relatively small wave heights can slow the boat down. Unless you are able to accelerate sufficiently to get the boat to rise up and aquaplane on the surface, you will be very limited as to the kind of conditions you can go out in and still make sensible progress. A keelboat is not designed to aquaplane and will rarely do so.

Once the dynamic LWL exceeds 9 metres a real improvement in performance is found even in quite lumpy seas. Another metre and it gets even better and so on.

Comfort

It will be obvious that the smaller the boat the lighter it will be, and thus, the more it will bounce about as the sea gets rougher. Heel will be more dependent on crew position. More importantly the small boat, having less inertia, will react more easily and rapidly to small changes in surface movements. A larger heavier vessel will tend to damp out some of this shorter period motion. Movement below decks in a small boat will be more rapid and more violent whilst the restricted space makes all crew movements more difficult.

A boat whose length exceeds the natural wavelength of the sea by a reasonable margin will spend most of its time supported by two waves and will tend to pitch less. It is the pitching that creates most wave resistance and thus most markedly affects boat speed.

Whilst a few intrepid sailors have been round the world in some very small boats – Shane Acton's *Shrimpy* was barely 5.5 metres long – it cannot be denied that creature comforts are severely restricted in such a boat. Headroom, stowage space and washing/cooking facilities are all likely to be less than adequate.

Safety

I am not suggesting that small keel boats are no use. They can be fun to learn on and are often the start of an enduring love of the sea. It is simply that the small yacht will be more limited by sea conditions. Because of these limitations, its usefulness will diminish as your experience grows and you want to venture further afield.

The small yacht will also become less than safe much earlier than will a larger vessel. For this reason, if for no other, it is wise to start with as large a boat as possible.

The upper size limit will depend on the depth of your pocket and on the crew you can muster. Anything above 12 metres will really need more than two competent sailors for comfortable cruising. It will also need to be fitted with aids to overcome the greater size of all the control gear if it is to remain safe when operated by perhaps a couple with or without children. If you want easy sailing you start having to consider furling and self tacking headsails, furling mains, powered winches and so on.

Size is by no means the only consideration when choosing a boat. Chapter 2 looks at some of the others.

2 BELOW THE WATER LINE

Hull shape

When one thinks of boats as 'different', it is usually either the shape of the hull or the way they are rigged that constitutes the difference.

The shape of the hull below the water line has a marked effect on the performance of a yacht and also affects what you can do with it. The keel largely determines this shape.

Functions of the keel

The keel has two purposes. It acts as a counter weight, to balance the heeling moment produced by wind on the sails, thereby providing lateral stability. Through its surface area it also provides resistance to sideways movements in the water, called leeway. Both the weight and the surface area of the keel are thus important.

Fin keels

A fin keel is short in relation to the length of the boat but goes down rather deeper in the water than a long keel (see Figure 2.1a). It makes the boat more manoeuvrable in confined spaces, which is what many people want. Such a boat will turn almost within its own length. This is a very useful characteristic if you are going to operate in confined waters such as marinas or small congested harbours.

With modern small but deep fin keels, reduced surface area is compensated for by the fact that the keel is working in deeper water, below the main effects of surface drift. Surface drift is the tendency of the surface water to move in a direction down-wind.

Lack of sufficient weight in the smaller size fin keel can be a problem. The stabilising force provided by the weight is greater as its distance from the centre of balance increases. Hence the current keel designs which tend to bulge at the bottom. The extreme example of this is seen in the latest keels with a horizontal fin as an extension to the base. Such keels have considerable advantages in reducing leeway even at steep angles of heel. They move the main mass away from the centre of effort and they can also be used to help lift the yacht at higher speeds.

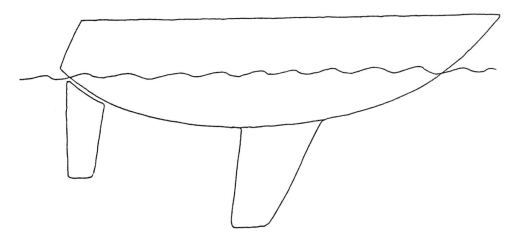

Fig 2.1a Fin keel

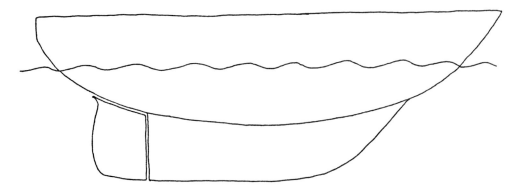

Fig 2.1b Long keel

Deep or shallow?

Many designers now offer fin keels in two profiles, deep and shallow, particularly when they are the bolt-on variety. With production boats, the ability to offer deep and shallow draft or even bilge keel versions on the same hull design, without recourse to additional expensive moulds, is an advantage. The difference in draft between the two profiles may be as much as 35%. In practice, the deeper draft will reduce leeway and make the vessel stiffer in a blow allowing more sail to be carried and giving improved sailing performance.

The shallow keel may be longer horizontally in order to increase efficiency. It will be possible, with shallow draft, to visit some harbours not accessible to a deep fin. It can also mean less time waiting to get in an out and allow anchorage in shallower water which may well give more protection and more options to choose from when selecting shelter.

The best choice depends largely on whether or not you intend to race and thus, how much speed or windward performance matters to you. For cruising, the lesser draft (with access to more places) will be more practical. If you intend to operate in areas where shoal water is common, a shallow draft is more sensible.

Cast keels

A cast keel can be a single solid appendage or it can be a hollow, cast case filled with more dense material such as lead. The latter method provides a way of improving on the weight problem since more of the dense material can be inserted low down, sometimes in a bulge at the base of the keel. Because of its high cost however, lead is tending to be replaced by solid cast iron. Cast keels are bolted to the bottom of the hull.

Cast keels are cheaper to produce than moulded keels and arguably, give a somewhat stronger method of yacht construction, provided the attachment method is designed to cope with the considerable bending moment generated at the hull/keel junction. Offering several profiles of keel design for a single hull mould has marketing benefits. It also gives the advantage that hull and keel can be transported separately during the manufacturing stages.

Disadvantages

The separate keel does not produce such a clean hull line and attachment can create problems. Stress distribution is difficult to control. Keel bolts can rust and weaken so need regular periodic checking. To do this, two or more must be withdrawn for examination, or the keel has to be X-rayed. Either method is costly. The hull/keel seal must be good or leakage will result. Bolt on keels result in round bilges so water that collects slops about and is difficult to pump out. Nevertheless the cost saving of the bolt on method makes them very popular.

Moulded keels

With GRP construction moulding the keel as a part of the hull makes some sense. Once moulding is completed, the hollow keel is filled with small steel punchings, cast iron sections, or lead pellets. These are protected from corrosion and kept from moving, by pouring in resin to fill up all the small spaces. Punchings are a waste product of the steel industry and so are not as expensive as might be expected.

A moulded keel produces a cleaner hull shape with no sharp angles. The problem of leakage is much reduced and internally it is easy to incorporate a bilge sump into which bilge water collects and is thus more easily pumped out. The little that remains, being confined, does not slop around.

Disadvantage

Any water finding its way into the ballast is well nigh impossible to remove. Iron ballast will rust; rust occupies a much greater volume than steel. This can, in extreme cases, split the keel. Stress damage can occur due to the increased rigidity of the moulding at the junction with the filled section. The density of a moulded keel is lower than that of a cast one; its intrinsic strength is less so it has to be bigger in order to get the same weight advantage.

Careful design and construction should avoid most of these problems but, if they do occur, the cure is both difficult and expensive.

Long keels

A long keel is quite a different concept from a fin. Length here refers to the horizontal plane. Such keels are usually an integral part of the hull rather than bolt-on. They often start just aft of the stem and continue to the point where the rudder is hung so that the rudder forms an extension of the keel as in Figure 2.1b.

The design provides more inherent lateral stability since it is both heavier and has a greater surface area. It therefore needs less draft than a fin keel. The extra length gives greater directional stability which means less work on the helm to keep a straight course. This makes the yacht a lot more comfortable and easy to handle on long sea passages, particularly downwind.

On the negative side, the greater length, which makes turning more difficult, reduces manoeuvrability in tight situations. This is the major reason for the long keel's lessening popularity in the face of increasing congestion afloat.

Another problem is increased drag which is largely a function of surface area. Coupled with the greater weight, this cuts down on potential speed, particularly in lighter winds and is why the design has virtually gone from racing fleets.

Twin keels

Often the builder will provide the option of one or two keels. Twin keel boats are called bilge keelers. By dividing the keel into two parts, each can be smaller and so the boat will draw less water. An important advantage of this design is the ability of such a boat to stand upright on its two keels.

If you are intending to do a large part of your sailing in creeks or estuaries or where sand banks are common this can be a great advantage. A mud mooring which dries out at low tide will normally be much cheaper than a deep water mooring and, in some parts of the country, be much easier to obtain. A twin keel boat is ideal in this situation.

Of course, a twin keel boat has disadvantages also. In particular its performance to windward is not as good as that of a single keel. Although the total surface area may be greater, the leeward keel provides most of the lateral resistance. As the boat heels, the resistance from the leeward keel increases whilst that of the windward one decreases. There is some net benefit until the optimum heel angle is exceeded. Remember also that the effect of surface drift is greater on the shallower draft. A number of manufacturers are now claiming that their twin keel designs perform as well to windward as the fins but I have yet to be convinced.

Any unintentional grounding of a twin keeled yacht is more difficult to reverse and, although the yacht should stand up, such a situation can be dangerous in heavy weather.

Lifting keels

A boat that can adjust its draft to anything between half a metre and two and a half metres to suit conditions seems, at first sight, to be the best of all worlds but I suggest that you temper enthusiasm with caution.

Several clever keel designs are available that lift up and down to give this facility. One problem is that a lifting keel can not easily have the same weight as a fixed keel, particularly on a larger boat. For most people the mechanism and power needed to lift, say, two tonnes would be impractical in terms of both cost and space.

The bulk of the counter weight must therefore be fixed to the hull, with the moving keel blade providing mainly lateral resistance (Figure 2.2). Simple mechanics will tell you that the closer you put the balance weight to the fulcrum or pivot point, the more weight you will need. The difficulty now becomes obvious.

A further problem is the strain put on the lifting mechanism and on the keel itself. If the lift is achieved by pivoting the blade about a fixed point, the lifting force is reduced but the loads on the pivot are great. The fan design helps, but does not solve, this problem. When the keel is raised and lowered by sliding, friction becomes a concern. A

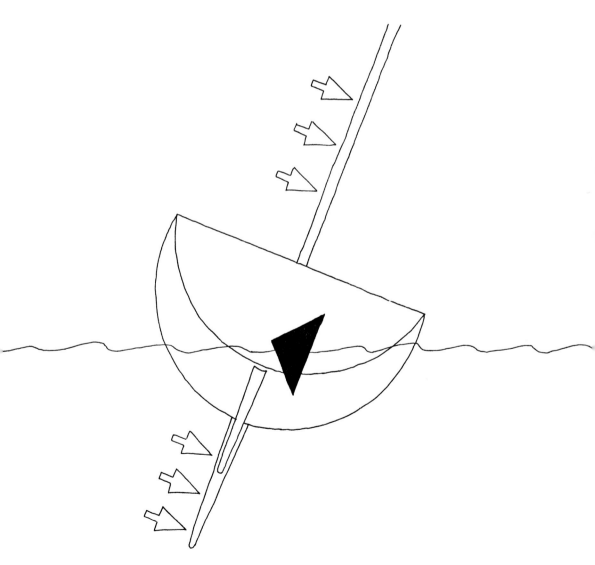

Fig 2.2 Moments of force on a sailing yacht

boat regularly taking the ground will accumulate debris in the keel box. Sand and small stones can work their way between the sliding surfaces greatly increasing both friction and wear.

Rudders

The rudder is not just the means of steering the boat. It is also part of the underwater profile and has an effect on the boat's performance and general handling. Its shape, position and how it is hung all have their own effects.

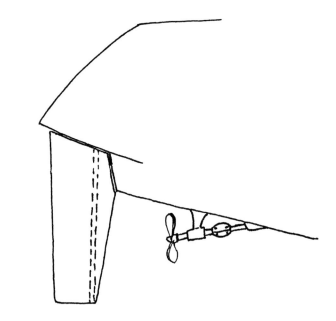

Fig 2.3a Modern spade rudder

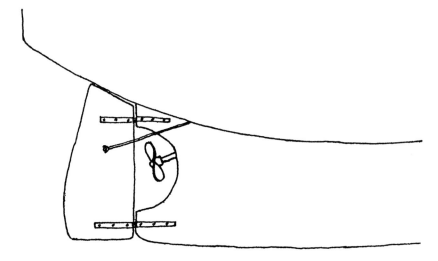

Fig 2.3b Traditional keel-hung rudder

Traditional rudders

The traditional rudder was shaped something like the one in Figure 2.3b. On a long keeled boat it made sense to make the rudder an extension of the keel. The keel provided lateral stability. Changing its shape, which is what these rudders did, provided the steering effect. The keel also provided good strong points from which to hang the rudder. Fishing boats and some commercial vessels still use the method.

Transom hung rudders

In the early days of yachting, rudders were hung either from the keel or from the transom. They had to be, to make them strong enough. Some modern boats have transom hung rudders. Light displacement hulls with broad beams often have very little of the transom actually under water; indeed the centre lifts above the water when the yacht is heeled. Such a rudder must extend a good way below the transom to have any real effect.

Balanced rudders

With the advent of short fin keels new methods had to be sought. At first the transom hung rudder continued but its disadvantages were many. It was vulnerable to damage. Because it had to be pivoted from (or slightly in front of) its leading edge, great force was needed to turn it causing considerable stress. From this came the idea of the balanced rudder, Figure 2.3a.

The balanced rudder is pivoted some way back from its leading edge. Part of the force applied by the water when the rudder is off centre, acts forward of the pivot. This assists the turn by reducing the torque load so that less effort is needed on the tiller.

Skeg or single mounting

Some modern rudders are hung from a skeg, a small fixed extension from the hull, which takes the strain. This reduces hull efficiency but increases strength. Becoming more common is the skegless rudder supported only on bearings within the hull. Such rudders are very efficient but need strong mountings and construction since the loads on them have to be supported at one end only. On a ten metre boat the supporting shaft of such a rudder is likely to have a diameter of 55 mm or more and be made from stainless steel.

Skeg or no skeg is a common talking point. A skeg increases lateral stability and strength, and reduces the risk of snagging but it also reduces efficiency and increases drag. No skeg increases efficiency but needs more strength in the mounting and increases the risk of snagging on nets or floating debris. I have had both and am not ready to come down strongly on either side.

3 INTERIORS

The way a yacht interior is organised has a considerable bearing on the whole crew's safety and enjoyment. In any discussion relating to choice of vessel it is crucial. Since you will not be able to alter things much on a production boat you must look critically at what is offered.

What follows, in this and the next chapter, is not meant to be a complete survey of yachts. It is intended as a guide to getting the would-be owner thinking along the right lines. The interior layout of a yacht is important but it is also very personal. What you want depends so much on how you will use your boat.

Sleeping quarters

If you expect to sleep on board for more than the odd night, make sure that berths are big enough. A six footer needs a minimum of 1.9 metres. Width should be at least 60 cm at the shoulders but one can accept a little less at the feet. Recently I was on a new boat with a so-called pilot berth that was 175 cm long, barely 44 cm at the widest and just under 28 cm at the narrowest part. I say, with feeling, be warned.

Foam cushions need to be 10 cm thick at least for any real comfort. Lee cloths, too, are a must. Not only do they make it possible to sleep without falling out of bed at sea; they also make for more comfort in harbour. Falling out of a pilot berth is no fun for the faller or for the unfortunate person on the lower berth.

Boat sales-people seem to think that the more berths they can cram in, the more marketable their product will be. To the inexperienced potential buyer this can be misleading. Ten people in a 9 or 10 metre boat is ridiculous in practice. There is not enough cockpit room or stowage space. A number of yachts around the ten metre mark claim to be ten berth. Double berths are impractical for use by two people at sea, however friendly they are. They are not ideal in harbour either. Personally I don't like a double berth, even when on my own in it. Except in a very calm marina, you can't keep in one place. Split cushions with a centre lee cloth can help if you are stuck with doubles. It is better to consider each as a single when deciding on crew numbers for passage making.

In general these ideas hold good for chartering too. If you can see, or already know, the kind of boat you are going to operate it helps. With few exceptions a six or seven berth boat will only be really comfortable with four or five aboard.

Bedding

Sleeping-bags are easier than blankets. They take up less room and keep you warmer. Stow them in bin liners to keep them dry and use sleeping-bag liners of cotton for comfort and hygiene. I have been amazed at how warm the so called 'moon bags' are. They take up half the space of a conventional bag and are well worth buying. If you tend to feel the cold, use two; they will still take up less room than one conventional bag. The bulky down-filled bags favoured by mountain climbers are both impractical and unnecessary on a boat unless you are sailing in the winter.

Pillows are a pleasant luxury but will have to be taken home. It is difficult to prevent them absorbing moisture and becoming unpleasant if kept on board for too long. Like most bedding, pillows take up a great deal of stowage space. Will you have it? If not, consider using domestic or saloon cushions with cut-down pillow slips. Blow-up cushions save space but are less comfortable.

Eating

Cooking at sea is covered in Part 7. When choosing your boat make sure that the galley can be used at sea, even if you only want to make a cuppa. Is the galley gimballed and can you put cups down where they will stay put? Fiddles at least a couple of inches high are needed. How efficient are the cupboards and work surfaces? Imagine the boat heeled at 45° (it doesn't have to happen for long!) and think about what will happen to the galley contents. If you don't think about it now you may find out later.

I like to eat in the open air if it is at all possible. It is not difficult to make a folding cockpit table. This adds a lot to comfort but could you stow one if you had it? Whilst about it, can everyone on board sit round the saloon table or does someone have to sit on the steps (or in the head!)?

The heads

Delicacy often prevents one asking about such things. I have been on yachts where it was impossible to sit on the loo and shut the door; where there was no door; where a man could not stand up to use it, even in port, and where it was mounted too low down for practical use. On one yacht I delivered it could not be used on port tack because the wretched thing flooded as soon as the sea cocks were opened; a very inconvenient convenience. Equally important is how it is ventilated and how the area can be cleaned. A wash basin that can be used under most conditions, and somewhere to put the soap, towel and loo paper are quite important considerations.

Shower

A shower is a luxury for some, a necessity for others. If the waste water is drained into the bilge and pumped from there, the risk of rot in any exposed timbers is high. Fresh water does more harm to wood than salt and soap makes it worse.

Not many people are keen on cold showers so consider how the water is heated. Electric heating takes battery power. A long shower or even a leaky tap can flatten the battery and waste a lot of fresh water. Heaters run off the engine often require it to be on for prolonged periods. Most marinas, quite rightly, restrict the use of engines. If you can only have hot water out at sea, the practical problem of using the shower there will probably deter you.

Storage

When you have spent a week on a boat with five or six other people you will know just how much room is taken up by personal gear, food, bedding, oilskins and so on. If you haven't done so yet, try imagining it, or think of a teenager's bedroom. If you double what you thought of, you will have some idea of space needed. A boat at a boat show, containing nothing but a vase of flowers and a diminutive salesman, may look roomy but imagine it under realistic conditions.

Construction

There is an unfortunate trend in some new yachts to skimp on the materials used for bulkheads and internal fittings. Various explanations have been given to me such as, 'Better hull design means bulkheads are not stressed so much', and 'Its done to make the yacht more spacious'. The truth is, I suspect, 'We're saving money at the expense of strength'.

The point that concerns me is not the hull integrity. It is the ability of the lighter internal structure to take the knocks and shock loads that it will be subjected to at sea. Boats should not be built for marina use only. At sea people are thrown off balance, they fall, they grab at things. If hand holds become fewer and lighter, panels are made from thinner material and so on, I suspect the life of such interiors will be shorter than it should be, and the risk of injury from structural failure will also increase.

4 ON DECK

Cockpit

The cockpit is the control centre of the vessel, so the design must be workable under any conditions. It will be impossible to alter much of it so it must suit your needs from the start.

For my money, in a cruising boat, the cockpit should be large enough for everyone on board to be able to sit comfortably. Even when all the crew are present the helmsman must still able to operate. It reduces cruising enjoyment when someone has to be banished to the foredeck or stay below because there is not enough room in the cockpit. When purely racing it is more a matter of having sufficient space for those who need to be there.

Shelter

The cockpit should have adequate shelter so that in a moderate sea, very little water comes in. It is difficult if not impossible just to look at the boat and decide whether or not the layout will keep you dry – too many factors are involved. You can only check this by trying it out. Coamings and good run off lines are important but difficult to assess. Canopies and spray dodgers help a lot but can not make up for design inadequacies.

Ergonomics

For the most part the ergonomic design of modern yacht cockpits is good as regards such things as seat shape, height, rake and depth. The positions of winches, cleats and the like are usually acceptable. Decisions over things like these must be made at the drawing board stage and are not so dependent on other factors.

It is in things like sheet leads and the positioning of the main track in relation to the boom attachment that I notice design deficiencies. One new and otherwise well designed yacht, has a main sheet track-to-boom position which makes it impossible to gybe whilst the helmsman is standing up and difficult when sitting down. I wonder what would happen during an involuntary gybe in this boat?

I do not doubt that this positioning can result from the need to make use of inbuilt strength points. I have the feeling that, in this case, it was a result of not having determined boom length when the cockpit layout was decided. Either way it is still poor design.

On one production yacht which I delivered, the cockpit was so wide it was impossible to brace my six foot frame in a sloppy sea. Sliding on my backside under the tiller produced only laughter at the time but, in some circumstances, it could have brought down the mast.

If more people comment on such things perhaps boat builders will adapt to suit the people who actually sail. I suspect that expediency regarding costs of production tends to override good design principles in some cases.

Sprayhoods and dodgers

A good sprayhood can be a great benefit and also a curse. When beating the windward in a nasty wet blow it is nice to be able to keep out most of the elements. Crouching under an ample canopy has its advantages.

The difficulty is that, if it is big enough to give much shelter, the sprayhood will also be big enough to restrict the helmsman's vision and to encourage the crew not to keep an adequate look-out. This can be a recipe for trouble. On clear sunny days the hood will usually fold down but it is actually in bad conditions that an adequate all round look-out becomes most important.

A further problem is lack of access to the foredeck. Sprayhood canopies are often taken right out to the toe rail. This makes moving forward more of a hazard than it should be. A compromise, worth consideration, is a small hood which simply covers the sliding hatch to the saloon. This will not protect the crew so well but prevents water going below whilst only marginally reducing the view. Access forward is unaffected.

If control lines are all led to the cockpit they will have to pass under or through the canopy so it will not keep out the weather as will a fully sealed canopy.

Dodgers

Dodgers provide so much comfort with very little disadvantage that I am very much in favour of them despite the extra windage they provide. Filling the space from about the sheet winch position back to the quarters they are a boon. Taken any further they reduce the view astern without much gain in protection.

Dodgers should be laced to the upper guard rail and to the stanchions. Be careful if they are also lashed down to the toe rail, that the lashings do not get in the way of mooring lines or spinnaker gear. If you dip the side deck under, a dodger secured along the rail may be carried away. A 10 cm gap between dodger and rail can prevent this.

The yacht's name or sail number on the outside of the dodgers helps identification whilst a few pockets for gear inside can increase their usefulness.

Stowage

Most of the deck gear not in use and all of the mooring gear, such as fenders and warps, will usually be stowed in the cockpit lockers. Sails also, will often have cockpit stowage. This means that lockers must be accessible and usable at sea.

Locker lids must be capable of being secured in both the open and closed positions. Most lockers are vast, deep caverns with access through a diminutive opening. Their use can be greatly improved by good organisation. If the locker is very deep try fitting a false floor. Under the floor you can stow items which are seldom used, spare ropes and the like. Hooks to take fenders can sometimes be fitted to the ends of the bolts holding the deck moulding to the hull. This uses up the otherwise lost space under the side deck and saves valuable stowage room.

Another idea, if the locker is deep, is to hang all spare sheets, guys, preventers etc on rope loops. It saves time and space. It also serves as a check that everything has been put away, and makes finding something in a hurry much easier too. Figures 4.1a–c show some ways of doing this.

In making a critical choice of boat always consider the stowage provided everywhere. Ask yourself, is it adequate? If not, can it be improved? Any boat where the answer is no to both questions would be one I could not live with.

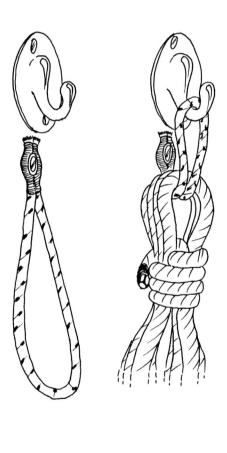
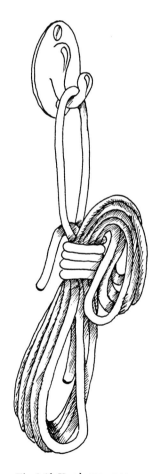

Fig 4.1a Hook-and-loop stowage   *Fig 4.1b* Hook stowage

Fig 4.1c Hook-and-line stowage

Deck layout

The deck layout will have been determined, particularly on a GRP boat, before you get
to it. There is often little you can do to alter it so you have to take a philosophical view.
It is best to look at the situation from the point of view of the various tasks to be
completed. Consider each task in turn and decide how it will be performed, both in
easy and more difficult conditions.

Sometimes you will think of a change that you can make that will make a task
easier. If any task seems to be impossible you will have to decide whether it is you or
the boat that is deficient. It is seldom the boat but it can be.

Fittings

It is difficult to be specific about fittings and equipment since so many variations of
layout work but I suggest that looking at them from an engineering view point can be
useful.

Most of the possible problems will become apparent whilst you are solving the task
situations mentioned above. Things like adequacy of cleats or fairleads both in
number, strength and position may be overlooked. Consider also the positioning and
securing of lights, sockets and wiring, the stowage for spinnaker poles and any other
infrequently used items.

Check how the stanchions are fitted, particularly the bases. Stanchions are often subjected to loads that have not been considered in design. They can bend and even break. It should be possible to remove them without dismantling the whole boat and the base should be sufficiently substantial that it will always be the stanchion that breaks, not the base or the deck.

Where guard rails run through stanchions are these adequately protected against chafe? If the rails are plastic covered wire, it pays to check them carefully. Look for signs of rust at the ends. If in doubt, replace them. Plain stainless wire makes it much easier to see any defects but is more prone to chafe. The tensioning lashings which, if fitted, should be at the aft end of each rail are best replaced each season. Ultraviolet damage may have made them brittle.

Guard rails are not too well named. If you fall against them with any real force they are likely to come away or the stanchion break. Even if that does not happen, their height is such that it is well below your centre of balance. Never clip safety harness to guard rails, which are only as strong as their lashings. These must be kept tight and in good condition to be any use.

Access

A point of particular importance concerns fittings. This is the ease or otherwise with which faulty items can be replaced or even loose ones tightened. In my experience most manufacturers give little thought to this problem. Headlinings that cannot be removed, backing nuts in inaccessible voids, rudder bearings bonded into the support tube, sheaves that cannot be removed individually from multiple boxes or blocks are examples of bad design.

When looking at deck items try to consider how easy or difficult they would be to repair or replace. I have owned a boat on which no provision whatever had been made for replacement of any deck fitting. On the best run boats, things break occasionally. If this happens the practicability of repair at sea, with limited facilities, could be crucial.

Every yacht skipper must learn to be a mechanic for his or her own safety. Basic repairs are as necessary a part of skippering as is plotting a course or steering it. More will be said on this subject later.

The final test

All the things suggested in this chapter have advised looking and considering from a static viewpoint; in harbour, ashore or in a marina. Hopefully you will have tried to think of how things will be at sea. Before you actually buy the boat you must be sure of how they will be. The only way to do this is to take the boat out and try it. Stay below (if you can!) for at least part of the time and see how it all feels.

PART 2
Rigs, sails and wind

Ask a European child to draw a sailing boat and you get something with two triangular sails hung, point upwards, from one mast. The bottom edge of one sail might be supported on a more or less horizontal rigid pole. Vessels like this, usually referred to as sloops or sloop rigged are, by far, the most common seen in European waters.

There are, of course, many variants of this model. A few of the more common are: a second, shorter mast aft (mizzen) which makes the yacht a ketch or yawl; a second spar holding the top of the mainsail making it gaff rigged. With a second staysail forward of the mast, it becomes a cutter. Cutters sometimes have a bowsprit, a spar which protrudes from the bow on to which headsails are tacked. Much less common, is a similar spar over the stern, called a bumpkin.

Other designs, often regional and very different, exist. A Chinese child would draw a junk, while an Arab child would draw a dhow. The main effect of the differences is to redistribute the sail area so as to change the handling characteristics and capabilities of the vessel.

5 SAIL DYNAMICS

To understand how your own, or any other, rig behaves you must first understand how a sail works. It is only comparatively recently that the dynamics of sails have been fully understood. Even now there is still some argument over detail. Until quite recently, it was a matter largely of trial and error as different rigs evolved. Now however, designers are able, with the use of computer models, wind tunnels and other technical devices, to predict the behaviour of different systems with considerable accuracy.

We have no such technology available when sailing. Instead, we need to understand the basics, combining these with both observation and intuition to get the best from our sails.

The aerofoil

When air flows over its surfaces, the sail works in the same way as does an aeroplane wing. It is an aerofoil. It does no harm to think of a sail as a single wing mounted vertically. Confusion can creep in here however.

Aerodynamics was originally concerned with aeroplanes. In aeroplane aerodynamics, an 'up wash' or 'up draught' is a movement in the logical direction, ie from below the wing upwards. A 'down wash' is the opposite direction. When the wing is turned through ninety degrees to form a sail these terms stay the same but the 'upper' surface now becomes the 'lee' surface. Thus, in texts, you may find a movement towards the lee is called 'upward' and one into wind is 'downward'. It is important to remember this. Figure 5.1 illustrates the point.

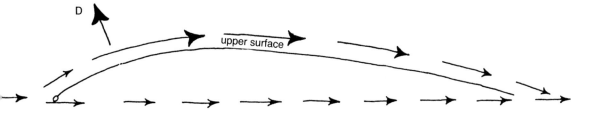

Fig 5.1 Air flow round a sail

When the free flow air hits the leading edge of a sail it divides. Some of the air passes in front and some behind the sail. The sail is not flat. The air flows at the leading and trailing edges in opposite directions, towards and away from the sail respectively. The velocities of the separated and recombing masses must be about the same. The paths travelled by the two lots of air are different lengths. All these things result in the velocities of the air masses, as they flow round the sail, being different.

Look at Figure 5.1 again. The edge of the sail that is closest to the wind is the luff. This is the edge that actually parts the air. The trailing edge of the sail where the two lots of air recombine is the leech. In the ideal situation the separation and recombination must be smooth from luff to leech so that no turbulence is created.

Turbulence

Turbulence is the movement of the air in rapidly changing directions. The term should strictly only be applied to the air in the layer closest to the surface of the aerofoil but I shall use it to describe any air that is in a disturbed state as opposed to smooth flowing. Turbulence that extends away from the immediate surface results in separation of the smooth air stream from the aerofoil. Since any such separation will reduce the effectiveness of the sail it is to be avoided.

Intuitive behaviour

Let us now look at the situation from an intuitive point of view; remembering that air is a fluid and behaves in the same way as any other fluid.

You will be aware that when a fluid approaches an obstruction it starts to change direction, to go round the obstruction, *before* it actually arrives. Think of the surface patterns that you see on the upstream side of a buoy for example. This is a very important point to remember. It happens because the particles of fluid coming in contact with the obstruction tend to pile up so to speak. The result is an increase in density which sets up a pressure wave. This wave is transmitted back through the fluid very rapidly. Sound is an example of a pressure wave and sound moves at over 700 miles per hour in air at sea level, faster in water. A lot faster than your yacht is moving!

Intuition confirms two more factors. One is that individual particles of a fluid will take the shortest possible path they can round an obstruction. The other is that even a fluid has some friction. As it passes the obstruction it will pull at, and be pulled by, the material of the obstruction. Think of the wind on your face.

Air flow

The next two points that we need to understand are not intuitive. First, the air flow round an obstruction such as a sail can be represented mathematically by two components, one is the linear flow similar to the free flow of unobstructed air, the other is called the circulation flow which moves round the obstruction. The two

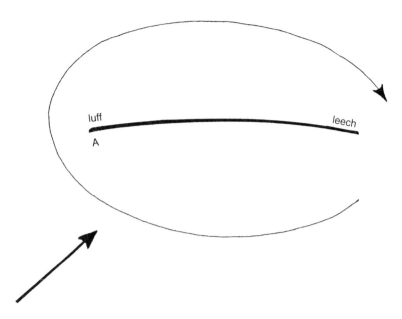

Fig 5.2 Circulation and linear flow round a sail

streams are shown in Figure 5.2. These two streams have both speed and direction ie they are vectors, just like tides, and can be combined in the same way.

Second is the fact that the pressure exerted by a fluid is inversely proportional to the square of its velocity. This is called Bernoulli's principle after the man who discovered it. Put simply it means that when the air flows faster it exerts less pressure than when it is moving slowly.

Driving force

Now you have the keys to understanding what happens. Figure 5.1 shows the two streams combined to find the net result. The sizes of the arrows indicate the velocities in the same way as those on a tidal chart. It can be seen that the stream on the lee side of the sail is faster than that on the windward side. The pressure on the lee side is therefore reduced and the sail will try to move in the direction D. This is what drives the boat along. To get the greatest benefit, the flow velocities on each side of the sail must have the greatest difference between them. Again intuitively, this suggests that the more we can do to increase the circulation stream velocity until it approaches the linear velocity, the better things will be.

Unlike a rigid aircraft wing, the sail is soft and must rely mainly on pressure differences to keep its shape. The air flowing over the curved surface has a higher velocity than does that taking the more direct route. Because the pressure is lower in the faster moving air stream a pressure difference exists between the front and back of the sail. It is this pressure difference that causes the boat to move. That is just a restatement of what has gone before but think on a bit. What happens at the leech?

Once the lee and windward streams pass the leech there is no cloth to separate them so that any pressure difference cannot be maintained. Air would rush from high to low until the pressure was even. This suggests that the velocities of the two masses must be equal, or nearly so, by the time they reach the leech. Remember the pressure waves we talked of earlier. If the recombining air streams are at the same velocity, the air passing over the lee side of the sail must have been slowing down. Let's see what effect this will have.

Luffing and stalling

Drive (or lift in aerodynamics) depends on pressure difference. These differences result largely from the angle between the apparent wind and the aerofoil. Think of a very thin flat aerofoil.

If the aerofoil is perfectly in line with the airstream there will be no difference between the pressures on the two sides, because the velocities will be the same. A sail in this situation, not being flat or rigid, will not be able to hold its shape and will collapse. In practice this collapse will happen long before this point is reached. The collapse starts at the luff since the pressures there will equalise earlier. Hence this condition is called luffing.

Now think of the same aerofoil rotated at right angles to the stream. This will be a pure obstruction producing, if it is not moving with the stream, high pressure on the upstream side with severe turbulence on the downstream side causing high drag. It will tend simply to be forced down stream with no discernable luff or leech, no lift and no movement in the plane of the foil. If it were actually an aeroplane wing, gravity would take over and it would simply fall out of the sky.

Actually, long before the rotation is completed, the drag force will begin to approach the lift force. At this point the aerofoil is stalling.

Somewhere between these two situations the aerofoil, in our case the sail, will behave as we want it to. In fact there are quite a few degrees change in the angle of attack (the angle the sail makes with the wind) between the luffing and stalling conditions for a sail, but only a small range when the lift is at maximum.

6 THEORY AND PRACTICE

The objective

Efficient sailing means maintaining the greatest pressure difference between the two sides of the sail. This will occur when the air on the lee side of the sail is moving at its maximum speed, without turbulence, and that on the windward side is moving so slowly that it almost stops. It sounds simple but lots of things work against this ideal situation.

Unfortunately the ideal, like most ideals, is impossible to achieve. By increasing the angle of attack beyond the luffing angle it is possible to increase the velocity of the circulating flow. Indeed at some point it will exceed the velocity of the non-circulating stream at the luff. When this happens, air actually flows from the windward side, round the luff, to the lee side so that separation of the stream can occur at about point A in Figure 5.2.

This means that more air is diverted on to the lee side of the sail and thus its velocity is increased still further. The problem is that all this air must decelerate fairly rapidly as it approaches the leech (remember both streams have to be moving at about the same speed when they recombine). This deceleration produces turbulence which encourages the lee stream to separate from the sail. Put another way, you could say that when the angle of attack is too great the stream flowing round the luff is incapable of following the line of the sail and so, separates. When this happens, drag increases rapidly and drive is lost. The sail in fact stalls and, if the situation is uncorrected, will collapse

Boundary layer

Turbulence is always present close to the surface of the sail due to the drag produced by the sailcloth and, near the luff, by the mast. Such drag is made worse by any seams, cringles, hanks, in fact anything in the way of the flow. This thin layer of air is called the boundary layer. It always exists, but provided it stays thin, we can live with it. If it thickens, separation occurs, lift is lost and the sail loses drive.

True and apparent wind

A further complication is the fact that the effective wind over the sail is a function of boat speed. The true wind is that which is felt relative to a fixed point on earth. The wind one experiences on a moving vehicle or vessel is the resultant of the true wind vector and the velocity vector of the vessel. Figures 6.1a–d should make this more clear.

   Confusion often exists as to the changes that occur in apparent wind as a result of boat speed. Some conclusion can be drawn from Figures 6.1a–d:

1 Apparent wind speed will always exceed the true wind speed when the true wind direction is forward of the beam.
2 As the angle between true wind and heading increases, the true and apparent wind speeds will become equal. Thereafter the true wind speed will exceed the apparent wind speed. In practice this point is reached at about 10–15 degrees abaft the beam, depending on the relative velocities of wind and boat speed.
3 Apparent wind direction will always be forward of the true wind direction unless the true wind is from dead ahead or dead astern.
4 Apparent wind speed will increase as boat speed increases when the true wind is forward of the beam.
5 The angle between apparent wind direction and the boat heading will decrease as boat speed increases save for the exceptions of 3 above.

If any of these points are unclear consider the following. Imagine driving down a straight road in your car towing your boat at 30 mph on a completely calm day. If you had an anemometer mounted on the boat it would read 30 mph. If you stuck your hand out of the window you would feel a 30 mph wind. The only wind you would experience would be the apparent wind created by your car.

   If, instead of complete calm, you had a steady 10 mph wind blowing from behind you would measure and feel only a 20 mph wind. You would not expect to feel one wind on the back of your hand and another on the front but only the difference between the two winds. With the 10 mph wind coming from your right, instead of behind, again you would not measure or feel two separate winds but only a single combination of them both. This example explains the speed changes. The changes in both speed and angle are shown in the diagrams.

The tell-tale signs

It should be apparent from what I have said earlier that, for effective sailing, it is important to know how the air is behaving as it passes over the sail. An easy way to do this is to use tell-tales. Short lengths of wool or light ribbon attached to the sail serve this purpose.

   It is no good putting tell-tales too close to the mast on the mainsail because the very presence of the mast generates turbulence. You should get a pretty good idea if some are positioned about a quarter to half a metre from the mast and some more are

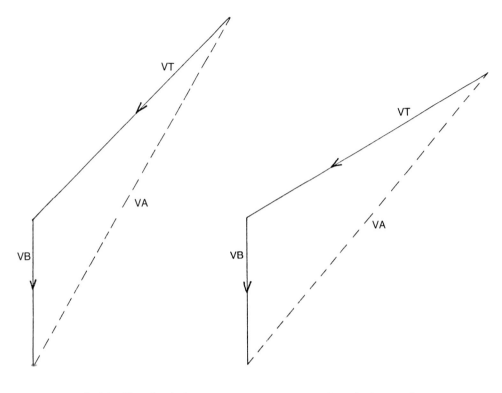

Fig 6.1a Close hauled

Fig 6.1b Fine reaching

VB = boat speed vector
VT = true wind vector
VA = apparent wind vector

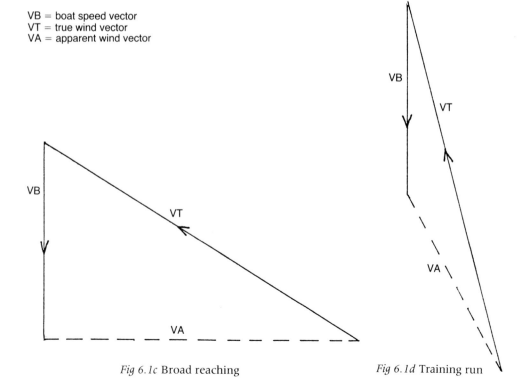

Fig 6.1c Broad reaching

Fig 6.1d Training run

attached to the leech. The height of the tell-tales matters too. Most mainsails are pretty inefficient close to the boom and also very close to the head. If the top most tell-tale is about a fifth of the way down the sail and the bottom one about a fifth up, with two or three others spaced equally between, you will have some useful idea of what is happening. Tell-tales on a headsail can be a lot closer to the luff because they have no mast to get in the way; about 15 to 20 cm is close enough.

Reading the signals

In crude terms you want the angle of the sail to be set so that all the tell-tales, particularly those on the lee side of the sail, are streaming out parallel to the deck. In practice you will find that it is difficult to get all the bits of wool to behave as you want them to. For example, there is always a turbulence bubble on the leading surface of the lee of the sail.

Combining sails

So far what I have said has referred to one sail at a time, main or jib. In practice we are likely to be using two sails together most of the time so what happens then? In fact the various streams round the two sails interact with each other so that the net result is more like one composite and complex single aerofoil. I shall not go into very great details here. Figure 6.2 shows the idea. Many specialist books on the subject are available. A few points are worth making however.

Consider first what happens, in practice, when a second sail is added. A genoa added to the main for example. I do this because you will probably have experienced this in changing headsails. Several things should have been noticed. First you find that you

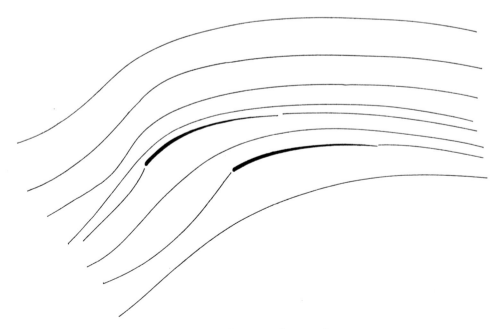

Fig 6.2 Air flow round two sails

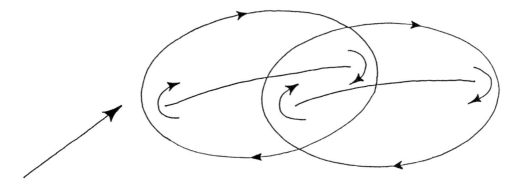

Fig 6.3 Circulation and linear flow round two sails

can point higher, ie sail closer to the wind. You may also have observed that, on a given heading, you will need to have the main sheeted in tighter. You should be moving faster and with less weather helm. A more subtle point is that, although you have less weather helm, you may notice the tendency to broach in gusts has actually increased. Why do these things come about?

First let's dispose of the popular idea that the 'slot effect' somehow increases the velocity of the air between the sails. If you follow that argument through to its logical conclusion any venturi effect between the sails would mean that the action of the jib would oppose that of the main.

Actually the presence of a headsail causes the stream to be parted earlier so that some of the air which would have been passing over the lee side of the main is diverted to pass on the lee side of the genoa. This increases the volume of air flowing on the lee side of the genoa and also its velocity. The velocity of the air over the lee surface of the main has actually decreased.

Look at Figure 6.3; since this shows that the circulation flow round the two sails is opposed, the mean velocity of the stream between the sails, ie over the lee of the main, *must* actually be less than it is with one sail alone. The pressure differences over the main are therefore reduced. At the leech of the genoa however the air is moving faster than it would without the main, since it is still decelerating towards the leech of the main. It follows then that the main helps the genoa's effectiveness but loses some ot its own. Since the gain is greater than the loss, the combined result is a benefit.

What about reduced weather helm? The centre of effort on the main alone is aft of the mast. That of the headsail, forward ot the mast. Combining the two gives better balance thus reduced weather helm. This is course, helps the speed since whenever the rudder is off centre it acts as a brake.

Broaching

The velocity differences between the lee and windward streams are reduced over the main and increased over the genoa respectively. If a broach starts to occur this will mean that the wind will stall first on the genoa. The drive being maintained longer on the main, it tends to accentuate the broaching tendency. As the broach starts, more weather helm is experienced so the rudder is moved to counteract this. The rudder then tends to stall and the broach develops further. Rapid easing of the main sheet is the only effective counter action. The situation is more noticeable on a fractional rigged boat owing to the relatively larger main.

If you look carefully at the flow lines in Figure 6.2, you will notice that the flow off the genoa has to reach the main at a very shallow angle. If it does not, the mainsail will be backwinded and start to stall. The ideal situation is when the two sails remain parallel over the greater part of their area, only closing very slightly. From this point alone, it should be apparent that the two sails are interdependent and so must be adjusted together.

7   SAIL TRIM

Control of the flow

When you adjust a sheet to alter the angle of the sail to the wind you are altering the pull on the bottom aft corner, the clew, of the sail. Easing the sheet thus tends to raise the clew as well as move it away from the centre line of the boat. This is so even on the main with a kicker set. The leech therefore tends to open out at the top so that the angle the sail makes with the wind is smaller at the foot of the sail than at the head.

With a fractional rig this is no bad thing because the part of the mainsail above the forestay attachment acts as a single sail which needs to be more open. On a masthead rig it is less desirable.

To counter this effect, the pull needs to be more down than in. This can be achieved for a headsail by moving the jib sheet lead block forward. This will also bring the clew closer to the tack and thus increase the curvature of the sail. A leech line can be used to tighten the leech but should never be left tight when close hauled because it tends to produce leech curl.

Mainsail controls

The mainsail has more controls available in addition to the sheet tension. The mainsheet track position can be moved more to leeward to exert greater leech tension for near close hauled positions. However, as the boat moves further off the wind, this will no longer work. You simply run out of track.

Increasing the tension on the kicking strap will help and modern yachts can have sufficient power in the kicker for this to be effective. The outhaul can be tightened or the mast can be straightened. All these things will increase leech tension, although they do other things as well.

Overdoing the leech tension can defeat the object by causing the leech to curl. If this happens on the mainsail when beating, part of the drive force of the sail will be deflected so as to disturb the linear flow off the sail and thus reduce boat speed. This is a real danger because the sail looks to be setting well with a good smooth shape. The thing to avoid is a curl to windward. Excessive downward pressure can also distort the sail cloth and do permanent damage.

The effect of excessive leech tension in the headsail is to cause backwinding of the main. This is due only in part to the slot shape. Backwinding is also caused by the increased angle that the flow of the headsail leech makes with the main. It is better to let the head of the genoa open a little by easing the sheet, even to the point where it is just luffing. This helps to maintain the parallel lie of the two sails lower down where the camber depth is greatest and so most drive is produced.

Sail camber depth

The greatest camber depth is where a line drawn, to the sail, at right angles to the cord of the sail is longest (see Figure 7.1). The position of this point can be moved forward in several ways. Increasing luff tension, either by tightening the halyard or using a Cunningham downhaul will do it as will tightening the clew outhaul or bending the mast with the backstay tensioner.

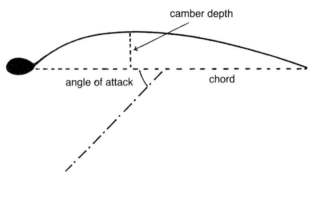

Fig 7.1 Sail shape terms

In any close-hauled or reaching situation the greatest cord depth must be forward of the centre-point. The centre-point of the cord moves closer to the mast with increasing distance up the sail, since the cord length is reducing.

For maximum drive it is generally accepted that a point somewhere between one third of the way from the mast and the centre of the cord, measured at the mid-point vertically on the sail, is about right. The greater the wind strength the flatter the sail must be and the closer this point should be to the mast.

Battens

Battens are fitted in the leech of a mainsail to prevent leech curl. Leech curl is more likely in a mainsail than a headsail for several reasons. Firstly, leech tension will be greater in the mainsail since the kicker, and most of the sheet tension, act downwards. Secondly, the mainsail is often cut with a curved leech, called roach, to increase the width of the sail at the point where it has most drive. The battens help prevent the roach from rolling in and are not intended to compensate for excess leech tension however.

Battens are often of uniform stiffness but, since the tendency to curl is greatest at the edge of the sail, tapered battens may be used. To gain the required sail shape, these must be fitted with the thicker end at the leech. If tapered battens are incorrectly fitted they will not work properly and will prevent a smooth curve to the sail and also damage the sail cloth by putting unfair stress on it at the inner ends of the batten pockets.

Halyard adjustment

Correct halyard tension is important. Halyards are often set up taut and left for the duration of a passage whatever the wind. From what I have said earlier, it should be clear that luff tension needs to be altered to suit conditions. Tightening in strong and easing in light winds will improve performance. The tension needs to be sufficient to prevent crows feet, small horizontal wrinkles, forming in the luff yet not so tight that a vertical fold starts to form close to the mast. Look at Figures 7.2 and 7.3 to see what I mean. In Figure 7.2 the luff has been wound in too tight for the wind strength and in Figure 7.3 it is too slack. The optimum is somewhere between these two points.

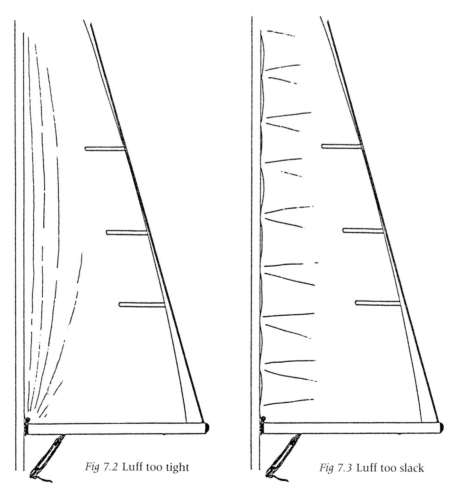

Fig 7.2 Luff too tight   Fig 7.3 Luff too slack

The exact tension needed depends on the required position of maximum camber depth. This is related both to wind strength and point of sailing. A racing yacht will usually have a Cunningham hole fitted in the mainsail. This is a cringle about 30 to 40 cm up the luff. A line attached to the foot of the mast can be passed through this cringle and back down to a cleat for making luff tension adjustments. This is a lot easier than altering the halyard when racing hard. Try experimenting for yourself and you may be surprised at how much you can improve the yacht's performance with correct halyard tension.

Mast bend

Most racers and many cruiser/racers have a deliberate mast bending capability. This is done by adjusting the backstay tension. Since the forestay stretch is minimal, shortening the backstay causes the masthead to be lowered aft forcing the centre of the mast to move forward.

Small amounts of mast bend can be induced in any mast but care should be taken since several potential problems result. Tension on the backstay increases downward pressure and so giving compression loading on the mast. If the spreaders are not, either angled back or arranged to swivel, sheer loads can be induced that can stress the mast to the point of damage at, or close to, the spreader fittings.

Effects of mast bend
When the mast is bent forward at the centre several things happen. The camber of the sail changes with the sail becoming flatter. The leech is softened so that the head of the sail opens. Upper shroud tension is reduced whilst lower shrouds may be tighter causing the top of the mast to bend away to leeward. The headsail luff is tightened.

8 DISTRIBUTING THE WIND

One sail or more?

Most yachts are designed to use at least two sails at a time. There are several reasons for this. First, any sailing boat needs a certain sail area to make it go in a particular wind. Dividing this area between two or more sails makes each sail smaller and thus easier to handle. Next comes the problem of balance. A conventional single masted yacht will have its centre of effort, the point about which it pivots, on the fore and aft centre line, more or less at the place where the mast is stepped, or just a little behind that position.

This means that the force acting on a sail set behind the mast tends to turn the yacht into the wind whilst force on a sail set forward of the mast turns it the opposite way. Think about this for a moment. Distributing the forces between two sails means that the yacht can be more easily balanced so that it will sail straight, or very nearly straight, with the sails correctly set.

Having two sails, particularly if they are slightly overlapping, gives another advantage. As mentioned earlier, the presence of a headsail actually increases the wind velocity over the front of the *combination* of the two. This increases the pressure difference overall and, improves the drive that the combination provides.

Dividing the driving area into three or more sails makes each easier to handle. The other benefits are still present but the law of diminishing returns begins to set in if you go too far. You finish up with lots more control lines, also the edges of any sail are less effective than its centre. This can mean that you can have a more complicated but less effective system.

The ketch rig, with only a mizzen and a small head-sail set, is a particularly stable configuration in heavy weather conditions and so is popular with ocean voyagers. I go no further into the relative merits of various rigs here since many books have been written on the subject.

Reducing sail area

Deciding when to reduce sail is a vexing question for many skippers, and yet has a relatively simple answer. No yacht is fully efficient if it is over-canvased. All you get is a wetter, rougher, more uncomfortable ride. You put unnecessary strains on the rigging, sails and gear and also on the helmsman and crew. Racing crews will accept this although I have, on occasion, won races by reducing sail area. When cruising it is neither necessary nor sensible to be over-canvased.

Sometimes a wind increase can be temporary, possibly just a gust or short squall. You may shortly be going on to an easier point of sailing. If this is so you can briefly hold on to excessive sail by spilling wind. This works quite well with the main (even when it appears to be luffing quite badly) and helps to reduce excessive heel. If the increase is going to last for a while however, you will have to do something about it quickly.

It is impossible to lay down hard and fast rules because boats have different characteristics. The thing to remember is that your boat has been designed to sail at a variety of wind strengths. Full sail is for light winds. If your 10 metre boat will sail at six knots with full sail in a force 2 wind you can be sure that it does not need full sail in force 4. If you have to motor to keep going when the wind is less than force 3 you will probably be able to carry full sail up to force 5.

Heel as an indicator

Another approach is to look at the heeling angle. Modern light displacement hulls will sail best at angles of heel around 20 to 25 degrees. If, with the sails correctly set, your heel angle is consistently more than 30 degrees, you probably have too much up. You should do something about it, because both weather helm and drag are starting to reduce the boat's performance quite apart from the strains on the rig and on the crew.

What to do depends on several things. Full main and a medium genoa close on the wind in a force 4 could be uncomfortable, particularly with wind over tide. The same sails in the same wind on the beam and from offshore, would give exciting and enjoyable sailing. Down wind in the same conditions, you might be considering increasing the sail area.

Weather helm

This is the condition you get where, if you let go of the tiller or wheel, the boat will turn up into the wind. To keep straight you will have to pull the tiller towards the weather side of the boat. A little weather helm is desirable since it means that if you let go accidentally, you will come up to wind and stop. Too much weather helm and you are starting to put the brakes on.

Lee helm

Lee helm is the opposite of weather helm. It should be avoided. If your boat has lee helm and you let go the tiller it will career away down wind until it gybes. It will then steady again before gybing on to the original tack and so on. This is both unpleasant and dangerous.

Balance is what it is all about. Remember what each sail does. If you have a great deal of weather helm, maybe even tending to broach in gusts, it is high time to adjust the sail trim. If adjustment is not sufficient, you probably should have done it earlier and you will need to reduce sail. Lee helm is seldom a problem of handling, more one of design. If you find that a boat you try has marked lee helm in a moderate wind, you will be better off finding another boat.

Headsail size

When beating to windward in a heavy sea it will be useful to reduce the headsail if waves are frequently breaking over the bow. A large volume of water thrown into a big genoa makes everyone sit up and it can split the sail. A working jib, with the foot cut higher, will help to avoid this. You may find that with the jib up you will need to take in a reef in the main to restore balance. Students sailing with me are frequently surprised when, on having done this, the boat speed increases rather than decreases.

Over-canvased

This fact is not actually difficult to understand. A big headsail tends to push the bow down so that the yacht hits, rather than rides, the waves and thus, slows down. The increased heel provided by the larger sail area does two things. It allows wind to spill off the top of the sails and it also pushes the curved side of the boat down into the water. These things increase weather helm and also water resistance.

Excess heel will reduce rudder efficiency. The rudder must be held well off centre to counter the weather helm keeping the boat straight. This is like putting the brakes on. The result is less speed with more effort. Carrying too much sail for too long is also bad for the sails. The cloth of a light air sail is not strong enough to take the strain in a blow and can pull out of shape. Such stretch damage is usually irreversible.

Making the best course

Provided the wind is more than about 50 degrees on one side of the desired course to steer and not so far aft that it comes from dead astern, the best course will probably be that course. Leeway has been taken into account and the vessel is sufficiently far off the wind not to be pinching when beating. If the wind is anywhere from a fine to a broad reach we shall be very happy. The problems arise when the required course is not within these parameters.

The fundamental problem under sail is that the wind is never constant, even in very settled conditions. Both the force and direction change continually. When the wind strength increases, particularly in a gust, the direction changes in a fairly predictable way. The basic wind (in the northern hemisphere) tends to veer in a gust and to back in a lull from the mean value. The reverse occurs in the southern hemisphere.

Using gusts
People sometimes say that gusts are not so important when cruising. In a stable air stream a gust or lull can last perhaps a minute. In unstable streams gusts may well last

for ten or more minutes so they do matter. Quite apart from the need to take correcting action in a strong gust, considerable advantage can be gained from both noticing and using them.

Think about the last two paragraphs in relation to the tack you might be on in northern waters. If you are sailing close-hauled on port tack, any increase in wind will reduce the attack angle since it will come more from the bow. The drive will thus drop as the headsail begins to luff. The heel force will not reduce and, in a strong gust, may increase.

Bearing away in the gust may not seem right but in fact it will keep the boat driving and maintain speed. It may be necessary to ease the main sheet but the maintained drive in the headsail will help avoid any tendency to broach. The boat will move down wind of the desired course.

On a starboard tack any wind increase will result in an increased attack angle hence giving increased drive and much increased heeling moment. Instinct will probably cause the helmsman to put the helm down and harden up to windward to reduce the heel. The boat will move up wind of the desired course.

From the foregoing it can be seen that when tacking in a wind from directly ahead of the desired course, a starboard tack will be more beneficial than a port tack. Life is not as simple as this however; sea conditions matter too. More will be said on this in Chapter 41 but it is worth making the point here.

Downwind

The problem of directional variation on a dead run is that the wind appears to change sides as the strength changes. When running, the sails are likely to be set goosewinged ie on opposite sides. In this condition a preventer should always be used.

Consider the situation on a starboard tack with the wind dead astern. In a strong gust the resulting veer will bring the wind over the port quarter. Thus a starboard tack, with the main boom on the port side, will mean that the boat is sailing by the lee in a gust. The drive on the headsail increases and that on the main decreases. The boat will thus tend to turn to port. An involuntary gybe becomes a distinct possibility.

On a port tack the wind moving from astern to the port quarter as it increases can generate a turning moment also to port since the force on the mainsail increases faster than that on the headsail. In this condition a broach is possible as the main, boomed well out, takes over.

It is often better to tack downwind. This gives better control whilst also allowing the sails to behave more as aerofoils. The apparent wind velocity decreases more slowly for a given increase in boat speed. The result is an increase in both boat speed and stability. Although the actual distance over the water is increased by a tacking course, it is probable that the other factors will outweigh this disadvantage.

9 DOWNWIND SAILING

Most of what has been said so far has been concerned with sailing close hauled or on a fine reach. Once the sails are freed off different factors come into play. Most people will tell you that a broad reach is the fastest point of sailing. This is true but may be not so much due to dynamic principles as to the fact that most helmsmen are less than effective when sailing to windward.

Broad reaching

The last statement is true in dynamic terms for several reasons. Once the true wind is abaft the beam by about 20 degrees the point of sailing is a broad reach. The apparent wind will be at right angles to the boat's heading and from now on will be less than the true wind. At this point, the dynamic force of the wind on the boat will not only be less than it would be under the same wind conditions when sailing upwind; it will also decrease as boat speed increases.

The advantage is that now heel force is reduced without the drive having changed much. This makes it more efficient. With the lower heel force, there will be less actual heel. As the wind comes further aft leeway becomes less. All these things result in greater hull speed because the drag forces have been reduced relative to the drive. Equilibrium can thus be achieved at a higher boat speed.

Camber shape

Now consider the sails. The importance of camber was mentioned in Chapter 7. As the wind comes aft, sheets are eased to correct the trim. This produces more curve in the sails. This increase in camber actually produces a large increase in the drive potential. At the same time it reduces the heel force. Provided the camber is not increased too much, the angle of attack becomes less critical since the drive force is more or less flat over a wider range of attack angles. The result is the helmsman thinks he is getting better!

Increasing the camber further will give improved drive but at the expense of increasing the criticality of the attack angle. Racing trimmers will do this nevertheless because they must maximise the drive. When they do so however, good helming becomes more crucial.

Attack angle

The commonest fault off the wind is to have too great an attack angle. Although it makes little difference to the driving force in cruising terms, it will increase the heel force dramatically. As a result, drag is increased, weather helm is experienced and the speed benefit one should be getting is lost. It is a common belief that increased heel means increased speed. This is wrong. The *feeling* of speed is greater but this is an illusion. Leeway, hull drag and weather helm *are* all greater. The speed made good is actually lower.

Too small an attack angle wastes potential speed but is less common since the boat tends to feel dead in this condition.

Sail twist

The greatest problem off the wind is that, with a more open sail, the boom will lift and the head will twist open so that efficiency is lost despite the increase in camber. Some twist is inevitable and even beneficial. It is the excess that must be avoided. The remedy is to move the traveller fully to leeward so that the main sheet angle is as steep as possible and to ensure that the kicker is tightened in order to hold the boom down before the sheet is eased.

Mast drag

The disturbance of the air flow at the luff, caused by the presence of the mast, is more of a problem when sailing off the wind. Short of changing your mast there is not a great deal you can do about it except trying to avoid clutter which will disturb the flow. If maximum speed matters to you then move spare control lines, halyards, spinnaker boom lift and so on, away from the mast and tack them down to the pulpit or the toe rail. The effect of mast drag is to reduce drive and to increase heel so it is worth trying to avoid the worst of it.

Strong winds

Downwind in brisk conditions it is usually more beneficial to cut down drastically on the mainsail rather than the headsail. This reduces the risks both of and from a gybe. The larger headsail tends to pull the boat downwind reducing the risk of a broach, whilst a small area main reduces the force in any gybe that does happen. The loss of speed is often small in relation to the improvement in comfort and safety.

Avoid a dead run

A dead run, with the wind directly astern, is not a good point of sailing although it may seem so. It is actually the slowest and least stable point.

With the wind directly astern the aerofoil effect on the sails is minimal. It is still present but is small. Most of the drive results from the resistance of the sail acting in the wind stream. This resistance is greatest when the relative velocities of wind and boat speed are at maximum difference. Since the wind can be assumed to have a constant mean velocity the drive will be at maximum if the boat is not moving at all!

As boat speed increases the two velocities will become closer and closer until, in theory at least, they are equal. At this point the drive will cease. In practice this never happens. What does happen is that the drive reduces until it is equal to the resistance of the water. At this point the boat stops accelerating.

Typically this point will be reached when the boat is moving at little more than one third of the wind velocity. In a twelve knot true wind the maximum boat speed will thus be about 4 knots and the apparent wind about 8 knots.

There is a further problem. Just as the instantaneous wind velocity varies about the mean so also does the wind direction. This is why people who sail on a dead run find they experience unexpected gybes. A preventer will stop the gybe and will help to keep the boom down but it will not trim the sail.

Preventers

Whilst on the subject of downwind sailing it is appropriate to mention preventers. A preventer is a piece of stout line used to hold the main boom both forward and down when sailing off the wind.

Some years ago I used to sail with a chap who hated preventers and would not allow them. The reason for his dislike was the way he had learned to rig them. He would take a line from the outer end of the boom up on to the foredeck where he would lash it to a cleat. Any subsequent adjustment meant that someone had to go forward and release it.

It is a good idea to fit an eye in the centre of the boom. The preventer is taken from this eye through a block on the toe rail at the shrouds and thence back to the spinnaker winch in the cockpit. In this way the preventer can easily be adjusted or released under control without anyone going forward. A cleat can be used if you have no spinnaker winch but a winch gives more control. The attachment point is chosen to give maximum downward pull on the boom. When you wish to release the preventer on gybing it is both simple and safe.

An alternative is to have a snap shackle fitted to the lower end of the kicker tackle. The shackle can then be moved from the mast base to the toe rail when sailing down wind to serve the same purpose. With this system however the strain on the gear is greater and someone needs to be forward to re-position it when gybing. During the actual gybe there is no restraint on upward movement of the boom.

When running I regard a preventer as essential. When reaching in light winds on a sloppy sea it is also very useful. It prevents the boom moving with the swells and spilling wind from the mainsail. A separate preventer provides much greater control and, pulling both down and forward, helps to take the strain off the kicking strap as well as adding considerably to safety and improved sail shape.

10 STANDING RIGGING

The rigging on a sailing vessel should be seen as an integral part of the propulsion system. A failure of any part of the rigging can, at times, prevent you from continuing to sail. The failure of certain items can, quite simply, make the mast fall down. Winch failures can be dangerous and for the most part need not happen.

With the foregoing in mind, the need to check and to look after these items of equipment regularly should not need mentioning. My experience however suggests that it does. In this chapter I shall concentrate on explaining what the standing rigging does, how to check it and how some of the possible problems can be reduced or avoided.

Standing rigging is what keeps the mast up. The failure of even one item can be catastrophic so it is worth knowing what to check and what signs there are to indicate potential problems. What to look for depends, to some extent, on what kind of rig you have but general principles apply. Unless you have an unstayed mast, the mast must be supported in a minimum of three and usually four directions, fore and aft and at both sides.

Wire rigging may be stainless or galvanised. The first indications of potential failure in both types can be a broken strand or strands. On the nineteen strand wires usually used for stainless steel rigging, a broken strand is normally fairly easy to spot. This is because it is usually one of the outer strands that goes first. This strand, once it is not under tension, will tend to untwist a little leaving the two ends slightly separated at the break. The broken strand then stands slightly proud of the main twist and can often be spotted by looking closely along the wire.

Swages

The places where breaks are most likely to happen are at joints or where the wire changes direction such as at the spreader ends. Roll swaged joints, if badly done, can actually *cause* a weakness, since each of the outer strands can be nipped slightly. It is virtually impossible to identify a poor swage although one in which the end of the wire does not emerge from the ferrule will be weaker. These joints all need to be given the closest attention. Someone will need to climb up the mast to examine them properly.

Bends

At a bend, the most likely strands to fail are those on the outside of the curve due to uneven stress. The inner ones may be subject to chafe so need to be looked at also. Spreader end caps, if fitted, should be removed when checking to ensure that all is well underneath as should any boots or other anti-chafe protection fitted at the chain plates.

End fittings

Forks and eyes on end fittings, and occasionally chain plates themselves, are subject to fatigue failure. They can also fail if the alignment with the wire is even slightly out. As well as for wear, these fittings should be checked carefully for any signs of cracking or distortion. Clevis pins must be checked for both wear and straightness. Any suspect pin should be replaced by one of the correct diameter and length.

If you are forced to make a temporary repair using a shackle, use the largest available and do not over stress the rig whilst it is in use; it will never be as strong as the correct item. Mast tangs and keyhole eyes in the mast should be tight and show no signs of elongation or distortion.

Galvanised stays

Galvanised wires are usually the so called 7 × 7 variety. Such wires are made up from seven bundles each with seven strands. The strands are much thinner than the 1 × 19 more common to stainless rigging. With 7 × 7 a single broken strand is not easy to spot, though it may make itself felt if your hand catches it. Stainless wires may be in 7 × 7 on the lower sections of split backstays with tensioners, due to its much greater flexibility. It has greater stretch than 1 × 19 also and is therefore seldom used for full length stays.

The first sign of trouble on galvanised wires or fittings is usually a rust stain which is relatively easy to spot. Rust signs should always be investigated. Some stainless fittings are not as stainless as they should be and these can show rust stains also. Look for them particularly where the cable enters a fitting.

Testing for weakness

Gentle flexing of the fitting joint when not under tension can cause a weak strand to part. This is better than waiting for it to happen at sea. Take care not to distort the joint too much causing a permanent kink.

If you spot any signs which you have doubts about you can usually get a rigger to have a look for you. I work on the rule, 'if in doubt replace', on the basis that this is money well spent if it will stop my mast falling down.

Choice of materials

You will have little choice over the materials used initially for your rigging, even if you are buying a new boat. When you replace any item however it will be up to you what you use. This is very much a case of getting what you pay for. It is always best to go for quality since any failure here will cause costly damage to other parts of the boat and/or crew. Whatever you do, do not reduce sizes. The builder will not have used anything larger than he needed to; if you cut down, your rigging will have inadequate strength.

Most modern boats now use stainless rigging because of its long and relatively maintenance free life. If you still want galvanised rigging you will have to accept that it needs more maintenance to last its full potential, although faults are easier to spot.

Rod rigging is becoming more common on racing yachts because of its low stretch and high strength properties. Potential failure is very difficult to spot. Actual failure will almost always be catastrophic.

Protecting the sails

At any point where a sail in use is likely to rub against rigging (or anything else) it should be protected. Plastic end-caps for most spreaders are available. These simply snap into place. A tennis ball suitably cut will often do just as well. If these places cannot be protected, and even if they can, it is worth having your sailmaker sew a patch of cloth on each side of the sail where rubbing occurs. This will save the main fabric of the sail. The same is true for headsails where they rub on the pulpit. Bind the rough areas with tape or have patches or both.

The bottom of the shrouds is often a place where sheets can snag as they run. The best thing here is a short length of thick plastic hose fitted over both the shroud plates and bottlescrews. It is cheaper and just as effective as custom made boots. You only need them on the outer pair of shrouds. Instead of cutting the tube, slip it on to the shroud before connecting to the fork or bottlescrew and then slide it down after fitting. It may need taping in position. I also fit a length of hose on my forestay to protect it from the anchor chain.

If the genoa touches the shrouds when sheeted hard in, fit lengths of thin tube here too. Patent material is available for this purpose which comes in two halves that can be snapped on to the wire. It is more expensive than hose but is easier to use and lasts a lot longer because it will rotate on the shroud as a sail pulls over it. This further reduces wear; it protects the sheets too.

Rigging tension

Most people who set up their own standing rigging seem to be afraid of pulling things too tight. On a cruising yacht this is virtually impossible with hand tools and far more damage can result from having the rigging too slack.

There are no hard and fast rules to guide you but make sure that the inner and outer shrouds have even tension on both sides and that the mast is not pulled out of shape or to one side. The upper shroud, being longer, will have more stretching available than the lower. If the shrouds are not tight enough, the mast head will fall off to leeward when the boat is pressed.

This can cause the mast to bend to windward, further decreasing the angle at the head. In extreme conditions this could cause the mast to buckle, especially if the spreader end can ride up the shroud. Correct tensioning is therefore very important.

The spreader ends often clamp on to the shrouds. If so, they should be checked both for tightness and for position when setting up the rigging and at least once during the season.

A straight mast

One way to make sure that the mast is upright is as follows. Choose a very calm day with the boat afloat, or ashore but set absolutely level; use a spirit level or clinometer. Make a plumb line with a large fishing weight (the larger the better). Haul it up the mast using the main halyard. With the boom to one side or removed, adjust the length of line so that the weight hangs just above the deck. If it swings too much let the weight dangle in a bucket of water.

Once this is done it is fairly easy to adjust the mast for both straightness and verticality in relation to the beam plane. Remember that most masts require some rake and often some bend in the fore and aft line for optimum performance. If you have the original builder's instructions they may well tell you how much rake and/or bend is needed. You can then set this up by adjusting both the shrouds and the stays. If not ask another owner, your yard or the makers for advice.

Another method is to take the main halyard down to the chain plate on one side. Adjust its length until it is hand tight, then transfer it to the other side. If the mast is straight it should be possible to attach it in the same position without readjusting the halyard length. This method works best on moulded hulls since it depends on the profile being exactly uniform on both sides.

Sailing checks

When setting the sails at sea, make it a habit to glance at your rigging. Potential weaknesses are often more apparent when the gear is stressed than when you are looking at it on a mooring. If the mast is twisting or the lee shrouds are over slack, perhaps on one tack only, ask yourself why? Whilst you are deciding, ease the sheets and/or reduce sail to reduce the stress and you may well prevent a serious mishap.

11 SPARS

Spars are the masts and booms including the spinnaker pole and or whisker poles. Most modern yachts have spars of aluminium alloy, a few are resin bonded carbon fibres, still fewer Kevlar and either glass or carbon fibre combinations. On more traditional craft wooden spars are normal.

Aluminium is an ideal metal in some respects. It has a high strength to weight ratio, particularly when alloyed with other metals. It is fairly easy to extrude into quite complex shapes and is not over costly. Its main drawback is its corrosion properties in salt water. Untreated it will break down quite rapidly in the presence of salt. It is also high on the galvanic table (next to zinc which is used for sacrificial anodes) and is thus very susceptible to electrolysis.

Anodising

Fortunately a treatment is available which markedly reduces corrosion in aluminium. Anodising is a process whereby a hard, corrosion proof coating is formed on the metal. The coating is extremely durable and can actually be produced in a range of colours although spars are generally limited to silver, gold or black.

What is less well appreciated is the fact that once the surface coating is breached, corrosion can set in. Aluminium oxide is hard and will form quickly. This, in dry air, will prevent or inhibit further corrosion. It is actually the oxide that salt water attacks. Oxygen in the water is then able to react with the metal and the process, instead of stopping, continues rapidly.

If the metal stays dry and salt free, corrosion is slow. Spars tend to corrode more readily when salt water is trapped and remains in contact for some time. With aluminium spars even small small scratches in the anodising can lead to deep pitting. Such problems worsen if the spar is constantly wet such as at a mast boot or gaiter (see also page 58).

Electrolysis

This is similar to corrosion in appearance and is often confused with it but has a different cause. The problem arises when any two different metals are in contact in the presence of an ionising liquid called an electrolyte. Salt solution is an excellent electrolyte.

The effect is the formation of a voltaic cell, a 'battery' as it is commonly and erroneously called. In such a cell one metal, the more positive one in the Galvanic Series, is eaten away and the metal is converted into a metallic salt. The further apart the two metals are the more rapid the action. Only magnesium is more positive than aluminium.

The Galvanic Series
+

Magnesium
Aluminium
Zinc
Iron
Stainless steel*
Lead
Copper
Bronze

—

*Stainless steel comes in various grades. The least reactive types of marine grade stainless steel may be below bronze in the table. Any stainless steel item attracted by a magnet should assume the higher place.

So called inactive stainless steel is commonly used for connecting spars to their fittings. This produces some electrolytic action (sometimes called galvanic erosion) with time and some authorities suggest that either aluminium rivets are used or that each screw should be coated with zinc chromate before insertion.

Bronze is some way down the table and if a bronze fitting is to be used it must be separated from the aluminium by an inert barrier. This means that a non-conducting material such as 'Tuffnol', well oiled teak or silicone rubber should be used to separate the two metals.

Care of fittings

Aluminium alloy fittings can sometimes give rise to troubles apart from those mentioned above. Cast items can fracture and should be checked for cracks. Poor casting is virtually impossible to spot unless a void reaches the surface. The best defence against this, which does not always work, is to buy only those castings made by a reputable manufacturer. At least you will get redress from such a firm if something does fail. Boom and mast end fittings, also any cast cranks such as are sometimes found on kickers or backstay tensioners, are the most likely items to suffer from fractures and cracks.

I once found a bronze fitting that failed having been mounted in position with an aluminium packing piece under it. The aluminium had started about 3 mm thick but, by the time I found it, had almost completely eroded away in the area in contact with the bronze.

12 RUNNING RIGGING SYSTEMS

In Chapter 10, fixed rigging was discussed. The wires and ropes used to raise and lower sails and spars, collectively called running rigging are almost as important. Fore-thought about running rigging failure can reduce the potential problems to inconvenience rather than disaster.

Halyards are usually made from wire with rope tails on boats from about 6 metres up. On smaller yachts they may be pre-stretched polyester but the give in such halyards prevents them being made up tightly enough for larger boats.

Wire ropes

Wire ropes are normally restricted to halyards. These are always 7×7 rather than the stiffer 1×19. The first sign of potential trouble is the appearance of broken strands. Since these wire ropes consist of many thin strands, once again, breaks are not easily seen. They are usually felt first! Broken strands stick out of the main rope like small needles and are equally sharp.

Strand breakage
Whilst the breakage of only one or two strands will not cause failure of the halyards, even a single strand can do serious damage to hands as well as indicating that the item is past its best. It is usually better to replace them at the first signs of whiskering. When whiskering starts at a place that can be touched it will often mean that more serious damage has occurred aloft where the wire rope runs over a sheave.

Wire to rope splices

Wire to rope splices are normally made in halyards. This is mainly so that the tail, to be held by hand and to be run round a winch, is more comfortable to handle and provides greater friction. Wire rope has little stretch, consequently the part of the rope tail running through a jambing cleat or round a winch tends to be the same part all the time. This is where most of the wear will occur. Wire ropes put a great load on pulleys and fairleads and a worn pulley can greatly increase the rate at which a wire rope wears. So, incidentally, can a pulley of incorrect size.

Rope chafe

Chafe will produce a woolly matted appearance in the surface of plaited rope at wear points. Most of the strength of this type of rope is in the core, so quite severe surface damage will not markedly affect the strength. It is often possible to shorten the wire portion of the halyard when chafe damage is first noticed so that different parts of both rope and wire are in contact with the chafe producing items. This will change the wear pattern of the whole assembly. It can prolong the life of the halyard and thus save money but must be done before the worn area has become weakened.

A good wire to rope splice should last the life of the halyard but it is worth examining all splices from time to time for signs of wear or movement. Such splices are not easy to do without a lot of practice. Since you are unlikely to get that practice, it is better to ask a professional rigger to make up any new halyards unless you are very sure that you can make a good job of it.

Kevlar

A modern material which is becoming more common is Kevlar. This is a man-made fibre which is immensely strong and virtually free from stretch. It is much lighter than steel but is more brittle than most man-made fibres. Its stiffness makes it difficult to handle and it cannot be spliced. It is however tough enough to take roll swages which is the normal way to end Kevlar halyards.

The outer, protective sheath will not be Kevlar, most probably polyester. It is important that this sheath is not breached because the strong core is easily damaged and weakened by chafe. Kevlar cannot be heat sealed, unlike most other man-made fibres. Good tight whipping, preferably sailmakers, of all ends is thus essential.

Nylon

Nylon is not practical for running rigging, even on the smallest boats, since it has too much stretch and should never be used.

Plaited rope

Plaited ropes are easier to handle than laid ropes although more expensive. They also generate more friction and so hold better on winches and cleats. Most jamming cleats are not really suitable for laid ropes at all because they tend to open the lays as they grip.

Braid on braid

If you can use only plaited rope for rigging you will find it well worthwhile. There are two kinds of braided line. The older style uses a twisted core with a braided outer sheath. The more modern and rather stronger version, called braid on braid, has a braided core and outer sheath. Brain on braid tends to have rather more stretch than cored rope.

Colour coding

Most modern ropes come in a variety of colours. It helps considerably in the deck work if you adopt a colour code system for your ropes. I personally do not like ropes in plain colours since they tend to fade, and show the fading, more quickly. Instead I prefer white rope with colour markers. Such rope is readily available from most chandlers.

There is no set pattern of colours to be used for halyards. A blue trace for headsails, red for spinnaker sheets and green for guys, plain white for the main and a yellow tracer for spar supports such as the topping lift is one such system adopted by a number of boat manufacturers. Red invariably fades to orange in time so avoid using orange as a key colour with red. The main thing is to create a system that avoids confusion.

Stopper balls

Stopper balls are used to prevent a swage or an eye fitting from pulling into a sheave block and causing damage. If these are in the same colours as their respective ropes, they can be used to identify the wire ends of combined halyards to complete the system. If sheets are in the same colours as halyards, perhaps with a different shade, it makes life in the cockpit much easier.

Sheaves and fairleads

Any change in the direction of line of a piece of running rigging will mean that a sheave (the roller in a block) is used. The life of the rope will be largely dependent on the quality, cleanliness and smooth running of these sheaves. They should be checked regularly with this in mind. When you do so, look for cracks as well as the general condition. A cracked sheave will shatter sooner or later if not replaced and, when it does, the wire will often jamb in the block. This can lead to a potentially dangerous situation quite apart from the inconvenience. More information on this subject can be found in Chapter 38.

Fairleads do just what they say. They lead the rope in the best possible line to the next point of contact. A sheave and block may be used, it may be a low friction rubbing contact or, as in the case of many mooring line fairleads, simply a cast fitting. In every case any roughness or lack of free running will be a source of wear and potential failure. Such defects also increase the effort needed to tighten the line. Keep this in mind when making your checks.

Tackle blocks

Whilst on this subject, it is worth remembering that a block and tackle with several sheaves may be used to provide a mechanical advantage. For example the mainsheet is often run through several sheaves to make it easier to take up the strain. To calculate the *theoretical* advantage, count the number of rope sections linking the pulleys. Any friction in these pulleys will severely reduce the mechanical advantage, sometimes to the point where little or no actual advantage is gained. This makes life a lot more difficult and increases the risk of breakage.

It is false economy to buy cheap blocks. Since quality varies a lot, even with good makes, a new block should always be checked for easy running before purchase. If it is even the slightest bit tight refuse it.

Check the maker's instructions regarding lubrication. Many modern blocks are so-called self-lubricating, that is, they are made from materials having particularly low friction properties. Oil or grease put on such bearings will often increase friction and can sometimes damage the material permanently. Salt can cause stiffness and thus, undue wear in sheaves. Make sure they are kept clean and free from salt deposits.

13   CARE OF RUNNING RIGGING

Care of your rigging is not just a matter of good seamanship. It will repay you handsomely by giving it a longer life and lessening the risks of failure. Care will also improve your sailing performance and make your sails more efficient.

Organising the surplus

Once a rope has been used to hoist something, a large bundle of it is left at the lower end. Particularly if all your lines are lead back to the cockpit, these need organising. Bags made of heavy fabric, fitted with drain holes and fixed to the vertical surfaces close to cleats are useful for this purpose, or you can use simple shockcord loops. Failing these, try coiling the spare ends and hanging them from the winches or cleats. Make sure that they can be freed off quickly and easily if need be and locate them so that they do not interfere with any cleat or winch which you may need in a hurry. A method of making up these coils is shown in Figure 13.1.

A rope not in use should always be coiled away. It may be a chore but it is worth it. Loose rope lying around is a hazard to crew movement. Also it can become tangled and fail to run out at the crucial moment or, catch on something or someone and be released inadvertently to cause an accident.

Spare ends at the mast can be stowed in the same way. If you use cloth bags attached to the mast, beware of poultice corrosion. This is a particular form of the electrolitic erosion mentioned in Chapter 11. It results from salt water being kept in contact with a break in the anodising for prolonged periods. It can result in damage amazingly quickly.

Before dropping a sail, the coiled surplus rope should be removed completely from its stowage so that it will run out freely. In the cockpit it helps to throw the surplus down the hatch before starting to lower so that it will run easily. Watch where you are throwing it though.

When control lines end at the mast, it is particularly important to use stopper knots in the free ends. These prevent the lines running out completely. If the line is lead through the mast, a simple figure of eight knot will suffice. If, however, halyards run outside the mast, it is a good idea to pass the free end through the back of the respective securing cleat before tying the figure of eight. This will prevent it from being able to run right up to the sheave at the top of the mast when released.

Fig 13.1 Stowage of tails of ropes in use

Grit in ropes

The life of any rope is much reduced if small particles of grit manage to work in between the fibres and cut them. With man-made fibres, which have less inherent friction and are continuous filaments, it is a particularly serious problem. This ingress of grit is much more likely if the rope is being trodden on. It is not so likely if the rope is stowed away properly when not actually in use.

Sand is the curse of the sailor and should be avoided like the plague. It can easily be brought aboard after a run ashore or by children who love it. Be sure to wash away any from feet or boots before coming aboard.

Reducing wear and damage

On many boats that one sees in harbours and on moorings, more wear is taking place on the running rigging during the time that the sails are stowed than it ever does whilst sailing. The 'marina symphony', that cacophony of slapping rigging that anyone who has spent a night in a marina knows, is a prime cause of wear.

Any item of running rigging not actually in use should be sweated up tight. Try to find a point of attachment for the lower ends of halyards so that they are not slapping the mast. Apart from the unwelcome noise that slapping halyards make, every noise represents a release of energy. That energy, not only keeps you awake; it may well be knocking the anodising off the mast, wearing away the sheaves, wearing the halyards itself or, more probably, a combination of all three.

Headsail halyards can be taken down to the stemhead fitting or to a strop on the pulpit. Spare halyards need a fixing point that will not cause them to rub against any sail that is hoisted. This can be achieved by making the attachment well forward on the pulpit. The main halyard should be taken to a point on the toe rail, if the boat has one, or to a short strop on the guard rail. Do not attach the snap shackle directly to the guard rails because this will cause wear on the shackle, the rail or both. Make sure that the attachment point is sufficiently far aft to avoid the halyard fouling the spreaders when it is taken up tight.

A suitable strop for securing halyard ends can be made from a short length of 6 or 8 mm laid rope short-spliced into a continuous loop. This can be left permanently on the pulpit or guard rail. Shackles can then be fastened to it. A loop avoids the attachment always being made in the same place which will shorten the life of the strop.

If your halyards are not fed through the mast you will need to have a means of pulling them away from it to silence them. This can be done with a sail tie to the shrouds or more easily, by making up a length of shockcord with a hook at each end that can be clipped to the shrouds. Use nylon hooks which will not damage the shrouds.

Jury halyards

A broken halyard at sea causes a problem as climbing the mast at sea and reaving a replacement is too hazardous for most people to attempt. A little advance thought can avoid this need. The spinnaker halyard on a fractional rig may serve to hoist a small jib. It will not work with a mast head rig, however, because the point of entry of the spinnaker halyard into the mast is well below the top of the forestay. Many yachts have twin foresail halyards so a spare is available. If not, it should be an easy matter to fit a spare.

The mainsail halyard seldom, if ever, has a duplicate but what about the topping lift? If you make your topping lift substantial enough to take the mainsail you then have a spare halyard. You will need to be able to hold the boom when the sail is lowered but this can often be done with a strop on to the backstay. If you use a backstay strop for a boom support do not forget to detach it when the sail is hoisted.

Sails can be damaged by the topping lift chafing on the leech of the main. It is possible to dope the leech stitching so that both its strength is increased and its friction lowered. Otherwise you will have to adjust or reposition the topping lift so that it is always clear of the sail.

It is the running rigging not in use that needs checking most at sea because it tends to be overlooked. Make sure that all of it is stowed tight and secure, that no chafe is occurring. Adjust the topping lift tension for different points of sailing to keep it free of the mainsail leech. Keep the free ends coiled and stowed.

Sheet leads

On a long leg off the wind it is often worth releading the genoa sheets so that they pass between rather than over, the guard rails. When close on the wind, a cruiser's headsail sheets are almost invariably inside the rails but off the wind they may be rubbing. A similar consideration applies to preventers. Do not forget that the track position may need altering with the wind strength and will almost certainly need it when the point of sailing changes.

If you cannot get a lead that is clear of the rails it may be possible to fit a length of tube on the rail for the sheet to roll over.

PART 3
Sail management

Life is much easier when sailing a yacht if you know what to do in a given situation. Whilst it is obviously impossible to provide textbook solutions to every sailing problem that can arise, this section is concerned with tried and tested practical techniques for running a yacht under sail. Some may well be familiar to you, others may not.

Any action you take will be easier if you have planned it in advance and effective planning requires practice. Especially with a new or inexperienced crew, practice gives a chance to make sure the plans will work when needed. It also provides an opportunity for refinements to be made at a non-crucial stage. It makes sense, for example, to practice reefing and sail changing, in relatively light winds at first. You can then work up to doing it in stronger winds so that you, and your crew, become confident. Any new ideas should always be tried first in easy conditions on *your* boat and with *your* crew.

14 LOOKING AFTER THE SAILS

Identification

Every new sail is supplied with its own bag for stowage. The bag is usually, but not always, marked with the identity of the sail it contains. If each bag is not clearly marked with the *name* of the sail that it should contain then this is well worth doing. Some sail makers use a colour code system. If so, the crew must learn it, but the name, 'Working Jib' or 'No 2 Genoa' etc, written on the bag, is far less likely to cause confusion. Some people also have the head, tack and clew named on each sail. This is a matter for you but is useful if you sail a lot with novices. For those who do much night sailing it is worth considering a touch system using buttons or leather tags.

Stowage

I prefer to have one locker used only for sails. This is not always possible but, if it can be done, it makes life so much easier. Sails should, when not in use, be stowed in the sail locker properly folded and bagged. If, for some reason, folding and bagging cannot be done immediately after use then the sail should be properly stowed as soon as possible.

Folding sails

When sails are to be put away in their bags, other than during a sail change, it is worth folding them properly (see Figure 14.1). Modern synthetic fibres are pretty robust and

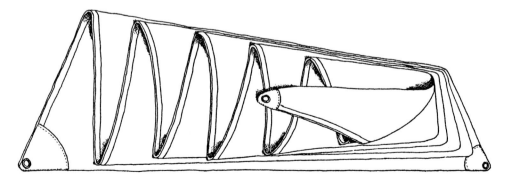

Fig 14.1 Folding a headsail

will stand up to a lot of abuse but, with care, they can still be made to give better service than they would do otherwise. Folding away is part of this care.

Another aspect is space. If you simply stuff your sails into the voluminous bags provided not only will they get badly creased but will also fill the bags! By the time you have four or five headsails stowed in this fashion, it becomes impossible to move down below. A properly folded sail lasts longer, is easier to handle, avoids twists on hoisting and takes less than a tenth of the space that a crushed one does. It may be a chore but it is a worthwhile one.

Flaking

Headsails without a luff wire should be flaked, concertina fashion, as in Figure 14.1, with the folds roughly parallel to the foot. Make the folds 70 to 100 cm wide and when you get to within about 2 metres of the head, fold the head back along the length of the flakes towards the tack. If the sail is then rolled from the clew it will make a neat bundle with the tack outside. Try to avoid the folds coming at exactly the same places each time since this can cause local weakening of the cloth.

Rolling

If a luff wire is fitted, it is best to roll the sail from the head to the tack keeping the coils large enough to prevent strain. Once the tack is reached the sail is then rolled towards the clew. The second roll must be kept sufficiently loose to prevent the luff wire from being kinked. Keep the tack at one end so that it can be got at without unrolling the sail.

Preparing to hoist

When preparing to hoist, from either method, the tack should be connected before unrolling the sail. With a flaked sail, a couple of turns unrolled will expose the head which can then be attached before going any further. It makes hoisting from a pitching foredeck much easier and there is much less risk of a foul up quite apart from the ease of stowage. Either way, the sail is joined to the boat before the wind has a chance to take over.

In light airs, there is a further bonus to be had from hoisting a properly flaked headsail. The only pronounced creases in the sail will be parallel to the air flow. This can make a big difference to performance when the wind is insufficient to blow the creases out. Racing crews please note.

Wet sails

Try to avoid stowing any sails when wet, particularly tightly rolled ones. If you do stow them wet they will be slow to dry and will start to smell. If left for long like this they will develop black mould spots which can be very difficult to remove (but see Cleaning, page 66).

Wet sails are best packed loosely in their bags and left to drain until they can be properly dried. If in harbour or at anchor, in wet or dry weather provided the wind is not strong, the bags can be stood on the foredeck and tied to the top guard rail. Rain will help to remove any salt from the sails. Provided there is some wind and it is not actually raining, sails left like this will dry fairly quickly.

The quickest way to dry a wet sail is, of course, to hoist and use it. Do not, however, be persuaded into the common practice of hoisting sails upside down to dry when on a mooring. With no sheets attached they will flog and wear even in a light wind. As a sailmaker friend once told me, the only people who gain from this practice are sailmakers. It causes considerable damage, particularly if the sail is wet with salt water, since the dry salt crystals can actually cut into the fibres of the moving fabric.

If possible, rinse salt-contaminated sails in fresh water and hang them up in still, dry, air to dry naturally. This is the ideal but is seldom practicable. On a good warm day it will do no harm to take your salt contaminated sails on to the pontoon or ashore and hose them down. They will soon dry again if stowed loosely on deck.

If you have the space you can take sails home to dry, either laid out on the lawn or hung up. When hanging sails to dry be sure to hang them from the luff, which is strengthened, to avoid stretching the cloth.

Sail care when laying up

When laying up at the end of a season, sails for storage must be thoroughly free from salt and perfectly dry. It is worth taking your sails ashore and having them cleaned, or at least washed, to remove salt and any stains. They should then be passed to a sailmaker for any small repairs to be carried out well before the new season starts.

Some sailmakers will provide winter storage, either free or very cheaply, if you ask them to do the repair work. This is well worth considering because you can be sure they will be kept properly. If you intend to store your sails yourself, make sure that they are both clean and dry before you put them away in a dry, warm and airy place for storage.

Cleaning

It is generally easier to ask your sailmaker to clean sails since he has the proper facilities. If however you wish to do the job yourself, or to remove particular stains, a few points are worth noting. It is best to try first to remove any stains with a neutral solvent such as a liquid detergent.

The following suggestions have worked for me and are given with the best intentions but do be cautious because many cleaning products contain toxic substances and sail materials vary.

Don't be tempted into ironing sails. Sail cloth melts at quite low temperatures and softens at about 70 degrees Celsius, well below the boiling point of water. Ironing seems an unnecessary risk to me when one mistake can destroy a sail for good.

Nylon should never be cleaned with a strongly acidic cleaner since it can damage the fibre. This means avoid acid on spinnakers. Terylene is equally vulnerable to alkali cleaners (most washing powders). Having said this, modern fibres are pretty robust and although it is best avoided, will take some abuse.

Bleach should never be used on nylon but a 10% solution, by volume, of ordinary domestic bleach will remove mildew stains from terylene sails without adverse effects. Make sure that bleach is left on no longer than necessary and that it, and any detergent cleansing substance, is thoroughly removed with plenty of fresh water before drying the sail.

Rust stains

The best thing I know for removing rust stains is oxalic acid. A solution no stronger than 5% by volume should be used but it can be mixed in fairly hot water. It works on copper and bronze stains too and will also take metallic stains out of gell coat. Remember it works by breaking down the metal so do not spill it on metal fittings. Most proprietary cleaners for this purpose contain oxalic acid.

Remember to remove all traces, from the cleaned area, afterwards with plenty of fresh water. Also, wash your hands well since it is poisonous.

Tar

Tar can often be softened with white spirit (turps substitute). The resultant mess can mostly be removed with liquid detergent applied neat or by rubbing with one of the hand cleaning gells such as Swarfega. Tar often leaves a pale yellow stained area on polyester, even after the most careful cleaning, so try to avoid enlarging the original stain.

Lubricating oil or grease

Too generous oiling of piston hanks is often the cause of oil stains. The oil part can be got out using detergent or gell but this will often leave metallic residue which may need the same treatment as for rust. Carbon-based grease should never be used since carbon deposits are extremely difficult to remove. Bear in mind that grease left on a sail will trap carbon particles from the air.

Adhesive

Old sail numbers once removed can leave traces of adhesive which will collect dirt and discolour. Acetone will remove old adhesive but should be used with care and in the open since the fumes are toxic.

Reefing ties and temporary stowage

Although headsails are, or should be, removed and stowed away below decks after each use, the mainsail is less frequently taken off the boom. It will therefore need lashing down and protecting when not actually in use. Not just at anchor or when moored up but also when motoring under no wind or in harbour. Sail ties; short lengths of webbing, tape or cord, are used to restrain all sails when they are down, or partly down, and not removed from the deck. Soft webbing is much kinder to sails than cordage.

All reefing pennants and the outhaul should be slack before the sail is left so that the fabric is not stretched unevenly.

Some people have those fiendish devices consisting of shockcord loops with a plastic ball at each end for use on the main. They are supposedly easy to use but the number of black eyes, broken teeth and the like that they cause make them hardly worthwhile. It is better to learn to tie reef knots from the beginning.

It is a good idea to have the mainsail ties joined at intervals on to a length of shockcord with a clip at each end. This can then be attached to the boom ends. It leaves the hands free and avoids loss of ties over the side. Make sure to fit enough ties, so that you have at least one for each reefing cringle plus one extra at each end. It makes reefing very much easier and the whole thing can be removed when full sail is used.

Tying in reefs

Whilst on the subject of reefing ties, the first tie to be secured on a slab-reefed main should always be the one at the outer end of the boom. This should pass through the cringle that carries the reefing pennant. If this is not done, and the pennant should break or be accidentally released, the sail will snap back to the next tie and this can cause the sail to rip at the reefing cringle where there is no reinforcement. Such an accident is costly and could be dangerous.

Securing headsails

Headsails must be securely lashed if they are to be stowed on the guard rails. It is worth taking the trouble to roll them tightly into the foot before lashing (see Figure 14.2). If the sail is roughly flaked as it comes down, this job is made much easier and is well worth the trouble. The force of a wave hitting a stowed sail can be enormous and, if it is not properly secured, the sail can be damaged or even carried away. For quick stowage short lengths, about half a metre long each, of 6 or 8 mm shockcord can be permanently fitted to the upper guard rail. The free end is fitted with a nylon hook. This device can be quickly passed round a rolled sail and clipped back on to the rail. For a longer term job it is worth augmenting the shockcord with proper webbing sail ties, however.

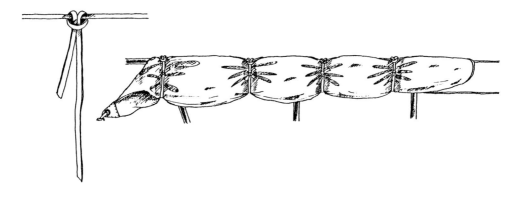

Fig 14.2 Stowing a headsail on the rails

Loose ties should first be attached to the top rail, using a larkshead knot, before securing the sail. They will not then blow away when untied and can be left *in situ*, whilst the sail is hoisted, to be retrieved later. If the larkshead is tied with odd length tails, the longer end can be brought under the rolled sail so that the securing reef knot is tied on top where it is easier to untie.

Foredeck netting

The fitting of netting around the pulpit and back to the shrouds is often done to help prevent lowered headsails from falling overboard. It can be useful, particularly when a headsail foil is used. I find, however, that it restricts movement on and off the boat when coming to or leaving a pontoon. Also, the ropes used for mooring and the crew can get caught up in it.

Fitting it round the entire guard rail is a sensible precaution if you regularly have small children or toddlers aboard however, since it converts the entire deck area into a giant playpen. In such cases the safety of the child outweighs any inconvenience caused.

Sheet stowage

It is an all too common practice to 'store' spare sheets, spinnaker guys and so on, in a heap at the bottom of the cockpit locker until needed. This means that someone has to hang head down in the hole sorting out the knitting. A much better practise is to organise the locker with shelves or hanging space for these items so that they can be coiled away and neatly stowed.

The same applies of course to things like mooring warps, fenders and preventers. It is quite amazing how much more space one seems to have and how much easier it is to get what you need quickly when cockpit lockers are properly organised. This repeats advice given in Part 1 but it is worth repeating.

15 REEFING AND SAIL CHANGES

When the wind strength makes the boat over-canvased on any point of sailing, reefing and or sail changes will have to be considered.

Slab reefing

A few years ago, many mainsails were reefed by rolling on to the boom. The tendency lately has been a return to slab or jiffy reefing. Such reefing usually has control lines as an integral part of the system. This method is both quicker than rolling and more efficient because what is left of the sail sets better.

When you have been obliged to reef, drive is reduced; this at a time when the sea state makes progress more difficult. Safety may depend on your ability to claw your way out of trouble so do not reef too much too soon. It is important that the sail left in use is working efficiently. With slab reefing the reefed mainsail will often set as well as full sail.

Roller reefing

Several things conspire to prevent a roller reefed mainsail from setting well. First, as you roll, the extra thickness at the leech spirals along the boom towards the mast whilst the luff rope and extra cloth in the luff tend to bunch up at the gooseneck Outhaul tension is difficult to maintain. These things, and the fact that the sail is not cut flat, often produce a wrinkled sail and a droopy boom, especially when the sail is deeply reefed. Having the free end of the boom low down in the cockpit is the last thing you need in a blow.

A partial solution to the problem is to increase the thickness of the roll at the outer end by rolling in a sail bag or by taking a large fold in before starting the roll. The latter is more effective but is hard to do in a blow. The sail is therefore less than fully efficient unless reefed by a very well practiced crew.

With reefs rolled on the boom, the kicking strap cannot be directly connected to it. To get round this you must either roll in a sail bag or use a boom vang, consisting of a prepared length of broad webbing with a cringle at one end for attachment of the kicker. A special claw saddle is sometimes used but these can damage the cloth.

Do not be tempted to sail without a kicking strap when reefed. Off the wind this would allow the boom to lift which can cause the gooseneck fitting to shatter, quite apart from making it impossible to set the sail properly.

In-mast and in-boom reefing

Systems are now available which reef the sail either into, or just behind, the mast. A good deal of experiment is still going on in this area. With the luff supported only at its ends great tension is needed to maintain the luff shape. The extra tension increases the compression loading on the mast. Reefing into the boom is also available which avoids this problem. With either system, sails need to be cut much flatter than is necessary or slab reefing.

A few electrically operated systems are marketed. These seem to me to be fraught with potential dangers since a failure could leave one with a sail set which could not be lowered.

Mainsail reefing techniques

Precise methods depend on the particular rig but some general points can be made. First the drive must be taken out of the sail. This is done by easing the sheet and the kicking strap. Before the halyard can be released, the weight of the boom must be transferred to the topping lift which must be well secured.

If it is normally held by an open jambing cleat try to secure it to a horned cleat also. When the sail is on the way down, crew are going to be standing on the coachroof gathering it in. They will thus only have the boom to hang on to for balance. The steadiness of the boom will depend on the topping lift pulling up and the mainsheet pulling down. If either comes free the boom will swing about so make sure this cannot happen.

It is not necessary to come head to wind in order to reef. It will often be more comfortable for the deck crew if the boat is held as close on the wind as possible whilst maintaining some drive in the headsail. This provides a much more stable platform from which to work and also allows the helmsman to maintain control.

A sail that is to be slab or jiffy reefed will only need sufficient sail lowering for the luff reefing cringle to be attached to the ramshorn hook on the boom. Once this is done, the halyard crew should sweat the halyard up tight again as quickly as possible. The reefing pennant, a line rove through the corresponding cringle in the leech, is fed through the boom in order that it can be hauled in, either at the mast or led back to the cockpit. Once the halyard is tight again the reefing pennant can be winched in as the main sheet is eased. It is particularly important that the mainsail is not driving at all whilst the reefing pennant is being taken in. It is also important that the boat is not put through the wind.

To neaten up, the slab which now hangs below the boom, is rolled into itself and tied to the boom out of the way. This last is not essential but it does make a neater job and reduces windage and wear on the cloth. A mainsail which is set on track slides, although it sets less well, is easier to manage than one which runs in a luff groove because the luff remains captive. Once again the crew member controlling the halyard must work with the deck crew for smooth and safe lowering. The lower slides will need to be removed from the mast track when reefing. Make sure that the track gate is closed after this has been done to avoid the whole lot running out when the sail is eventually lowered.

I like to make sure that a sail tie is secured through the reefing pennant leech cringle *before* the topping lift is eased and the mainsheet and kicker tightened home. The idea of putting this tie through the pennant cringle is that, should the pennant break, the reef is still held and damage to the sail (as mentioned on page 68) is avoided. The remaining ties can then be used to tidy the sail. The kicking strap should be tightened up again at this point, whilst still on a close-hauled course.

When the mainsail is roller reefed it will generally be necessary for one crew member to lower the main halyard whilst maintaining a slight pressure on it. At the same time, another member of the crew rolls the sail round the boom, taking the track slides out as required and dressing the luff on to the boom.

Headsail reefing

Roller reefing of headsails has become very popular over recent years and many of the early problems, most of which resulted from poor mechanical construction and a failure in awareness of the forces involved, have been overcome. Such reefing is still a compromise however.

Systems, though broadly similar, differ in detail. A large genoa cut rather flatter than usual is fitted with a bolt rope and this is fed into a slotted tube. The tube rides on the forestay and can be rotated round it, usually by means of a drum at the lower end. The sail is thus caused to wrap round the tube so that the area exposed to the wind can be continuously varied. From full genoa to storm sail simply by pulling on a line! It sounds too good to be true and it is.

What are the problems? A big genoa is a light air sail. If it is to work properly it must be cut from light cloth. It also needs to be cut full so that it holds the wind. A storm jib must take anything the elements throw at it. It needs to be cut from heavy, strong cloth and to be kept as flat as possible. It also needs to be set with its tack low on the forestay so that its heeling moment is kept down. No single sail can do both jobs well.

When a sail is to be rolled round a spar it must be cut flat if it is to retain its sailing ability when part rolled. Its foot must be low also because, as it is rolled, the tack will climb towards the centre of the spar. When it has only a small area exposed, the sail is working high up on the forestay and in front of it is a thick roll of cloth acting as a spoiler. The sheet lead also poses a problem. The point of attachment must be moved further and further back as the sail is rolled in. The roller reefing headsail is thus a compromise and, like all compromises, does not do as well as the real thing in any function.

It has become popular because of the ease with which it can be altered and, when short handed, there is no denying that it is a useful idea. I would not, however, have a rolling headsail without a separate storm sail that can be hoisted totally independently of the rolling sail without having to remove the latter. In practice this means an extra forestay either beside the original or perhaps a special inner forestay that can be quickly put into position when needed.

With a cutter rig the foresail can be fully furled leaving the staysail only for use in a strong blow. This is a big advantage.

Changing a headsail

Only in racing is it really worth hoisting one headsail inside another when making a headsail change. For cruising it is best to lower and secure the existing sail before attempting to raise a new one. To save time, have the new one ready on the foredeck. Make sure that both sail and sail bag are secured. It is usually easier to secure the tack of the new sail first so this should be the first corner to come out of the bag.

Preparation

If your sails are fitted with piston hanks, the sail should next be clipped on to the forestay, otherwise either lash it temporarily to the rail or leave the bulk of it in the bag. The lazy sheet can now be removed from the working sail and attached to the clew of the new sail ready for hoisting. This saves time between sails. Make sure, though, that the helmsman will not be tacking before the new sail has been made ready to hoist.

There is no need to come up into wind to change a headsail. To make life easier for the foredeck crew, either ease the main to reduce the angle of attack and thus the heel, or come closer on to the wind which will do the same thing. As the speed drops on lowering the headsail the apparent wind will move aft again. Remember we are not racing here.

When the foredeck crew is ready, the cockpit crew should ease out, but not fully release, the working headsail sheet before lowering the halyard. This takes the strain off the sail. Failure to do so can pull the luff right out of a foil or put unnecessary strain on piston hanks when the tension comes of the halyard. Leaving the sheet attached and just pulling makes it much easier to get the sail down without its going over the side. If the sheet has been eased first, the moment the halyard is freed off, the drive will go out of the sail and it will be a simple matter to pull it down at the luff.

Pulling down the sails must always be done at the luff, never at the leech. This mistake is made far too often. The luff is supported by a wire, tape or rope, whereas the leech is not. Pulling on the leech, particularly when the wind is flogging the sail, can put sufficient strain on it to cause permanent stretching of the cloth. It can also cause the untensioned luff to pull out of a foil if one is fitted. This causes damage to both sail and foil.

Stretch in the leech will prevent the sail from setting properly giving rise to leech flutter, often called 'motor-boating' because it sounds like a two-stroke engine at high revolutions. This is both irritating and distracting. It is also inefficient and increases sail wear dramatically.

Time to change

The decision as to when the change can be started must be made by the helmsman. The halyard however, should only be raised or lowered at the direction of the foredeck crew, both when dropping and hoisting a sail. Do not forget to release the sheet once the head of the sail is within reach of the foredeck crew since this will make the job of sheet transfer a lot easier.

If the headsails run in a foil it is often best to leave the new sail in its bag until the first sail is down and secured. Once the old sail is lowered secure it temporarily to the rail but do not disconnect the tack yet. Unhank the luff or slide it out of the foil and clip the head, together with the halyard, to the corner of the pulpit. Then secure the sail temporarily with shockcords or ties. Remove the second sheet and transfer it to the new sail. Now transfer the halyard to the new sail and get it hoisted. This gives the helmsman more control again.

Once the new sail is working, you can finish either securing or removing and bagging, the old sail. Be sure that the correct bag is used or you will get into a hopeless muddle.

Storm sails

A yacht that is to be used for anything more than local day sailing should have the means to reduce sail for storm conditions. The odd thing is, although many if not most boats have storm jibs, a large proportion of skippers have never tried them out. This is a failing. If the boat has a storm trisail it is even more essential that the crew know how to use it, well before they have to.

Storm jib

A storm jib should not be *just* the smallest sail you have. It should be specially made for the job. It will be cut flat, from heavy cloth and will usually have a wire luff. If you have a headsail foil you will need either a second forestay or lashing cringles fitted along the luff. In a full gale a storm sail can pull out of a foil unless well secured.

Practise hoisting the storm jib in a moderate wind and find the correct track point for the fairlead block. It should be such that the sail has almost even tension on both foot and leech when sheeted as flat as possible. A downward bias of about five degrees will prevent leech flutter from causing damage but don't overdo it. Make a note of the track position or mark the track. It is sometimes possible to sheet the storm headsail so that it is self tacking and this is worth trying.

Trisails

In storm conditions it must be possible to reduce the area of the mainsail to no more than 30% of the full sail value. If you cannot do this by deep reefing the standard main you will need a trisail.

Some people argue that a trisail should always be used in gale conditions since it is made for the job. This view, which can be justified at first sight in theory, neglects some practical considerations. In order to hoist a trisail the main must first be lowered and stowed. It has to be removed from the luff groove altogether if the sail has a bolt rope fed directly into the groove. It will also need to be fully or partly removed if you have track slides. That is, unless you have either a separate trisail track or a gate in the main track sufficiently high to allow the mainsail slides to be dropped below it. (see Figure 16.1).

Fig 16.1 Trisail track and switch

Removal of the luff of a main from the track in a gale is a task not to be undertaken lightly. A deep reef will be both easier and safer. If you have a trisail, consider what you would have to do on your particular boat in order to hoist and use it.

Let's assume for now that you have a trisail and can use it. The advantages are great. The sail is like a small main with the greater part of the foot cut away in a wedge so that the clew is well below the tack level when it is hoisted. It is set like a headsail, not on the boom. When it is used, the boom should be lowered and lashed down; the mainsail being either removed or firmly lashed to the boom. The topping lift must be detached from the boom and tacked down well aft so that it cannot foul the trisail.

The mainsheet is seldom used on a trisail. Instead the clew is fitted with two sheets, which should be led through substantial blocks, attached well aft to the toerails if no specific strong points are provided. The control needed is minimal. The spinnaker winches can be used for tensioning but the sail should be set flat and cleated home. It will be self-tacking.

The method described will differ in detail from boat to boat. In any event it is only common sense to be sure of the correct method to be used on your boat before you need it in earnest. The only way to do this is to try it out. You will have to do it in a wind strong enough to keep the boat going and under control with the reduced sail area.

PART 4
Weather

The biggest single influence on any sailor's course of action is the weather. It determines his decision whether to leave port or to stay at home. It will influence his choice of destination and often dictate it. The yacht's speed, the amount of sail it carries, its comfort, stability and, ultimately its safety are all influenced by the weather. Without a reasonably thorough knowledge of how to interpret, understand and anticipate weather patterns no one should be called a 'Yachtmaster'.

One needs to know in advance, the probable direction, duration and intensity of winds and the degree of visibility likely at different times. To do this takes certain skills. Many excellent books have been written on the subject some of which are mentioned in the bibliography to this volume.

The subject is covered in this section with broad brush strokes only. A general idea of how the weather is caused and how to anticipate it is given. For the finer details the reader is recommended to look to one or other of the authorities quoted and to progress from there.

16   THE FUNDAMENTALS

As the moon is the principal influence on the world's tides, so the weather is influenced by the sun. It is the heating effect of the sun on the atmosphere, the land masses and the seas that sets up global winds. These winds, moving over both sea and land, over polar ice-caps and tropical deserts, are the basic causes of the effects we experience in the atmosphere.

Three closely linked physical fundamentals are involved. These are: pressure, temperature and humidity. It is the changes in these three that drive the motors of the winds.

Pressure

Pressure within the atmosphere is not uniform. The atmosphere is held close to the Earth by gravity. Each particle of gas in the atmosphere is pulled towards the Earth and would actually reach it if it were not for many other particles in the way. Although each particle of a particular gas has the same mass, those lower down have the ones above pushing on them. The closer one gets to the surface of the Earth, the more the pressure increases because the density increases.

Imagine the situation in a rugby scrum that collapses. All the forwards are more or less the same weight but the chap at the top of the heap has only gravity pressing on him. The poor unfortunate at the bottom has gravity plus several other players on top of him so he experiences a much greater pressure than the one at the top. Those in between experience different pressures depending on how near the top they are, and thus, how many more bodies they have above them. The scrum is a lot more dense at the bottom of the pile than at the top. This is what it is like in the atmosphere. There is a steady increase in pressure as one gets closer to the Earth.

Atmospheric pressure is measured in bars. One bar is far too big a unit however so the figures quoted on weather maps are in millibars ie thousandths of a bar.

Temperature

Now consider temperature. Like the pressure, the temperature of air is not uniform with height. Instead it decreases as height increases. This is because temperature decreases as pressure decreases and increases as pressure increases. Have you ever noticed how the pump gets hot as you pump up the pressure in a bicycle tyre or a ball?

We all know that hot air rises. That is how a hot air balloon works. Thus the warm air near the Earth's surface will try to rise through the cooler air above.

Let's come back to the scrum analogy. Our chap at the bottom doesn't like being squashed. He struggles and gets heated under the crush, eventually he rises to the top. If the pile lasts long enough, another individual takes his place and gets squashed and heated in turn. The whole mass is in constant motion.

Humidity

Humidity relates to the amount of water, in vapour form, that a given mass of air can hold. This is a function of temperature. The hotter the air the more water it can hold. As a mass of hot, moist air cools, the water forms into droplets and falls out of the air. In the atmosphere this eventually becomes rain.

Humidity is a relative thing and is given as a percentage of the moisture that a mass of air contains in relation to the mass that it could contain at a given temperature. Thus, 100% humidity indicates that the air is saturated. Any cooling at this point will cause water to condense out.

The atmosphere

Pressure, temperature and humidity in the atmosphere are interdependent. If one changes, the others tend to change also. The system is dynamic since the sun provides an input in the form of heat which changes the temperature.

17 GLOBAL WINDS

The sun does not heat the atmosphere evenly over the whole globe, of course. It provides more energy at the equator and less at the poles so the air towards the equator gets hotter. This means that at the poles there is always a mass of cold air falling and becoming more dense whilst lower down, towards the temperate latitudes, there is a mass of hotter rising air. Pressure at these latitudes is lower so the colder, dense air moves in.

A general movement of air from the poles towards the temperate zones thus exists at the surface. This creates an air stream which is southward in the northern hemisphere and northward in the southern hemisphere.

The polar wind does not extend right down to the equator for several reasons. Instead, this air begins to heat up enough to rise at about the 60° latitude mark and a stream flowing in the opposite direction meets it. Figure 17.1 shows the situation in the northern hemisphere down to the equator. A similar pattern exists in the southern hemisphere but with all directions reversed.

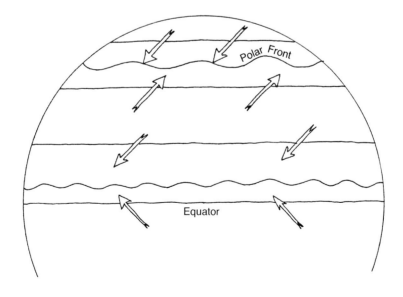

Fig 17.1 Northern hemisphere prevailing winds

Earth rotation

You will notice in the diagram that the winds do not flow due north or due south but at an angle.

The winds are formed by the forces described above but are modified by a further force. The Earth rotates on its axis in a direction from west to east. The atmosphere sits all round the Earth but is only tenuously attached to it. It is this that causes the winds to appear to flow at an angle. In fact we, as observers on the Earth, are moving beneath the winds as they move N or S. They are only dragged a little in an easterly direction by the friction at the surface. As we shall see later, the friction layer only extends to about 600 metres above the surface when it is flat.

Looking down on the North Pole one would see the Earth's rotation as anti-clockwise whilst looking in the opposite direction at the South Pole the rotation is seen as clockwise. This accounts for the apparent reversal of the winds in the two hemispheres.

Coriolis effect

A further effect needs considering at this point. If you were to stand on the Geostatic North Pole you would rotate but not go anywhere. If you moved 2 metres away you would move round the Pole on a circle of radius 2 m and thus move about 12.3 m with each revolution. At the equator the radius of the Earth is about 6,380 km so the distance moved during one revolution is about 40,000 km.

At the Pole all your motion would be rotational whilst at the equator you would have no rotation; the movement would be all linear. The rotational force must therefore decrease as one moves away from the Poles towards the equator. It is this effect that makes the bath water flow in the opposite direction in Australia to that in England and is the key to the behaviour of depressions discussed in the next chapter.

Polar Front

Where the Polar Easterlies meet the Temperate Westerlies a region called the Polar Front exists. This region moves a little with the seasons. Northern Europe sits astride the front and it is this fact that largely accounts for the unpredictable weather there. The polar winds are much colder than the temperate winds and it is this temperature difference that provides the energy for the depressions that are so common in these latitudes.

Air masses

The major movements of air are classified by where they come from and the route by which they arrive. In North European waters there are four masses that influence our weather. These are, from the north, Polar Maritime (mP) and Polar Continental (cP) depending on whether they come from over sea or over land. Similarly winds from the south are either Tropical Maritime (mT) or Tropical Continental (cT).

Pressure systems

From Figure 17.2 one might expect that all the winds around the United Kingdom would be either cP or mT winds. These global winds, however, are modified by pressure systems. Most of the time our winds are maritime in origin. This is why we tend to get what we feel is more than our share of rain. It is also, though, why we tend not to get extremes of temperature.

A pressure system is an area, often quite large, in which the mean pressure is either lower or higher than the surrounding air. The Siberian High and the Azores High are examples. The former gives us unusually cold winters while the latter is responsible for those elusive hot dry summers we sometimes experience.

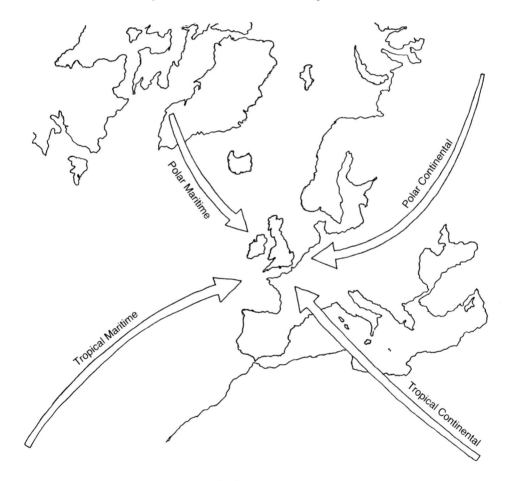

Fig 17.2 British Isles major wind influences

18 STRUCTURE OF DEPRESSIONS

The most common pressure systems that affect us are the lows that come sweeping across the Atlantic bringing rain and strong winds. Depressions (lows) are usually smaller systems than anticyclones (highs) and thus last for shorter periods but with greater intensity. Unfortunately we experience many more lows than highs.

What is a depression?

In the simplest meteorological terms a depression is an area of the atmosphere in which the pressure is lower at a given altitude than the pressure in the surrounding air at the same altitude. How this happens is complex but not too difficult to understand.

Most of our depressions develop across the Polar Front (Figure 17.1). When the two masses of air meet they have very different temperatures. The air coming from the south is a lot warmer and thus less dense than the cold polar air. As the masses come together a wedge of warm air gets scooped northwards into the colder air in much the same way that the surface of the sea is scooped up into the air above to form a wave.

The Coriolis force means that the area nearer the North Pole has a greater rotational, and smaller linear, moment than that lower down. If you like, the bottom of the wedge is moving faster than the top. The whole mass starts to spin. In the middle the warm less dense air produces an area of low pressure. One might expect the surrounding air to rush in and fill this space but the spin effect prevents this happening.

Think of a roulette wheel. When the wheel is spun, the ball moves away from the low point in the centre and rises up the high sides. This is what happens in the depression. The mass of swirling air is carried along by the prevailing wind, usually eastward, and the low centre does not fill whilst the spin continues.

Cloud is always associated with these spinning masses since the warm air in the wedge was mT air and thus contained a lot of moisture. The high humidity means that water will condense out as the air mass cools. It is this water that forms the clouds. Satellite pictures, now commonly shown on television, show the swirling mass of cloud clearly.

Isobars

A depression is a three dimensional phenomenon. From a point in space it appears as a spinning cloud formation, like a Catherine wheel. It can be, and usually is, represented

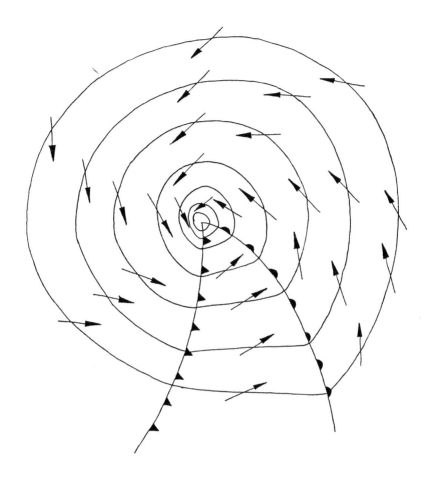

Fig 18.1 Plan view of a depression showing fronts, isobars and wind directions

diagrammatically as a series of equal pressure contours called isobars. These lines are the equivalent of height contour lines on a map or depths on a chart.

Isobars are normally drawn at 2 mb intervals. The distance between successive lines therefore gives an indication of the steepness of the pressure gradient and thence the wind that can be anticipated. Figure 18.1 shows such a diagram. Notice that the wind arrows drawn on it indicate that the winds are blowing in towards the centre at an angle. The arrows show the direction at sea level. At a height of about 600 m the friction effect of the water surface is gone and the arrows for winds at this height would be nearly parallel to the isobars.

The friction layer
Within the friction layer, the rotating winds of the depression are slowed down. This disturbs the equilibrium of the system and the winds start to move in towards the centre. It is this slowing that eventually causes the depression to fill. Think of the roulette wheel again; as the wheel slows the ball comes back towards the centre.

Sectors and fronts

A few more terms used in forecast information need explanation. The wedge of warm air mentioned at the beginning of this section is called the warm sector but this is relative and means only that the air on either side of it is cooler. This larger segment is called the cold sector.

Where two sectors meet is called a front. The warm front is the one at which a stationary observer will pass from cold sector to warm as the system passes over him whilst the cold front is that at the end of the warm sector. The warm front is always the one to the east of an east-going depression. In the northern hemisphere this is the usual direction of travel. The reverse is true in the southern hemisphere.

Troughs and ridges

A trough is an area where, to a static observer, the pressure falls then rises again fairly quickly. Its equivalent in land terms is a valley. A ridge is the reverse of a trough and uses the same name as its land equivalent. Fronts always result in troughs and are sometimes referred to as such.

The vertical plane

The slowing effect of the friction layer is important to understand since it is the cause of most of the effects experienced in a depression. Figure 18.2 shows a cross-section through both sides of the warm sector of a depression.

Notice how the fronts lean in the direction of movement of the system. This is due to the friction layer. The cold front leans at a steeper angle than does the warm front. It also moves faster and, if the depression lasts long enough, will eventually catch up with the warm front. This happens first near the centre of the depression where the warm sector is narrowest.

Occlusion

When the warm and cold fronts combine they are said to be occluded. By this time the warm air has been used up and the depression should be filling and becoming much less vigorous.

Intensity

The intensity of a depression, and thus how vigorous it is, depends on the temperature gradient between the two air masses initially. When there is little initial mixing the depression will tend to be *very* deep and *very* vigorous. It will be a small intense depression. An intense depression has *very* strong winds associated with it and can do considerable damage. This was what happened in NW France and SE England on October 16th 1987.

Depression weather

So much information is available about specific weather that it would be superfluous to repeat it here. I will simply show why certain inferences can be drawn from the existence of a depression if one knows its path and dimensions.

Fig 18.2 A cross-section of a depression in the vertical plane cutting both fronts

Consider again Figure 18.1 and 18.2. The warm sector consists of a mass of warm moist air which is both rising and cooling. Ahead of this sector is a mass of cool air which, if anything, is warming. This air may be wet or dry.

The warm front

We can be sure that the air in the warm sector is wet and condensing out moisture to form clouds. Remember where this air originated.

Since the top of the wedge advances more rapidly than the bottom, any observer at sea level will be under a part of the warm front before he is into it. As the clouds within the warm sector will cast a shadow over our observer, he will experience a reduction in temperature before the warm front arrives.

The ability of the air ahead of the warm front to hold moisture will depend on its origin but we can be sure that this ability will reduce the closer one comes to the front. In addition, the part of the warm front above this air is rising and cooling. As the front approaches, therefore, we might expect rain. It may be only light at first but will increase as the front gets closer. With the increased humidity experienced we can expect visibility to reduce.

Long before the front arrives the very top of the wedge will be into the upper atmosphere. Here it will catch the high speed winds and any cloud in it will be dispersed or streamed into thin wisps. Our observer will see this as high altitude haze or thin streamers of cloud downwind or both. Thus altostratus or altocirrus clouds will indicate the approach of a warm front.

As the observer comes closer to the wedge the cloud base will move down so that the cloud is now forming in less strong winds. The cloud will thus appear lower and will be thicker and less broken. It will be seen as cumulus, small as yet, but by the time the rain starts the cloud layer may well be complete.

Between fronts
On the arrival of the warm front the observer will be in or under the cloud and visibility will be poor or, at best, moderate. It will be raining steadily now.

The wind may have been steadily veering as the front approached with a more distinct veer when it actually arrived. The temperature will probably have dropped and then risen again as the front arrived. The wind velocity may have decreased a little after the front passed but will be slowly increasing now as the isobars close up.

The cold front
What can the observer expect as the cold front gets closer? Above this front will be clear air. As it gets closer the cloud layer will be thinner and may even become thin enough for the rain to stop. The pressures at the front form a trough so we can expect a temporary drop as the front passes. The isobars are quite close together both at and behind the cold front so the wind will increase. A large veer will take place because the isobars behind the front have changed direction quite a lot.

Behind the front the clouds will be broken but some may be thick cumulus. Sometimes they may build to thunder clouds. Heavy squalls may occur as these clouds pass over. The stronger, higher winds will be forced down in the squalls so they will run more nearly parallel to the isobars. Thus the strong gusts will result in a rapid but temporary veer.

After the cold front
As the cold front moves away the clouds will become more scarce and smaller until the sky is clear. The temperature will have dropped as the front passed over. The observer is now in the cold sector. After the strong squally period, the winds will gradually decrease. If no further depression is on the way we may expect the wind to back slowly.

The effects of land
Since the friction layer is quite thin, you would expect that anything that sticks up into it will modify the behaviour of pressure systems. This is true and even quite low hills can have a marked effect.

Diversion
In general, the moving air masses take the line of least resistance and so are diverted along channels and around land masses. A small shift, in global terms, of the Polar Front can change the weather in Britain out of all proportion. In the summer of 1986 for example it moved about 80 miles south. This resulted in the usual summer depressions that are normally diverted north round Ireland being diverted south instead. The result was a dreadful summer in England out of all proportion to the global shift.

The other factor relating to land is that of temperature. Land is a much worse conductor of heat than water though a better absorber. The sea thus acts like a huge storage heater. It takes a great deal of heat to change its temperature. This means that the land warms up much more quickly in the absence of cloud and also cools much more rapidly. The sea temperature may change only a few degrees between summer and winter whilst that of the land may frequently exceed this seasonal change between one night and the next day.

Sea breeze

The effect of these differences is to create a local temperature gradient similar to the global ones. This is most commonly seen as a sea breeze in summer. This breeze blows onshore by day reaching its maximum by mid afternoon and occasionally reversing at night to create a much weaker offshore wind a short while after nightfall. The offshore breeze rarely occurs in European latitudes. From the sailor's point of view this is important because a sea breeze can cause quite strong winds close to shore on a warm afternoon.

19 WEATHER FORECASTS

Official forecasts in general, and shipping forecasts in particular, are the basic sources which sailors use to make weather decisions. These decisions will be modified by local knowledge and experience but the forecast information will certainly be the major influence.

In the last chapter we gained a general picture of the forces involved together with the effects they produce. These general ideas are applied to specific situations. In particular they are used to interpret the kind of information you receive in a shipping forecast. It is in the use of such information that you can anticipate what is likely to happen over the next few hours or sometimes days.

Forecast periods

Forecasting is not an exact science. If it was life would be very different for all of us, but there are far too many variables for it to be exact. It is more an art; the art of the possible perhaps. Most of the time, even in the unsettled weather patterns of northern Europe, it is possible to make reasonably accurate predictions over six to twelve hours and to a lesser extent over the next twelve.

Beyond a twenty four hour period the predictions become fairly unreliable except in very settled conditions. That is not to say they are no use. The general pattern with the positions of fronts, depressions, highs and so on will be there. The inaccuracies come more in trying to predict the size, intensity, movements and timing of the various influences at a local level.

The form of the forecast

In this part of the world the form used to transmit a forecast is the same whatever country is broadcasting it. This is useful when trying to receive a forecast given out in another language or by someone who does not naturally speak English. English is the official language of international telecommunications but not all weather broadcasts are made in it.

Shipping forecasts

These are the special forecasts intended for sailors. Each broadcast starts with the time of origin of the forecast. It is important to note this time because, when interpreting the information, it will be necessary to advance the positions of any systems from then to get the current situation. The information from coastal stations will be for a different time to that of the area forecasts. Since this difference may be several hours it is important to note also. The two times must be advanced to one common time to make any useful predictions.

Gale warnings

The first weather information given is a list of the sea areas in which winds in excess of force 7 on the Beaufort scale may be expected during the forecast period. It is useful as a warning but the information will be repeated in detail for each sea area. The general synopsis which follows is more important.

Recording the forecasts

Maps of the forecast areas are available together with a grid of boxes to be filled in. Use of one of these is almost essential, unless you are very experienced, as the forecast is broadcast by the BBC at conversation speed. Figure 19.1 illustrates the form available from the RYA.

Standard abbreviations are published but are not vital to learn. You can easily develop your own, but whatever system you use must be easy to read afterwards and should be totally unambiguous. The following table gives some of the more useful standard symbols.

Meteorological terms and symbols

Beaufort scale

	Term used	Velocity	Sea condition
0	Calm	< 1kn	Mirror-like sea.
1	Light air	1 to 3	Ripples only in glassy sea.
2	Light breeze	4 to 6	Small wavelets with glassy look.
3	Gentle breeze	7 to 10	Large wavelets, a few crests break.
4	Mod. breeze	11 to 16	Small waves, some white horses.
5	Fresh breeze	17 to 21	Pronounced waves, many white horses and some spray possible.
6	Strong breeze	22 to 27	Large waves, many foam crests, spray.
7	Near gale	28 to 33	Tumbled sea, breaking waves with foam.
8	Gale	34 to 40	High waves, breaking crests, much foam.
9	Severe gale	41 to 47	High breaking waves with rolling tops, constant spray affecting visibility.

Pressure changes

Term used	Change
Steady	Less than 0.1 mb in last 3 hours
Rising/falling slowly	0.1 to 1.5 mb in last 3 hours
Rising/falling	1.6 to 3.5 mb in last 3 hours
Rising/falling quickly	3.6 to 6.0 mb in last 3 hours
Rising/falling rapidly	more than 6 mb in last 3 hours
Now rising/falling	trend reversed in last 3 hours

Visibility

Term used	Range of visibility
Fog	less than 1 km
Mist or haze	1 km to 2 nm
Poor	1 km to 2 nm
Moderate	2 to 5 nm
Good	more than 5 nm

Weather

Term used	Symbol Beaufort	plotting	Meaning
Rain	r	.	continuous falling droplets
Drizzle	d	,	fine droplets slow falling
Snow	s	★	crystaline ice flakes
Hail	h	△	ice pellets
Shower	p	▽	intermittent precipitation
Thunder	th	↖	electrical cloud discharge
Squall	q	↡	short term strong wind
Mist	m	=	suspended moisture particles
Haze	z	∞	suspended dust particles
Fog	f	≡	as mist but more dense
Precipitation			water particles state undefined

Note: Capital letters are used to indicate 'heavy' rain etc.

Wind: Strength is given in Beaufort notation. Direction is given in cardinal points and half points from the source.

Sea State: numerically stated in terms of wave height in metres.

Calm	less than 0.1	Smooth 0.1 to 0.5	
Slight	0.5 to 1.25	Moderate 1.25 to 2.5	
Rough	2.5 to 4.0	Very rough 4.0 to 6.0	

General synopsis

This is an overall picture of the weather systems both within and approaching the forecast area. The position and intensity of each system is given, together with any changes expected during the period. Movement trends are indicated by direction and rate. The special terms which are used are given in the tables above. This information will be needed to provide the data for bringing your weather map up to date.

R. MET. SOC./R.Y.A. METMAP

GENERAL SYNOPSIS   at .... GMT/BST ....

Gales	SEA AREA FORECAST	Wind	Weather	Visibility
	Viking			
	N. Utsire			
	S. Utsire			
	Forties			
	Cromarty			
	Forth			
	Tyne			
	Dogger			
	Fisher			
	German Bight			
	Humber			
	Thames			
	Dover			
	Wight			
	Portland			
	Plymouth			
	Biscay			
	Trafalgar			
	Finisterre			
	Sole			
	Lundy			
	Fastnet			
	Irish Sea			
	Shannon			
	Rockall			
	Malin			
	Hebrides			
	Bailey			
	Fair Isle			
	Faeroes			
	SE Iceland			

COASTAL REPORTS (Shipping Bulletin) at .... BST GMT	Wind Direction	Force	Weather	Visibility	Pressure	Trend
Tiree						
Butt of Lewis						
Sumburgh						
St Abb's Head						
Smiths Knoll Auto						
Dover						
Royal Sovereign						
Channel L.V. Auto						
Land's End						
Valentia						
Ronaldsway						
Malin Head						
Jersey						

7/90

COASTAL REPORTS (Inshore Waters) at .... BST/GMT					
Boulmer					
Bridlington					
Walton on the Naze					
St Catherine's Point					
Land's End					
Mumbles					
Valley					
Blackpool					
Ronaldsway					
Killough					
Orlock Head					
Larne					
Corsewall Point					
Prestwick					
Benbecula					
Stornoway					
Lerwick					
Wick					
Aberdeen					
Leuchars					

Fig 19.1 RYA Metmap form

Rather than trying to write down all that is said it is often easier to mark the position and movement of each system directly on the map. It is a quick and accurate method but you will need a good knowledge of where the various sea areas are located or you may miss something whilst looking for an area.

Area forecasts

Specific forecasts for each of the sea areas round the British Isles and northern Europe are given. These start at the top of the North Sea and continue clockwise around the British Isles.

The area information should be recorded in the boxes as fully as you are able. Don't neglect rainfall and visibility in areas away from your own because this detail makes it much easier to fix the positions of any fronts. Only if you can do this accurately will you be able to decide when and if a particular weather pattern will affect you.

The information is often given in considerable detail. The following is an example: 'South west veering west 4 to 5 increasing 6 or 7 for a time then veering north west later and decreasing 3 to 4. Rain then showers becoming fair. Visibility moderate, poor in rain becoming good later'.

Try writing that all down as it is said! The annoying thing from the beginner's point of view is that it is only when the weather is unsettled and you particularly need the detail that these long forecasts occur. Add to this the fact that the poor reader has to deliver it in the same amount of time!

The answer is practice; practice and a bit of guile. Look at the example again and compare it with the following:

SW v W 4–5 (6–7)/NW L 3–4 R/S/F M(P)/G L

It actually says the same thing. You could leave out the 'v' for veering since the wind is hardly likely to 'back' from south west to west. If it did use a 'b'. I use brackets to mean 'for a time'. Those round the 'P' I can easily associate with the showers. The '/' is used for something equivalent to 'and then'. An 'l' can be used for 'later'. Notice that I have no symbol for 'decreasing'. It is obvious anyway.

Fortunately most countries broadcast weather information in English at least once or twice a day. More importantly, almost all repeat the information at dictation speed after the first reading so that it is not too difficult to get the gist of it, even in an unfamiliar language.

Weather maps

Unless you are fortunate enough to have a weather Fax recorder on your boat, or perhaps a TV, you will need to turn all the information you have written down into a synoptic chart for yourself. This feat is becoming less popular nowadays with so many sources of weather updates available but can be worthwhile nevertheless.

Start by noting on your map form, the locations of the 'lows' and 'highs'. Their direction of movement is given in the general synopsis. You will need to advance them to fit with the coastal station report times. Next do the same with all the pressures given for the coastal stations and weather ships. Put beside each a line in the direction of the wind and mark on it the little flight feathers to indicate the wind strength.

Now join places having the same pressure with very light lines. Try to make the lines form smooth curves and remember that the wind direction will be crossing these isobars at about 20 to 30 degrees angled towards the centre of the low pressure. You may need several attempts before you get a good line but persevere. Once you have got the isobars on you can start locating the fronts. This is the point when I wish that our forecasts included temperature, it makes it so much easier. However they don't so we have to do without.

Your isobars, and the synopsis, moved to the same time, should be able to give you the centres of any lows. Fronts will mostly start there and trail southward (in the northern hemisphere) whilst curving to the west.

Rain and visibility information will help to position the fronts. Remember from the last chapter that showers ahead of a warm front will be turning to more steady rain with much less well defined cloud and that visibility will be going down as the warm front approaches. It will probably be raining in the sector between a warm and a cold front. It will be showery just behind a cold front but clearing with well defined clouds and visibility will be getting better.

Fronts are troughs in the general pressure pattern. A dip in pressure can thus be expected, accompanied by veering and temporary wind increases as a front passes a point. Hence comments like 'now rising' or 'now falling' which indicate a change in pressure movements are useful clues.

A useful practise at home is to listen to the 1750 forecast on Radio 4, draw your synoptic chart and then compare it with the TV weather map after the six o'clock news. Do this a few times at home and you should find it improves your performance a lot.

Some newspapers publish synoptic charts and they can be useful. The problem is that they will be rather old by the time you get them. At least twelve hours and probably more. They can still provide a useful check on your own attempts and will again help to improve your performance.

Anticipation and planning

The point of all this forecasting must not be forgotten. It is to make it possible to anticipate what is likely to happen. Once you have a pretty good idea of the weather you can expect you will be able to plan accordingly.

You will want to know four basic things. How strong is the wind going to be? From which directions will it blow? How long is it going to last? What will the visibility be like?

Things like, 'Is it going to rain?', and, 'How hot will it be?' are useful but not critical. Other things like the probable sea state and so on can be deduced from the basic information.

These are the sorts of considerations you will need for passage planning. Forecasting must always be done with these aims in mind to be useful. If your passages seldom last more than 24 hours you should be able to avoid the worst that the weather can do to you.

The table of meteorological terms on pages 91–92 gives some facts and figures which can be used in conjunction with weather forecasts to assess the probable times at which particular weather may arrive. An understanding of the terms used in forecasts is essential in order to use them. These are also given in the table.

What to do if you get caught out is covered in Chapters 41 and 43 in the section called 'When things go wrong'.

PART 5
Resources

A yacht at sea is a miniature world, dependent entirely on its own resources. Once away from shore, what you have with you is what you must survive on.

You have finite quantities of everything: fuel, water, power, spares, skills. The only way you can make sure you do not run out of essentials is to plan ahead and to keep checking and replacing your resources as they become depleted. The boat, and the crew, depend on the skipper to keep going. If you are the skipper, that means you. You can't fetch a doctor and you can't opt out. Until you have actually skippered a boat this may not be obvious. When you have, for the first time, you will be very aware of it.

In this section resources refer to all the material things that one takes so much for granted when ashore. Also involved though, are the personal abilities of skipper and crew. These are equally important resources to be managed on any vessel at sea and are covered in detail in Part 7.

Most resources can come under the heading 'fuel'. Either fuel for the boat (diesel, gas etc) or fuel for the crew (food and fresh water). The other material resources are the things that help to conserve these fuels (waterproofs, bedding etc even your sails can be included). All the material resources must be provided before departure, stored safely and kept in good condition so that they are available when needed.

20 ENGINE FUEL

Most yachts which cruise, even very small ones, have an engine to provide power when the wind does not oblige. Most inboard engines now run on diesel while outboards still uses a petrol/oil mixture. Although these two fuels have very distinct differences the care and control of both have things in common.

Fuel tanks

For an inboard engine, the size of tank fitted and thus fuel capacity will, apart from spare fuel in cans, have been determined during the yacht's construction. The capacity will be given in the builder's specifications. You should know how much fuel the tank holds and also how fast the engine uses it under a variety of conditions so that you can determine the range of your vessel under engine alone.

Tank size

If you do not know the capacity of your tank you must find out; by measurement if necessary. One litre is 1000 cubic centimetres ie a cube measuring 10 cm on all sides so for the capacity in litres of a rectangular tank simply measure the height, width and length in centimetres, multiply them together and divide by 1000. To convert the result to gallons divide the volume in litres by 4.55.

Dip stick

If you do not have any built-in method of measuring the quantity of fuel in the tank, a dip stick is a good idea. Do not forget that, if it is to work, it must reach the bottom of the tank every time it is used and the tank must be level or nearly so. A dip stick is easy to make from a length of 10 mm dowel.

Measure the height of the tank and mark this point. If you know the volume and, provided the tank has straight vertical sides, the rest is easy. Since the divisions will be equally spaced, simply divide the volume in litres by 5 and divide the height marked on the stick into that number of equal parts. It is now an easy matter to mark the dip stick permanently at the five litre intervals so that you can check how much fuel you have at any time. Burn the marks on the stick with a hot wire or old knife; it is more permanent and does not contaminate the fuel.

A round-ended tank is a bit more complicated to measure and an irregular one almost impossible. It is easier to find the volume of either by filling it using a 5 litre measure. Start with it empty, then pour in five litres at a time marking each change in height on your dip stick at each fill using a soft pencil. Laborious but worth it in the end. You cannot use a metered pump for this because the foam produced by the pump will obscure the actual divisions unless you are able to wait for 5 minutes or more after each 5 litres before dipping. Once the job is done, make permanent marks as described earlier.

Sight tube

Static fuel tanks are often fitted with sight tubes which show the fuel remaining against a scale. I have come across yachts with them but, unless the vessel is pretty large, they are of limited use since you can't get to read them easily, particularly when you are at sea.

Electronic fuel gauge

An electronic fuel gauge is convenient and easy to read but check it to make sure that it reads accurately (many do not) by the same method using a dip stick as for an irregular tank.

Reserve

You should always carry a reserve of fuel in a separate can. If your main tank leaks this will be invaluable to you. It can also be used to top up the main tank in order to extend your range.

Range

Once you know how much fuel you can carry, you need to find out how far this will take you. On a day when there is little wind and you need to motor, use the dip stick before starting the engine to find out how much fuel you have. After running at cruising speed for a couple of hours or so, check the level again. Divide the number of litres used into the number of miles run according to the log and you now have a consumption rate in miles per litre. If you repeat this exercise several times it will give you a fairly accurate indication.

Of course the rate will not hold good under all conditions but it gives you a starting point. Sea state will reduce your range if you try to motor in windy conditions. It is worth measuring this reduction when you get the chance. The information may be useful one day. It can be a lot more than you might think. If you are estimating, allow at least 20% reduction.

Alternatively, dividing the fuel used by the hours run will give the range in litres per hour. I like to know my range in terms of litres per hour when the engine is operating at cruising revs. In this way, by checking boat speed over the ground, I can estimate, in a whole variety of different conditions, how long I can keep going and from this, calculate how far I can get. This method is of more practical use.

The range found earlier is, of course, the range over the surface. Tide and drift will need to be taken into account if you want to calculate your range over the ground.

Water in fuel

You often hear people complaining about water in the fuel. It is obviously a problem since boat builders always fit one, frequently more, water separators in the fuel line. Most people blame the fuel supplier when they find water in the tank. In my experience this is usually unjust. It can often be your own fault, because you encourage the water to collect. Never! I hear you cry, but read on.

The problem

What happens is this. The fuel tank has a breather hole so that, as fuel is used, air can replace it. If it didn't, a vacuum would develop in the tank and stop the engine. This means in effect that the tank is open to the atmosphere. For reasons of economy in pipework and because diesel oil is not very flammable, fuel tanks are often fitted near the engine. These two things form the root of the problem.

When the engine is started from cold and run, the quantity of fuel in the tank reduces slowly whilst tank, fuel and air above it gradually warm up. All three expand. Instead of air being drawn in, the air in the space above the fuel expands much faster than tank or fuel so some is forced out of the breather hole. When the engine is stopped, the air cools down as do the tank and fuel. All contract but the air contracts most so air is drawn in from outside. It goes without saying on a boat, that this air will be moist. As the tank cools, the moisture condenses on the inside of the tank and runs down into the fuel.

Since water is more dense than diesel, the water sinks to the bottom of the tank and is trapped there. This cycle is repeated every time there is a change in the tank temperature: between night and day or when a warm day is followed by a cold wet one for example, or when the engine is run. Gradually this water accumulates until, if you do nothing about it, enough is collected to find its way into the engine fuel system. If it reaches the pressure side of the fuel pump it will stop the engine. The whole system will then need bleeding before you can restart.

Prevention

What to do depends on your system but the first line of defence is to keep your tank as full as possible. This has two advantages. It not only reduces the air space and thus the amount of condensation drawn in. It also reduces the amount of solid contamination that finds its way from the tank to the filters.

The other thing is to remove any accumulated water regularly. This is done by draining it, either from the tank, from the first filter or both depending on the system in your boat. Try to avoid it getting in too. If I have doubts about the quality of the fuel being supplied I run the first bit through a filter funnel.

Petroil fuels

A few yachts still have inboard engines which use petrol. You will need to be doubly careful, if yours is one of these, since this is a much more volatile fuel. If you have an outboard and need to store petrol-based fuel for it, the following rules still apply.

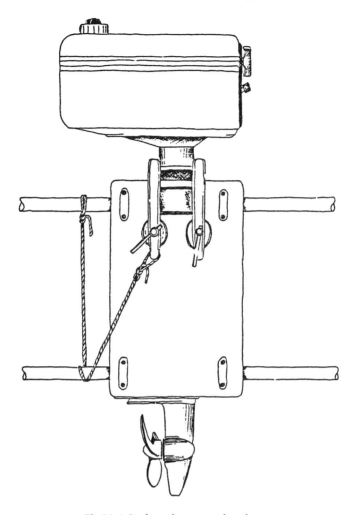

Fig 20.1 Outboard stowage bracket

Petrol storage

Store spare petrol only in metal cans, in a well ventilated position, preferably on deck, away from the engine and the battery. A small outboard for use on the yacht tender can, often enough, have it's tank filled before a trip so as to avoid carrying any spare fuel. If you still feel a need to carry some spare, use a small can and store it in a vented locker. Don't carry a small amount in a large can. If you do you will have a can containing mostly explosive vapour.

The outboard is best carried on the pushpit (Figure 20.1) rather than in a locker. It is easy to make a board for mounting it and this will avoid risks from spills or leaks as well as the build up of petrol vapour below decks.

Mixtures

If your outboard uses a petroil mixture be sure that any petrol you carry is premixed in the correct proportions before taking it aboard. This can avoid costly errors. Pure petrol used in a two-stroke engine will quickly destroy it.

Maintenance

Cleanliness is one of the most important things to remember where fuel is concerned. If you are in any doubt as to the state of the fuel going into your tank it is worth filtering it. Solid particles can be filtered out using an old pair of nylon tights. A large funnel with a fine gauze filter will not only remove solid matter but will also separate out small amounts of water from the diesel fuel going into it.

Your tank will need draining and cleaning occasionally, especially if it is made of mild steel. Rust can develop inside as well as outside such a tank due to condensation.

Another problem results from water in diesel fuel. The suppliers of diesel add a small amount of detergent to the fuel in order to prevent build up of sticky deposits in the engine. This is useful but can lead to problems at the other end of the system. The detergent seems to combine with any water present. This then reacts with the fuel to form a waxy emulsion which can clog filters and even the pipework. Regular removal of any water by draining it off, at the cock provided on the first filter, is the best prevention.

Leaks

When checking and cleaning filters be sure to look for leaks in the system. Loose glands or filter lock nuts are the commonest problem, although pinhole leaks in tanks can happen. Tank leaks will start small but can rapidly empty the entire contents of your tank into the bilges if not spotted early. A messy and annoying problem to say the least; a little diesel goes a long way. Loose fittings on the pressure side of the system can stop the engine but this is fairly uncommon.

If the leak is in a petrol system the result is extremely dangerous. Petrol vapour is heavier than air and will quickly gather in the bilges to become an explosive mixture with air. If not detected, a small spark such as from a switch or the alternator can be enough to set it off.

Incidentally, it is much easier to spot leaks early, both of fuel and oil, from a clean engine.

Other uses of engine fuel

There is a lot to be said for using the same fuel for heating and cooking as is used for the engine. If you intend ocean cruising, the ready availability of diesel throughout the world makes this a sensible, attractive proposition and is worth considering.

21 HEATING AND COOKING

Using the engine

Central heating on yachts is becoming increasingly popular. Most systems, either combined with water heating or alone, use the main engine as the source of heat. This is efficient when under way but does require the engine to be run for fairly long periods in order to get sufficient heat. This is inefficient, annoying and often impractical in harbour or even at anchor. It is sometimes not allowed in marina berths for obvious reasons. A better system for anyone expecting to need heating for extended periods would be to fit one of the drip feed direct combustion stoves or a bottled gas heater.

Kerosene

Kerosene, or paraffin, is a fuel just as easily obtained as diesel which can be used for cooking, heating and lighting. Whilst an effective fuel, it needs to be burned under pressure to achieve full thermal efficiency. This can be a fire hazard and does make for more complicated ignition; you need to preheat the kerosene using alcohol or a gas burner before lighting up. Despite these drawbacks kerosene is popular with many traditional sailors.

It is a much more flammable fuel than diesel and, because of its penetrating ability, much more susceptible to leakage problems than either petrol or diesel.

Bottled gas

Liquefied gas is by far the most popular fuel for cooking on boats with propane or butane used in Europe almost exclusively. Boat heaters for water and cabin warmth are now available that use this clean, efficient, quick to heat and easy to use fuel. These attributes outweigh its dangers. Both propane and butane are heavier than air so that any leakage tends to collect in the bilges where it can accumulate to produce an explosive mixture. Care in use is therefore essential.

The best way to prevent a dangerous build up is to make safety rules in the form of drills to be followed. These drills should consider the following points:

1 Always have the storage bottles stowed in a separate locker which drains overboard.
2 Never store bottles in direct sunlight.
3 After use, burn off the gas left in the plumbing system by turning the supply off at the bottle and burning at the appliance until the flame goes out.
4 Take care when lighting burners to avoid unburnt gas escapes.
5 Fit a gas detector but do not rely solely on it. Dry pump the bilges regularly to remove any accumulation.

A drawback with bottled gas is the lack of standard connections. You may well find that you are unable to get replacement bottles to fit your connectors, when you need them, away from our own country. Do not switch between butane and propane since each needs a different pressure regulator and adjustments may need to be made to your appliance by a professional if you have to change. .

In North America, liquified natural gas (LNG) is available. This is a much safer form of gas to use since it is lighter than air but again your apparatus will need to be altered. So far there is no sign that LNG will become widely available in northern Europe for some time.

Checking the quantity

Sight tubes and dip sticks are not possible with gas. You can still get a good idea how much is left in the bottle though, even without a gauge. Weighing is the most accurate method. The bottle will be labelled with its net weight and with the weight of gas when full. A spring balance will need to be carried on board.

Tapping with a coin or key will also work since a different note is heard according to whether the knock is made above or below the liquid level.

Another method can be used when the cooker is in use. Put your hand on the side of the bottle and slide your fingers down. At the point where the vapour stops and the liquid begins, a change in temperature can be felt. The bottle will often be cold enough to have condensation on it above this point.

Cooling effect

This effect is due to the cooling of the evaporating gas. In very cold conditions and when the rate of consumption is high, say the oven and a burner are on together, the gas can appear to give out. This is because the temperature has dropped to a point where no further evaporation occurs.

It is a potentially dangerous situation since the flame will go out. Once the bottle warms up again the flow may restart resulting in a gas escape. 'Flame guard' burners are usually fitted to ovens but not always to top rings on older cookers. The cooker, when in use, should be checked from time to time to make sure the burners are actually alight. If they are not, the taps should be turned off and the bilges pumped free of gas using a manual pump before relighting.

22   ELECTRICITY

All but the absolute purist will need electricity on board any cruising boat, if only for starting the engine and running lights and instruments. In practice it is virtually impossible to comply with the International Regulations for Prevention of Collisions at Sea lighting rules without a wired electricity supply on a yacht. This means rechargeable lead-acid batteries or something similar.

Circuitry

The primary battery circuit will supply power, via a heavy duty cut-out switch, to a fuse panel and to the engine starter. The alternator provides the power for recharging through a regulator, often along the same wires.

The wires feeding the starter motor must carry a heavy current and so are easily recognised by their greater thickness. These wires can not be fused due to the high current so it is important to switch off at the main switch when the system is not in use to reduce the risks of fire.

Master switch

In most systems it is important not to switch off the master switch whilst the engine is running. This is because the alternator must have a load all the time it is running. The battery via the master switch provides this load. If it is disconnected, even for a moment, the regulator and possibly the alternator too, will be destroyed.

Battery size

Yachts are usually fitted with heavy duty batteries. It is often a temptation to fit smaller ones since lead-acid batteries are both expensive and heavy. The capacity of a battery depends both on its physical size and its internal construction. It makes practical sense to have batteries with enough capacity for one alone to start the engine easily when 80% charged.

It is also a good idea to have sufficient power to run the required lights at night, ie navigation, compass and chart table as a minimum, without noticeable loss of illumination after 24 hours without recharging.

Capacity

The two requirements mentioned in the last paragraph need two related, but not identical, properties in a battery. The starter motor needs maybe as much as 300 amperes for a very short time whilst the lights need a much lower current for a much longer time. The former is concerned with the maximum discharge rate and the later with the overall capacity of the battery.

Available power

The battery manufacturer will supply information about the maximum discharge rate if asked. The overall capacity is stated in terms of ampere/hours, usually on the battery, but this figure is only an indication of the available power; you decide how you will use it. For example a battery rated as 80AH (80 ampere hours) could, in theory, supply 1 amp for 80 hours, 8 amps for 10 hours and so on.

Power requirement

Suppose you wish to run your masthead tricolour light with a 21 watt bulb, two compass lights at 3 watts each, a chart table light of 6 watts and a red cabin light at 10 watts plus instruments taking 17 watts in all. First add up all the wattages of all the equipment, in this case giving a total of 60 watts. Divide this figure by the voltage of your system (probably 12 volts). This gives a figure of 5 which is the current in amperes that you will be drawing from your battery.

The 80AH battery quoted above would, in theory, be able to supply this current for 16 hours maximum. After this it would need recharging. In practice the ideal is seldom, if ever, achieved so you should expect to need to recharge somewhat earlier.

If you have a lot of electrical apparatus, especially if this includes high consumption items like pumps, it is a good idea to have three batteries. Two supply the general electrical needs of the yacht whilst one is kept for starting the engine. Never use all the available battery power for the internal electrics. If you do, you may be unable to start the engine when needed. It is very difficult to start a diesel engine by hand cranking, although some will do it. It is even more difficult to bump start a boat!

It is incredibly easy to use up all the available capacity. You will, of course, be able to run the engine and recharge the others if you have been wise and kept one battery for starting. This will however, use part of your limited fuel supply. It is best to conserve the available power, recharging only when you *need* to run the engine, rather than the other way about. This is especially so on long trips when fuel replenishment is likely to be a problem.

Other power users

I do not like to have to rely on things like pressured water systems, electric bilge pumps and, still less, electric water heaters or fridges on cruising boats. All these things make living easier but are only really practical if you are able to run your engine for several hours a day. Manual alternatives make a sensible precaution. More will be said about this in the next section.

Charging rate

A mistake often made is the assumption that an hour or so of engine will recharge a flat battery, or more commonly, that a night's use of lights will be replaced in an hour or two. The lead-acid type of battery charge cycle differs, depending on how it has been discharged. When a heavy current is taken out of it such as for engine starting, discharge is rapid but so also is charging. This means that only a short time is needed to restore the battery to its fully charged state once the engine is running. If however, the discharge has been slow, say over 24 hours, then recharging will also be slow so that a much longer period will be needed to restore the charge.

Lighting

For general lighting, fluorescent strip lights are preferable to filament lamps. They are about three times as efficient and so provide a real saving. They can often produce interference in electrical instruments, particularly portable radio receivers, so be cautious. If only used in harbour this should cause no serious problem. It is a good idea to have at least one, low wattage, incandescent filament light in the main saloon however.

Fuses

As mentioned earlier, all the circuits feeding low current sources are fused via a fuse panel. The values of each fuse should be known and any blown fuse should always be replaced with one of the same value. Before a fuse is replaced it is wise to find out why it blew. A fire in the wiring could result if this is not done.

Wiring

Wires in boats are much more likely to fail than wires in houses for several reasons. Firstly electricity and salt water are not a happy combination. Copper wires will rarely be connected with copper terminals. Any wire carrying a current and getting wet will thus corrode away sooner or later if nothing is done. Patent waterproof greases are available for coating terminals and will help with this problem but not eliminate it.

If a circuit, say a light, does not work, check first the fuse then the bulb. If it still does not work suspect a terminal and check all connections. Sometimes they can become too dirty to work. On other occasions you will find the wire broken and will need to remake the connection to the terminal. This is not too difficult but if you are in doubt, consult an electrician.

The second cause of failure is more of a problem. Boats unlike houses are continuously on the move. If a wire has a long unsupported run, down inside the mast for instance, it will be continuously moving as the boat moves. This sometimes causes a break at a point where you can not get at it but more often causes the insulation to be chaffed away. If this happens a short circuit results and usually the fuse will blow and/or the item on the end of the circuit will stop working.

The only long term solution is to replace the wire. A temporary repair can sometimes be made with insulation tape if you can get at the damaged section. This must only be a temporary repair since water can now get in and corrode the wire. Wire sizes are related to their ability to carry current without loss of voltage. Never skimp on wire size because, although the circuit may still work, it will not work as well as it should. It is possible for too thin a wire to become overheated or even burn.

The third reason is that, sadly, wiring on boats is often done to a poorer standard than that in houses. Because the voltages are lower, the idea seems to be that risks of injury are less and so it is not so important. This is not just reprehensible, it is wrong. Low voltage circuits carry higher currents. This means that poor connections are more likely to result in circuit failure and that fire risks are actually higher.

Spares

The spares box should always have a selection of fuses of the correct values and of the correct sizes to fit the fuse holders, they are not all the same. It should also contain a spare bulb of each type used on the boat (more if several bulbs of the same rating are in use). Add a couple of rolls of different coloured PVC tape, a mast length of wire of the same size as that fitted, but never less than 1.5 mm cross-section, and you should be able to make a repair in most cases.

23 WATER

Possibly the most precious of all your resources is your supply of fresh water. Like the fuel, it is essential that you know how much you have available. It is also necessary to know how fast you are likely to use it. Novice sailors tend to use water at an alarming rate. As skipper, you must encourage water conservation early, even when it is not essential. As a crew member you must take care not to waste water.

Tank capacity

Water tanks are often built into odd corners of the yacht. They can be soft bags or rigid tanks in very strange shapes. If you do not know how much your tanks hold and can not find out from the boatbuilder check with the local agent for your particular design. He can often give you the answer for the price of a phone call.

    If all else fails, it is best to drain the tanks completely and refill them from calibrated cans so that you can measure the capacity. This can be a laborious process but could be well worth it in the future. In any event, complete replacement of your water supply occasionally will help to keep the tanks clean and the water sweet.

Hoses

The hose itself may not be of the correct grade of material for fresh water supply. Some rubber hoses are particularly bad in this respect. The clear plastic hose is probably the safest, or even better, carry your own. You will often need this in Europe where standpipes are frequently provided but have no hose fitted. Nowadays a soft, cloth covered hose on a reel is available. This takes little space and it certainly is a useful thing to have on board.

Purity

This is one of the most important considerations regarding the fresh water supply. You can not always be sure that the source of water from which you fill your tank is as pure as you would like. This may not be the fault of the marina but simply the lack of concern of previous users. The chap who lets the end of the hose fall off the pontoon into the fetid waters of some marinas is a menace. You will not even know that it has happened.

You can reduce this particular risk to some extent by allowing the water to run fast for a few minutes and by washing the outside of the hose before putting it in to your filler point.

Purification tablets
Water tends not to deteriorate too much provided your tank is light proof. Biological impurities however, once introduced, will still grow and multiply. It is thus a wise precaution to use water purifying tablets. Use them according to the maker's instructions. The exception to this is during winter lay up. I like to fill my tanks at this time and then use double the quantity of tablets, flushing the whole system out before the start of the new season and refilling. A thorough flushing will be needed to prevent the unpleasant aftertaste.

Bottled water

Abroad, where bottled water is cheaper than in the UK, it is common to carry bottled drinking water. In some parts of the world a skipper will prefer to carry all his water bottled rather than risk contaminating his tanks.

Frost

Beware of frost damage. If your boat has a chance of freezing up you could seriously damage your tanks. In this case it is better to let them overwinter empty and then go through the purifying process as soon as the danger of frost is passed.

Reserves

It is always sensible to carry a reserve of fresh water in clearly marked containers. Should your tank spring a leak or become contaminated, you will still have some safe water for essentials. Do not fill these containers completely so that, if the worst happens and you have to take to the liferaft they can be thrown over and will float.

Don't forget to change your reserve at regular intervals otherwise it may become a danger in itself.

Pressured systems

Whilst on the subject of water it is a good idea to consider the relative merits of hand pumping and pressured water systems. I do not like pressure systems since a simple thing like a dripping tap can deprive you of all your precious fresh water and flatten your battery into the bargain.

With hand pumping despite its relative inconvenience, there is far less chance of wastage. When you are actually pumping every drop, you remain well aware of what you are using. Turning on a tap implies, to most people, unlimited supplies. Either discipline your crew well or fit hand pumps.

Extending and conserving supplies

In a marina, river or estuary, and probably within a mile or so offshore, it is not safe to use sea water for any purpose other than washing the decks. In the open sea however, particularly on extended passages, it is well worth using sea water for cooking vegetables and for an initial rinse when washing up. The water should be reasonably safe and consumption of fresh water will be reduced dramatically.

If you swim in the sea you will probably take in more potential hazards than the routine I have suggested will give.

Sea water washing

Washing one's body in sea water affects people differently. Salt rash can be a problem. An initial wash in sea water followed by a wipe over with fresh water on a face cloth is a satisfactory compromise for most people. Don't forget, salt water soap is available.

Incidentally 'baby wipes' are relatively inexpensive and are excellent for personal hygiene.

Rain water

As an alternative, collect rain water. This is ideal for personal hygiene and can be used for cooking and drinking when well away from airborne pollution. This means some distance away from land, however. In the tropics rain can often be anticipated with sufficient time to get set up to collect it, in a sail or awning. This is sometimes true also in temperate latitudes. Do not retain the first part of a shower but use this to wash your equipment. Rain water will be cleaner after it has been falling for a while.

Quantities

How fast fresh water stocks will be used up is clearly important but unfortunately there is no ready answer. I find, when cruising, that if I allow a gallon per person per day for all purposes I seldom exceed this allowance. This is without the water saving hints already given. On a long passage, with judicious use of sea water, this consumption rate can be safely halved. This still implies little or no wastage so it is particularly important to make the crew aware of the need for conservation.

PART 6
Safety

Safe sailing depends on a great many factors. It is perhaps a tribute to the many people who go to sea in small boats that there are so few accidents. By looking at some of these factors and exploring ways of making a boat safer I hope that the odds can be further improved in your favour. Prevention is better than cure. This is a well worn cliche but is very relevant in the matter of safety.

Safety in relation to boats can be divided into two main areas. That of the vessel and that of the individual. The safety of the vessel itself, of course, affects individuals as well, but the practical needs of the two situations are actually different. There is also a third important safety factor of which a skipper must be aware – an accurate knowledge of his position.

24 BOAT CONDITION AND SURVEYS

Leaks

In Chapters 10 to 13, I have talked about checking the rigging regularly. The hull and machinery also need regular checking. Any signs of structural damage or leakage should be carefully watched for. If and when noticed, these must be investigated before they can become serious.

In all cases when you have any doubts about a leak that you cannot resolve it will pay to get a boatyard, and possibly even a surveyor, to check it.

Under water
Leaks below the water line are obviously the most important. In GRP boats particularly, the most common places for leaks are around the keel, skin fittings, 'P' bracket and at the shaft bearings. Leaks round the join between deck and hull are usually less serious but can indicate a possible weakness. These places are common problem areas in other materials also.

GRP
With GRP construction, any leak means a potential weakness. This is true, but less so, in steel or ferro-concrete boats. Boats in all three materials usually leak very little if well maintained. Wooden boats are rather different since they tend to have some inherent leakage which varies with things like changes of temperature, salinity and stress. With such vessels it is the change in the rate of leaks that should cause concern and it is specially important to be aware of any increases.

Hull fittings
Through-hull fittings are potential danger areas from leaks. Corrosion may not be seen easily and should be looked for. If the fittings are of metal, check the earth bonding for continuity and soundness (the sacrificial anode is discussed in Chapter 35). Plastic through-hull fittings can become brittle, so look for any surface crazing, discolouration or cracking of the material.

Above water
Above deck leaks are more of a nuisance than a danger as a rule but never lose sight of the fact that they may indicate serious problems. The actual source of a leak from

above deck can be very difficult to locate; suspect any deck fittings particularly chain plates and hatches. Water will often run along the deckhead before finding its way down so the problem may not be located where you see actual drips or stains. It may be necessary to remove the head-lining and it is a good idea to find out from the builders how this should be done before the need arises.

Wooden hulls always leak slightly as mentioned earlier. This is true even more of wooden upper work. The problem becomes worse when the boat is stressed in strong winds or has been allowed to dry out. Watch out for increased rate of leakage in either of these conditions. Through-deck fittings are suspect on any boat and should be checked periodically for both corrosion and tightness.

Mast boot leaks
A keel-stepped mast can often give the impression of a sizeable leak since water hitting the mast can be driven down any channelling or even inside the mast. The boot at the partners (where the mast comes through the deck) will not always prevent this.

Surveys

When buying a boat, unless it is brand new, always have a survey done. The cost will probably be worth it in the long run. When you receive the report, make sure you understand it; a good surveyor will be pleased to explain it to you. I like to be present when the survey is done but some surveyors discourage this.

Be clear at the outset on what you want the surveyor to look at. Unless you have specifically agreed it, he will not generally look at anything which requires the removal of any fastenings. Neither will he look at spars or rigging above head height, sails, electrics, instruments or loose cordage and equipment. Any comments on the engine are normally confined to general appearance.

This leaves a lot for you to check yourself. If you ask him to cover these things you must say so when you agree the price.

If at all possible, have the survey done whilst the boat is out of the water since it will, of necessity, be limited when the boat is afloat. When buying with a marine mortgage a survey is normally compulsory. It is primarily for the lender's peace of mind, but the buyer still has to pay for it so you should insist on seeing it.

Most surveyors are reputable people who do a good job. Some are less so, unfortunately. If possible, use one recommended to you by someone who has used him. Remember surveyors are not infallible. The YBDSA will advise on surveyors in your area and they set standards for their members and insist on their being insured. If subsequently you have a serious problem not disclosed by the survey you may be able to get redress from the surveyor or his insurers.

Seacocks

Before taking any boat out to sea for the first time, find out where all the seacocks are and check them. They should operate without strain and without leaking. Do not leave them until a hose splits before checking that they will close. Some have a screw plunger like your domestic water main. Others have a valve which consists of a tapered spigot with a hole through it which must be aligned with holes in the fitting. The latter is quicker to operate and usually has some form of adjustment but is more prone to failure. Any valve can seize up. Both types should be operated regularly to keep them free.

Sails

'A stitch in time saves nine' is an old nautical saying. It refers to the sails and is just as valid today as it was in the old days. Watch out for weaknesses that show up whilst sailing. Deal with them immediately if possible and note them in your defects book (see Chapter 31).

Reliable sails are a part of safety. Have needles, sail thread and a palm on board together with a piece of sail cloth of the same weight as your sails so that you can do a temporary patch if required. I have never found sail repair tape particularly effective, except on spinnakers, unless reinforced with stitching. If you do use it, your sailmaker will normally cut out the stuck area when making a permanent repair.

Unless you are racing, there is little point in overpressing the boat. Reducing canvas and or sailing an easier course is not only less uncomfortable, it reduces the risks of damage and increases the safety margins. As suggested in Chapter 8, it can also improve performance.

Engines

Reliability in the engine is part of safety, so carry out regular checks. Daily checks should include oil levels and the cooling system. The manufacturer's instructions regarding servicing and routine checks should be followed faithfully.

Each time the engine is started make sure that the cooling water is running freely. The weed filter, if fitted, should be checked at least weekly. More often if you run in weed-filled waters. When a boat is left on a mooring for prolonged periods, the green frondy weed can build up on the intake. This will not always prevent the system working when the engine is first started but may well become detached and clog the filter after the engine has been run for a while, so check the water outlet from time to time when running.

Instruments

Always take any opportunity that arises to check your instruments. Because the compass was swung when the boat was built does not mean that the deviation has not changed. Deviation can change just by having the boat ashore over winter or by fitting a new piece of equipment.

When at anchor, put a lead line over and check the depth against that indicated on your echo-sounder. Use measured mile marks to check your log and remember that an in-hull log's accuracy is seldom better than ±5%. Use the VHF to call the Coastguard when you leave port. Take a Decca fix or a bearing with the RDF set when you know where you are. In this way you will build up an idea of how reliable things are. It is too late to start guessing in thick fog off a hostile coast.

Anchors and mooring lines

Part of your pre-sailing checks should be the anchors, and the chains or warps for them, your mooring warps and fenders. Not only do you have to be able to get to your destination, you have to be able to stop when you arrive and to remain secured whilst there. See that any shackles are properly seized and that they, and the chain, are in good condition. Check the condition of all warps including any splices.

Make sure there is sufficient cable on the main anchor for the location in which you intend to sail. Don't forget that, if the tidal range is great, you will need more scope than you might think. You can never have too many warps anyway so it does no harm to carry an extra length.

25 PERSONAL SAFETY

Skippering

Any sensible skipper will assess the capabilities of his crew and try to match his demands on them to the abilities they possess. A *good* skipper will have a realistic idea of his own ability and limitations and will work within these boundaries using the skills he finds in others to augment his own and thus blending the skills of the whole crew to best advantage.

On any vessel there can be only *one* skipper. That person must be in charge at all times. Different people have their own way of running things but in my experience, the best skippers are those who show that they can be in charge of situations rather than people.

Being confident *and* correct is not always easy but the skipper who has the respect of the crew will be truly in charge. Confidence comes from knowing what to expect in the pending situation and being ready to meet it. It also comes from being able to accurately anticipate other people's reactions. These skills can be acquired with time but their acquisition can be helped considerably by planning and by training.

Knowing your position

The ultimate safety of any vessel depends on the skipper knowing his position accurately at all times. This may sound so obvious that it is hardly worth saying. The fact is, however, that the majority of groundings result from failings in this area. Also the majority of lost yachts are caused by grounding. Often because the skipper thought he knew where he was but was wrong.

In European waters your chances of hitting something uncharted are remote provided you have the correct scale charts for the area. It follows therefore, that if you know where you are and are able to control your boat, you should be able to avoid hitting anything that is fixed.

How to find your position is discussed in detail in my book, *The Shorebased Sailor*. In general it is a lot easier to keep track as you go along than to find out where you are when already lost.

Minimum records

The minimum record that a navigator should keep is a note of the average course steered and the distance covered according to the log. This information should be recorded in a deck log book together with all course changes. This should be done at hourly intervals when coastal sailing, two hourly when short passage making away from land. From such information a dead reckoning (DR) position can be found. It is most convenient to make such entries at watch changes. Twice daily positions are sufficient when ocean sailing.

Note that the course steered is the average course over the last hour or few hours, not the instantaneous compass reading when the entry is made. The navigator will be able to work up estimated positions (EPs) on the chart after allowing for tide and leeway.

Fixing position

On coastal passages, fixes should be made whenever the opportunity arises in order to check the calculated positions. Even when an electronic positioning device is fitted these records should be maintained so that, if it fails, you are not lost. Where such a device is fitted it makes sense to note the latitude and longitude readings from it each time the DR is recorded. Should failure then occur, a recent accurate position will be available from which to extend by manual means.

A skipper will seldom be exactly certain of his position, especially when on passage. Safe navigation is about reducing the uncertainty as far as possible. Use all the means available and never rely on one method alone.

Prevention

Boat safety often depends on taking early action and sometimes on action taken prior to sailing. The possession of the essential emergency equipment and the awareness of all the crew of how to use it can be critical.

Part 9, Chapters 38–44 entitled 'When things go wrong' describes in detail a number of possible danger situations and how to react to them. In each case it will be seen that the location of various items is critical. It is essential that each crew member knows where to find such items in a hurry. Only by preplanning can this be achieved.

Team work

A good crew performance can be achieved fairly quickly if the members are taught specific tasks in such a way that they can rely on each other. Practice as a team helps this. Most people want to do well. All can get personal satisfaction from achieving.

You can always spot a good crew working as a team. By inference you are also watching a good skipper. Watch a yacht as it comes into harbour. The sails come down neatly, not too soon and not too late. They are stowed tidily on to the boom and on to the rail so as not to interfere with the berthing operation. The engine is running with the yacht making steering way but not much more.

Crew are distributed along the vessel. Bow and stern lines are made fast and coiled. Fenders are spread along the correct side and at the correct height for coming alongside. As the boat comes gently alongside, the two crew with the breast ropes, standing amidships, step ashore comfortably and take the little strain left using the strong points provided ashore. The boat is secured so smoothly and with so little fuss that the observer hardly notices how it was done. Already the remaining crew are setting springs, the engine is stopped and the navigation lights are off.

What the observer notices, on reflection, is the lack of haste and the lack of noise. There have been no shouted orders; no fierce revving of the engine; no one leaping madly across six feet of water to the pontoon; no anxious owner on an adjoining boat fearful for his gelcoat.

It has all come together without fuss as though it was the easiest thing in the world. The team has got it together and got it right.

Of course it does not always happen like that! That, or something like it, is what we should be striving for. It is what a good skipper and crew can achieve most of the time. It is the best contribution to personal safety that can be made.

A good crew will be a contented crew. They will, one hopes, be sailing because they want to. If they are fed well, are not bored, get enough sleep and are warm enough they will only need one thing more: the knowledge that their contribution is appreciated. The skipper who bears this in mind should not go far wrong with his human resources.

Safety harnesses and lifejackets

Each member of the crew should have a safety harness for his sole use. It must be fitted before setting off and kept ready in a definite place. A personal lifejacket should also be available for each crew member. It is the individual's responsibility to make sure that these fit and that he knows how and when to use them. It is the skipper's responsibility to check the crew's awareness.

When a harness is worn it must be attached to both the crew member and to the boat otherwise it is worthless. Both harness and lifejacket must be tested and checked for damage frequently.

There is no hard and fast rule about when either harnesses or lifejackets should be worn. It is a matter of common sense. Nevertheless, on my boats, I make the following rules:

Harness must be worn:
1 On deck at night.
2 In heavy weather conditions.
3 By novices when on the foredeck.
4 By non-swimmers at all times.

Lifejackets must be worn:
1 On deck at night
2 When risk of collision is high (eg poor visibility)
3 When using a dinghy.
4 By non-swimmers at all times.

Either or both can be worn by anyone who feels nervous without them. Whatever you do, do not ridicule anyone for wearing safety gear however unnecessary it may seem to you. A good deal of safe behaviour depends on attitude of mind. The nervous crew member is seldom in danger.

Clothing for safety

Man, as an animal, has long since lost his ability to retain adequate body heat without protective covering. It is far easier to keep warm than to get warm; it is easy to lose body heat when sitting on the deck of a boat in a stiff breeze.

At sea, the air temperature will always be lower than on land except in winter. Adequate clothing at sea, even in summer, usually means a sweater, scarf, hat and so on. These items must already be on board before the need for them is apparent. Keeping warm and dry provides comfort and reduces risks. Warm clothes, together with oilskins and boots to keep one dry, are part of personal safety. Even in summer, cold can kill.

Clothing will also protect the body from excess sun. At sea, the ultraviolet radiation that causes sunburn is much greater than on shore. I sometimes have difficulty in convincing people of this until too late. The point is, not only is there clearer air at sea, but also sea water reflects most of the ultraviolet radiation so that you will get a double dose of it.

Safe handholds and strong points

Awareness of possible dangers should decrease both nervousness and risks. The skipper will need to point out safe handholds and strong points for safety harnesses; a well-found boat will have numerous strong points fitted. In the cockpit the minimum should be at least two, fitted low down so that in the event of pooping or a knockdown, the crew on deck are held within the boat. Extruded aluminium toe rails are now common. These can provide a whole series of strong points along the decks. Attachment to the toe rail should always be made on the windward side of the boat since anyone falling overboard normally falls towards the lee side. Separate jackstays are best, however, because these make it possible for anyone moving forward to do so whilst remaining attached at all times (see Figure 25.1).

Additional strong points should be fitted at the mast and on the foredeck. These are the most likely places for crew to be working with both hands. As far as is possible each individual should be attached to a separate point and should be responsible for the transfer of his own attachment.

Rigging and guard rails

It is never safe to attach your harness to any item of rigging, either running or standing, nor to the guard rails. The fact that such items may be carried away in the event of equipment failure is not always apparent to crew and may need pointing out. Quite apart from this, rigging is under tension; a sudden sideways snatch load can increase the end loading enough to cause it to break.

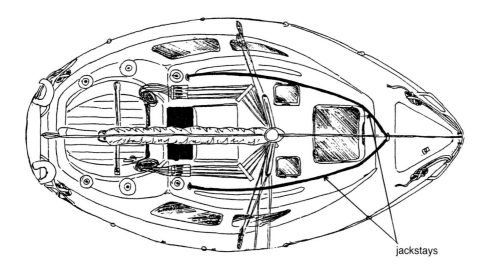

Fig 25.1 Separate jackstays run along the coach-house roof

Mutual care

One of the most useful ways of improving personal safety is to encourage the system called, in the services, the 'buddy-buddy system'. This is the system whereby each person in a team watches out for the welfare of the others on the basis that an observer is better able to spot potential dangers than are the participants. It is most useful when someone is working on the foredeck, at the mast or moving along the decks.

The observer will see such things as a potential gybe, or a loose rope that may not otherwise be noticed, in time to give a warning and thus save a possible accident. All crew members should be encouraged in this activity.

Man overboard

None of the items listed for recovery of a man overboard will be of use unless everyone on board knows how, and when, to use them. Practice this as an exercise regularly and always with new crew. Don't forget to practice getting someone aboard from the water when conditions are suitable. It is a lot more difficult than you might think so make sure they are wearing personal buoyancy. If someone actually falls overboard, the practice will ensure a much better chance of a successful recovery.

Man overboard recovery methods

The most reliable method is the so called 'reach-to-reach' method. I use a modified method which can be used by one person left alone on board. As soon as anyone goes over, things should be done as quickly as possible but safely and without panic.

The method I teach is as follows:

1 Call MAN OVERBOARD! Throw out the danbuoy and a lifebelt. Ease the sheets. If someone is available, he or she should point, and keep on pointing, at the person in the water. If Decca is fitted, press the MOB button.
2 The helmsman should put the boat on a *beam reach without tacking.*
3 At least one person should be getting a harness on if not already worn.
4 The best helmsman on board should take the helm. This is not always the skipper. Skipper should take charge of the action.
5 Prepare a line with a large bowline at the outboard end and secure the inboard end to a strong point amidships. Have ready the heaving line or patent pick up device.
6 If the spinnaker is up it should now have collapsed and be brought down. Lash it on deck or even cast it adrift. Do not try to bag it. Bring the halyard end back to the shrouds on the *windward* side. This will be the lee side when recovering the casualty.
7 Have the engine ready to start but do not start it until all lines are clear.
8 The helmsman now tacks on to a beam reach on the opposite tack. The person in the water should be roughly ahead (check where the pointer is pointing).
9 The person with the harness goes to the shrouds on the lee side with the rope loop and attaches himself on a short line. He then lies down on the side deck aft of the shrouds.
10 The helmsman should position the boat on a line about two to three boat lengths down wind of the casualty.
11 When the bow of the boat is about down wind of the casualty, bring up fast on to a fine reach to take off the way, adjusting the main as required.
    It is important to be on a fine reach and not head to wind since you must be able to control the boat with the main sail.
12 Move slowly forward until the bow is just abeam and up wind of the casualty and free off the mainsheet. Keep the helm to leeward.
13 The crew on the side deck can now lean down and pass the loop to a conscious casualty. If the casualty is not conscious, either clip the spinnaker halyard on to the casualty's harness or pass the rope loop round under his armpits to secure him, with extra assistance if necessary.
14 The helm should be positioned to maintain the hove-to condition whilst 13 is going on.
15 The spinnaker halyard can be used, with a winch, to assist in getting the casualty aboard. Take care.
16 Check for injuries then get the casualty below and changed from wet clothing into a dry sleeping bag.

Notes

a) Item one above includes several actions. These are deliberately included under a single number because they should all be done, as nearly as possible, at the same time.
b) Most light displacement boats will sail and will tack with the jib slightly aback. This is a great advantage if your boat will do it, because it cuts down on noise whilst the

manoeuvre is being carried out avoiding the need for shouting. With the lazy sheet secured as soon as the tack has been completed, it makes heaving-to much easier also.

This trick will not always work with a long-keeled boat. However this should all have been found out during practice; not when doing it for real.

c) The engine can be used to help the final manoeuvring but must be out of gear when actually alongside the casualty.

d) Whilst the method outlined above is a reliable one, it must be stressed that each boat handles differently and it is essential to test first.

e) The method as described sounds as though it needs several crew. In practice, since only one thing has to be done at a time, it can be done by one person alone if necessary.

The 'Quick stop' method

The quick stop method, variously called the Annapolis or American method, involves an immediate tack bringing the boat hove-to. This is fast and keeps the casualty close, the engine being used to come alongside. The boat will be upwind and the sails must be freed off in order to get to the casualty.

Gybe method

This involves an immediate gybe leaving the jib backed. It calls for skilled boat handling. It has the advantage of speed and the initial gybe turn will often bring the boat to a halt alongside the person in the water. The method needs very quick reactions and expert helming. I cannot recommend it for beginners.

PART 7

Looking after the crew

Skippering covers the whole business of running the boat. This book is about skippering. Looking after the crew is a part of skippering that is often neglected. That is not to say that skippers don't care about their crews. The trouble is they don't always think about them enough.

A client of mine was telling me of a skipper he sailed with on a weekend race. The start was delayed for reasons of weather and they dropped anchor in a bay. One of the crew decided it would be an opportune time for a meal. 'Where's the food kept?' he asked. 'Oh! I don't keep any food on board when I'm racing,' replied the skipper. The crew rowed ashore for fish and chips, I was told. One wonders what they would have done had the race not been postponed. This is extreme but not as extreme as you might imagine.

Looking after the crew rates fairly high in my terms. Keeping them fed and watered plays a big part in this.

26 FOOD

The subject of food fully justifies a chapter all to itself. Good eating is part of boat safety. A hungry crew is more prone to seasickness, tiredness, reduced responses and lower morale than a well fed one. The 1979 Fastnet Race Inquiry report makes this point very strongly.

In general, it is better to eat small meals frequently, especially on a long passage, than it is to have large infrequent meals. Small meals are more easily digested whilst maintaining stomach contents and energy levels. A full, or better, slightly less than full stomach is a great help in reducing the risk of seasickness. It may be hard to convince a beginner of this. The other thing about frequent meals is that they relieve boredom. When planning your food stocks it is worth bearing these things in mind.

Most trips will not keep you away from shore for more than two or three days but always have a good food reserve in case you get caught out. Do not overdo it though and rotate the stock so that older things are used first or you will be up to the gunwales in rusty cans before long.

The duration of the passage and the destination will have the greatest influence on what food stores to carry, both as regards quantity and content. Specific items are always a matter of individual taste but some general points can be made. For night sailing, particularly in sloppy seas, it is essential that preparation is kept to the minimum. This means ready prepared and instant foods.

Drinks

Soups, particularly the instant in-the-cup types, are a godsend to sailors. Have lots of varieties and ring the changes. Chocolate milk drinks and malted milk are more nourishing than tea or coffee. They can be made with powdered milk or be of the kind that only need to be mixed with hot water. Soups and milk drinks are not only nourishing; they seem to be more warming also.

For those feeling a little fragile, broth type drinks such as Bovril, Oxo or Marmite are more easily digested. Tea is better than coffee for those who don't like the idea of broth since coffee tends to bring on seasickness in at least some of those prone to suffer.

Whilst not objecting to alcohol in principle it can be a problem on board a yacht and you are better off without it. Alcohol not only slows reactions, it also reduces body heat. In the cold, wet conditions that often exist on a boat, both can be dangerous.

Snacks

Plenty of biscuits, both sweet and plain, should be carried. Dried fruit and nuts are good as are the crunchy type bars containing cereals mixed with fruit, nuts, honey or chocolate.

Chocolate biscuits and also bar chocolate give quick energy with no preparation. Some people are unable to eat chocolate at sea, however. Boiled sweets are often welcome, even by those who never eat them ashore. They help to prevent the dry mouth that comes with sailing.

Canned, dried or fresh food?

Some people have strong arguments for one or the other. I think there is room for all three on any boat. Dried foods take up less space but they use more water and need careful storage. Cans are quicker to prepare but are heavier to carry and take up a lot of space. On long voyages, cans lose their labels, and with them their identities, unless marked with paint or spirit pens. Tins also rust and become unsafe to use. Fresh foods, particularly vegetables and fruit, can make meals much more appetising but can be difficult to keep. On long voyages they are best hung in nets.

Canned foods

For the coastal cruising boat, cans are seldom on board long enough to cause the problems mentioned. I like to carry such things as meat and vegetables in cans. The best meals to include are the plain ones such as corned beef, tinned steak, ham and chicken. These can then have canned, dried or fresh vegetables added to make a greater variety of dishes. Ready-prepared canned meals such as Irish stew and steak casserole, to quote just two, are almost always a disappointment. They usually contain little meat and tend to taste canned.

I always include some canned potatoes in the vegetables, since they are so easy to use. Take also corn, green beans and peas – none of which can easily be carried fresh. Marmalade, jam and butter can all be found in cans and are safer than glass.

Canned tomatoes are useful but avoid large cans as they contain more than you need at one time and do not store well once open. Take tubes of puree so that you don't have to store open jars or cans.

I don't like the taste of canned butter but it does keep well. The soft margarines in plastic tubs keep well and are quite popular, as well as being much easier to spread than butter.

Dried foods

Vegetables such as onions, peppers and also mixed vegetables with pulses for soups and stews are best carried dried. Rice and pasta are also useful ingredients. I prefer dried milk on board. UHT milk takes up more space and does not make good tea. If taking UHT milk you will find the semi-skimmed variety tastes more like the real thing in drinks. Plenty of tea and coffee are a must. Tea bags and instant coffee make things easier. Fruit cake keeps well and so do muesli and porridge, which take up less space than patent cereals.

Last, but not least, on my processed list are spices and sauces, although these will probably be in jars. It is a mistake to think that only bland foods should be served on a boat. Food needs to be appetising when people are feeling a little jaded. Contrary to popular belief, my experience suggests that spiced foods do not promote seasickness as long as the seasoning is not overdone. It is rich rather than spiced foods that should be avoided. Ginger is actually a useful antidote to seasickness.

Fresh and frozen foods

Root vegetables are best fresh and will keep well if open to the air and in a dry spot. Hang them in nets if you can. Fruit keeps well if you buy it on the unripe side. The smells of both bananas and oranges tend to be pervasive, apples a lot less so and they keep better. Eggs keep well together with cheese and bacon, particularly if you buy these vacuum-packed in small enough quantities so that, once open, they can be used in a day or two.

Bread and bread substitutes
Few people are prepared to bake bread on board. The bread that comes in plastic bags will keep for about a week without going mouldy. Fresh bread needs to be kept dry but not sealed and can be freshened quite effectively by placing in a moderate oven for ten minutes. If the trip is to be more than a week without the chance to restock then take crispbread. Kept in airtight containers this will last a lot longer.

Keeping cool
If you are prepared to supply the power needs of a 'fridge you can carry far more fresh foods. A good cool box, however, can be almost as effective for up to a week. The trick is to freeze all suitable items hard in advance, including some patent cold packs, and be sure to pack the box full, with the different items in separate sealed containers. The food keeps cold much longer and tastes better this way. It is important that the cold box is full, to reduce air circulation, so put empty plastic boxes back again after their contents have been used. Ice can always be obtained on the continent and sometimes in the UK. It can be put into the empty plastic boxes.

Pre-frozen foods

Prepared meals in foil, or better still sealed plastic containers, freeze well. Sausages should be used before the contents of the box are totally thawed. If they are precooked and then frozen fast they will last longer. Bacon and butter can be frozen but eggs and milk do not freeze well. Fresh meat will need to be cooked before it has become thawed out naturally.

Cheese tends to go crumbly if frozen but otherwise does not suffer. You can freeze it to keep the cold box temperature down but it is best stored in a cool spot rather than frozen, since it keeps quite well anyway. If you buy it vacuum packed in smallish quantities, kept cool it will last well for weeks without freezing.

Bread and rolls freeze well. They help to fill the cold box if you have a large one although, once defrosted, bread tends to go mouldy quite quickly.

Food storage

Space is usually a problem, particularly on longer sea trips. Normally the problems result from the need to spread things about in various places. Whatever you do, have a plan and keep to it. Make a list with the location of specific items. If you don't, you will spend a great deal of time looking for a can of beans or that ham you know you have on board somewhere.

Canned foods can sometimes be stored below the cabin sole provided your boat is not a wet one. Goods in sealed plastic containers can fill up any odd spaces. Fruit and veg, and also bread unless frozen as mentioned earlier, need dry ventilated stowage. Do not forget that bread will absorb the flavour of anything stored with it.

Dried goods are best decanted into plastic containers with tight fitting lids so that they will keep dry. Again label the containers and plan their stowage. Aim to have opened stocks of the most commonly used items in smallish quantities. Keep these in sealed containers close to the galley. These can be replenished when convenient from the main stocks as they get low. This saves delving into lockers quite so often.

27 ORGANISING MEALS

Deciding choice and quantity

Planning meals for five or more people for up to two weeks can be a daunting task if you have never done it before. The way to tackle the problem is to consider each day separately. Think in terms of two main meals and at least three snacks; more if you intend night sailing.

Aim to make the meals varied but simple. Do not, for example, try to produce a meal at sea involving serving meat and several vegetables all cooked individually. You cannot cook or serve up such a meal easily nor can you keep it hot. All the effort will only generate frustration in the cook and disappointment for the crew. Go for one-pot main dishes such as stews, pies or casseroles, and serve one vegetable only. Spaghetti bolognaise or savoury mince and rice and such like are fine. Two pots are manageable, but anything more is risky.

Meals like those suggested above stay warm longer, take less supervision, use less fuel and save on the washing up. All plus points for cook and crew!

Utensils

Save the china for harbour use and serve in unbreakable bowls at sea. Vertical-sided saucepans with two small handles and well-fitting lids are easier to use and to stow if you can still find them. Buy them with all metal handles, including the lids if possible, then they can be used in the oven, too. The largest should be about 25 cm in diameter; choose the others so that they will fit inside each other; they take up less space that way. Three saucepans plus a frying pan should be sufficient.

Casserole dishes are fragile but worthwhile. Instead of buying expensive ones, ask your local delicatessen for old pate dishes. You can usually get them for a few pence so it does not matter if they break (provided they are not full at the time!). Have at least two large vacuum flasks; preferably one of them the pump type which is easiest for hot water.

Cutlery
You will need one plain and one straining spoon, a ladle (for serving soups and stews), wooden spoons, a spatula and a pair of kitchen tongs (for all manner of jobs). Add a couple of short, sharp, knives with one larger one, a good can opener, potato peeler and a cork screw (for wine when in port!). These should be sufficient for most jobs.

You will also need eating utensils but confine these to a basic knife, fork and spoon for each member of crew plus tea spoons and just a few spares.

Before a long day sail

Prepare rolls or sandwiches and store them in plastic boxes, foil or clingfilm. Cut cake and do the same with this. Make up a large flask of soup. Fill your second large flask with boiling water. This way you can feed the crew with hot and nourishing food at sea with minimum effort. Serve the soup in mugs and use the hot water to make drinks of the crews' choice. Fruit, nuts or biscuits can round off the meal.

Bad weather cooking

If your galley will take it, a pressure cooker is ideal in bad weather; you can tie it to the stove if necessary. It cooks food quickly and so is economical on fuel as well as virtually non-spill. A galley strap to give you both hands free is essential in heavy seas and a great help at any time.

When the sea is rough, one is very tempted to forget cooking but try not to. On a passage lasting less than one day it is acceptable not to cook but for longer trips hot food is important if not essential. It need not be elaborate; packet soups perhaps thickened with dried vegetables are often enough.

A stew made from canned ingredients will go into the oven in one of your all-metal saucepans. If necessary, wire the lid on and don't forget that it should be not much more than half full. Make sure your oven will stay shut too. It is quite amazing what weather conditions these precautions will withstand. I have had a casserole survive overfalls in a force 7 off the Channel Islands. Having a hot meal ready when conditions improved was greatly appreciated.

Kettles can be risky in these conditions even if you have good fiddles. The best kettle is one without a lid, filled through the spout and closed with a whistle. Stand everything in the sink to pour but lift each cup since your body makes a natural gimbel. Hold the cups over the sink so that what you spill (you almost certainly will spill some) goes down the drain not over your legs.

Serving

When serving to people in the cockpit put the food in bowls or basins. It keeps hotter and is less likely to be spilt. Give them a spoon to eat with; you can't really manage a knife and fork in the cockpit and it saves washing up.

If you are to have bread or rolls with the meal these should be cut and buttered by the cook before serving up the main dish.

Safety

Never attempt to fry anything in a frying pan whilst sailing. If you must fry, use a deep pan and never stop watching it whilst cooking. Always wash up pans whilst still hot, they are much easier to clean that way.

One point needs a further mention. Always wear oilskin trousers when cooking at sea to avoid the risk of nasty burns.

28 CREW ORGANISATION

Contentedness, competence and confidence are three qualities which, if possessed by all crew members, will make for a happy boat. The effective skipper will strive to achieve this ideal situation. How successful the attempt will be depends largely on organisation.

Contentedness comes from being well looked after. Food has been covered in Chapter 27 but contentedness is not created by just being well fed. It is a combination of being able to get enough sleep, keeping warm, feeling that everyone else is pulling their weight and feeling wanted.

When you join a new crew or, as skipper, take on crew you don't know, their initial competence is outside your control, but it does not have to stay that way. Part of the job of a good skipper is to improve the competence of the crew and it is as much a part of the job as any other. It is also in the skipper's own interest since it will make life easier and improve not only the efficiency of the vessel but also his own competence.

Some skippers, not always deliberately, make a mystery out of what is going on. Try to avoid this trap since a well-informed crew can be a great help. They will learn faster and be more willing to participate as part of a team. In addition, they will be more confident of your ability as skipper and will thus work more effectively.

Confidence is a difficult area. Self confidence without over confidence is a delicate balance. It is equally important to both skipper and crew. The skipper who can inspire confidence in his crew will need to be confident himself. He will also need to be right. More is said about this subject in Part 10.

Sleep

Insufficient sleep makes people irritable; it also makes them careless. If you are making a passage which is expected to last more than a few hours it is better to start watch keeping early. A routine established straightaway means that each crew member knows when they are expected to be working and when they can rest. By day, in gentle weather, it is not essential that a crew member off watch actually sleeps. Relaxing, reading a book or whatever, is enough for most people and if they want to sleep they can.

In bad weather and at night, sleep becomes more important. At first those new to sailing are reluctant to go below because they know that they are more likely to feel ill down there. They must be convinced that, once horizontal, they will feel OK.

Undressing

The need to get horizontal must not prevent the crew from getting out of oilskins and outer clothing before lying down. Lying on a bunk in wet gear not only makes the bunk wet and unpleasant for the next person to use it; it also means you will feel cold much more quickly. Oilskins can often be removed whilst sitting in the companion-way. Get someone who is happy below decks to find the sleeping bag, hang up the oilies and so on, so that time spent vertical down below is kept to a minimum. It is easier to sleep when warm. Once physical exertion stops, the body gets cold fast so it is important to actually get into the sleeping bag.

Watch keeping routines

The skipper should decide on watches based on the capabilities of the crew. He should know these or find them out very quickly.

At least one person on each watch must be capable of handling the boat and making basic decisions. Otherwise either the off watch crew or the skipper, will be continually interrupted to help out. If all the crew are competent I prefer a staggered watch system (see below).

WATCH KEEPING SYSTEMS

Number of crew	Note	Plan No.	Hour Number											
			1	2	3	4	5	6	7	8	9	10	11	12
Skipper + 2		1	S	A	B									
or		2	S	S+b	A+b	A								
Skipper + 3	(*3)	3	A	B	C									
or		4	S+a	S+a	B+c	B+c								
or	(*1&3)	5	A	A	b+c	b+c								
or	(*3)	6	S	A	A+c	B+c	B							
Skipper + 4	(*2)	7	A+B	B+C	C+D	D+A								
or	(*3)	8	A	B	C	D								
or	(*2)	9	A+B	B+A	C+D	D+C								
or	(*4)	10	A	A+d	B	B	C	C+d	A	A	B	B+d	C	C
or		11	A+d	A+d	B+c	B+c								
or	(*5)	12	S+b	S+c	A+d	A+b	S+c	S+d	A+b	A+c	S+d	S+b	A+c	A+d

Key

1 Capital letters indicate competent crew ie can hold a course and keep watch without supervision.
2 Each crew member is assigned a letter in order of apparent competence.
3 Where no letters are entered in a plan repeat from hour 1.

Notes

*1 Skipper sleeps during A's watch and supervises b+c.
*2 In easy conditions, first named is on helm and second below but dressed.
*3 Single man watches are acceptable if conditions are reasonable with competent individuals. Next man on is standby if needed.
*4 Once d becomes competent revert to Plans 7 or 9.
*5 Once b, c or d is fully competent revert to plan 11.

Staggered watch

It means that there is always someone on watch who is fully awake and aware of the situation. It often means that 'on watch' time is less than 'off watch' time. Each person also gets a chance to be in charge and this is good for morale.

If at all possible, the skipper should not be included in the watches because he or she will need to be available in a crisis. Crises can occur each time the skipper is off watch and if they do, he will soon get dangerously tired. A skipper not in the watch system will be available to give advice and to back up the deck crew for sail changes etc so that the off watch crew need not be disturbed.

The risk is that the skipper is in need of sleep too. In fact the skipper needs to be more alert than the rest of the crew. A wise skipper will sleep whenever the chance comes and, if he is in danger of getting too little sleep, delegate someone else to take over whilst he rests. A properly briefed crew will understand the need for this.

The mechanics of watches

How the watches are organised depends on both the strengths and number of crew. The table of watch keeping systems on page 139 gives several suggested systems that can be used with three to five crew plus skipper. The aim must always be to avoid anyone being on the helm for too long and to ensure that those off watch get long enough to have worthwhile rest.

You may disagree with the plans in the watch keeping table 1 but think about the advantages first. Two hours on watch is a comfortable time. It is also the minimum time off watch in which any worthwhile sleep can be achieved. In most of the plans suggested the time off watch is three or more hours, with longer rest times for the least experienced where possible. The plans take account of lack of competence by novice crew members.

It is not only bad for the individuals concerned but also dangerous for everyone else, to leave totally inexperienced crew on watch with no supervision. They will not learn much either. It takes only a few days to get beginners up to the standard of experience and competence where they can stand a watch and then you can revert to one of the more relaxed plans.

One point that needs amplifying. In plans 1, 3, 5, 6, 8 and 10, only one person is actually on watch at a time. This is satisfactory, as the note says, but should only be done with experienced crews. The use of self-steering is a great help in such situations since it helps in keeping a good lookout. With only one crew in the cockpit, he must be attached by his harness at all times. A single individual should not be on watch in heavy ship traffic, traffic lanes, bad visibility or heavy weather unless it is unavoidable due to crew numbers.

A watch keeping system is good for the crew since it demonstrates the value of each member's contribution whilst ensuring that everyone gets a fair share of the work and of sleep. Further benefit in crew harmony can be obtained by acknowledging the efforts of the crew.

General crew duties

When work is shared it is easier for everyone. The danger with sharing duties on a boat is, that unless jobs are allocated, some may be done twice and others forgotten. It is best to divide up the things that need doing and make it clear as to who is responsible for what. This is where checklists come in. Don't be afraid to make them. People who are unsure both like them and need them. Good skippers depend on them. It is the best way to avoid important things being forgotten.

Good habits should be introduced early, for everyone's benefit. Each crew member should be responsible for his or her own property, in particular making sure that it is stowed securely. Oilskins and boots should have a designated place and be put away every time after use; not dropped, wet, on to someone's bunk. Harnesses must be similarly located and should be individually adjusted before the passage starts.

With any general boat equipment item, each person should be aware of the correct location and be encouraged to replace it there after use.

Rules need to be kept to a minimum if they are to be observed. It helps if the reason for the rule is understood. Operation of the head to avoid blocking it or sinking the boat, for example, needs to be explained because you, as skipper, can not check each time it is used.

Try also to get your crew to look outside themselves. I have mentioned before that, when someone goes forward, a potentially hazardous situation may develop without the individual at risk being aware of it. Crew who watch for, and warn of, such situations are obviously of great benefit. This kind of mutual support, if not overdone, builds the right sort of confidence. Carried to excess however, it can undermine morale.

Duty rota

There are a number of duties or activities that must be carried out on a yacht. Some are more enjoyable than others, some are simply chores. There is a great danger that the distribution may not be even, or that it just seems uneven to one or more of the crew. Either way it can lead to discontent that is not always voiced but may spoil the enjoyment of more than one individual.

Rotation of all duties can avoid this problem but it can get a bit cumbersome. It is usually better to allocate the less onerous tasks and rotate the least attractive ones. You may be lucky and have someone who loves washing up or cleaning out the heads! If so let him or her take that job on by all means. Even so the attraction may pall after a while.

Cooking

Cooking and clearing up are jobs which I feel are prime candidates for sharing. I personally like cooking but many people do not, especially at sea. In practice it is best to expect the cook to wash up the preparation stages with someone else doing the after-the-meal dishes. Having the cook wash the pans is a great incentive both to keep the number of pans down and to avoid burning things.

Navigation

Navigation should not be allocated. Although some of it can be shared, it must always be someone's personal responsibility. Each watch leader, except on very short passages, should be expected to work up at least one position on the chart during his period of duty. All his data and calculations should be recorded neatly in a notebook in a form acceptable to the navigator who may wish to check it later.

Only the official navigator must be allowed to remove any markings from the chart, other than the plotter's own construction lines. This is very important and must be clear to all. If not, vital information may be lost.

Appendix 1 lists some of the routine checking tasks that a skipper could divide among the crew. Although this list is fairly comprehensive it cannot cover all the possibilities on any particular yacht. I include it to help you in compiling your own lists.

29 SEASICKNESS AND INJURIES

General health

If you have any health problem it is wise to consult your doctor before sailing and to advise the skipper of your condition and of any special treatment you might need. This makes sense but you should not be prevented from sailing by a disability.

Seasickness

A great deal is said about seasickness and a great deal of what is said is nonsense. Over some thirty years' sailing, much of it with novices, I have come to some conclusions.

When someone suffers a bout of seasickness there is no doubt that it can be a frightening and extremely unpleasant experience. On the part of the observer sympathy and understanding are called for. Non-sufferers often fail to understand this. The sufferers must not be allowed to let the problem get out of proportion, however.

Early stages
There are two distinct stages that are observed. The first stage, which precedes any vomiting, can creep up on the potential victim unawares. Initial symptoms may be confined to feeling hot or over-warm, a slight headache, dryness of the mouth and discomfort in the abdomen, bladder or chest.

These early warning signs are brought on by several causes. The most crucial is the loss of a fixed horizon either as a result of going below, closing one's eyes or staring at a disturbed sea. The symptoms are invariably more rapid in onset and more severe when one is hungry and/or cold or needing to urinate. Once these early symptoms are present it is extremely difficult to get the sufferer to eat. If you can, this will often limit or reduce the symptoms.

Observed symptoms
The onset off the initial symptoms always cause the sufferer to go quiet and to reduce bodily activity. If these signs are noticed, look for pallor with or without perspiration and for unusual irritability. A small job to do, a change of position so that the land is visible, a plain biscuit or bread or even a hot drink can reverse the process if the symptoms are noticed early.

Anxiety

Anxiety plays a large part. Activity such as taking the helm or obtaining bearings can distract and reduce the effects. Hard physical exercise particularly involving tension in the lower half of the body can accelerate the symptoms and should be avoided. Don't ask the victim to change a headsail.

The victim will be embarrassed by his or her own perceived weakness and loss of control and they will be reluctant to admit to any problem existing.

Second stage

Once the perspiration appears and the pallor takes on a greenish tinge, vomiting is almost bound to follow. Just before this starts the victim will start to loosen clothing and may move to a position close to the rail. At this time there will still be reluctance to admit to incapacity.

It is essential that the victim is attached by harness or is held firmly at this time since, once vomiting starts, he or she can easily slip overboard. The natural survival instinct is suppressed by the condition. During and after vomiting occurs, body temperature will drop and the victim will start to feel cold. Reluctance to go below at this time will be rational but if the weather is at all bad the skipper should insist.

Remedial action

Loss of body heat is rapid and overcooling can take place to the extent that hypothermia can start. Once below, the victim should be immediately placed horizontally, in a bunk and his outer garments should be removed in this position. If possible get the sufferer into, or at least wrapped in, a sleeping bag. A bucket will need to be provided although further vomiting is unlikely unless the sufferer attempts to move. If vomiting is frequent, water must be given to maintain body fluids. Seasickness is extremely debilitating and the patient should be encouraged to sleep as much as possible.

Cures

It has been said that the best treatment for seasickness is to stand under a tree. This certainly works! In my experience time and practice are the only cures that work afloat. You can assure any sufferers with confidence that the condition will not kill, despite what they may be feeling at the time, and that they will recover.

I have seldom met any sufferer who has not got over the problem by persisting in sailing. Each occasion will be less severe than the last and the occasions will occur less frequently. The major difficulty to be got over is the anxiety that results from having suffered or from anticipating the suffering.

Beginners should try to spend a few days sailing in fairly confined waters to get their 'sea legs' before venturing on to the open sea. Two or three days slow build up is enough to stop most people from suffering at all.

Prophylaxis

Many proprietary substances are on the market which, it is claimed, will prevent seasickness. Most are based on anti-histamines and all seem to cause some drowsiness.

They work best if the treatment is started at least 12 hours before sailing, so it makes sense to take a first dose before going bed the night before going aboard. This will have the added bonus of helping you to to get a good night's sleep.

Subsequent doses are less likely to make you drowsy. Continue with the tablets for at least three days before gradually reducing the dose and you may avoid the problem.

Pressure points

Bands to be worn on the wrist are currently available which have a stud to put pressure on a particular place. Great things are claimed of these bands but the results I have seen have been unconvincing. They may work for some people but cost as much as a two week course of tablets.

Injuries

A boat at sea is a fruitful source of injuries, due to the unpredictable motion in a confined space. Most of these injuries fortunately are not serious. Sensible precautions can avoid the more obvious hazards.

Burns and scalds

Risk of either of these injuries is present when cooking at sea and you should always take care. When cooking, trousers should be worn. At sea, waterproof trousers are best. They should be worn with boots so that any spills do not put the skin in direct contact with hot liquids.

Frying should be avoided on the move at all times. The use of large pans less than half full helps to reduce the risks since they are both more stable and less likely to splash over.

Any burn should be treated as potentially serious especially if extensive. The risk of infection is always high and sterile burn dressings should be carried in the first aid kit. Plenty of cold water is the best first aid.

Rope burns should be regarded in the same way as any other burn.

Fractures

Any fracture or suspected fracture should result in a change of plan in order to reach port as quickly as possible and any compound fracture certainly justifies a 'Pan Pan Medico' call. Shock in such an injury will be severe and must be anticipated. The patient must be immobilised to prevent aggravation of the condition

Other injuries

Other injuries will need to be treated on their merits but it is advisable for any skipper to complete a first aid course and to keep it current.

The 'Mayday' system (see page 188) can now be used in UK waters when a life is considered to be at risk. Each situation will have to be considered on its merits but try to avoid abusing the system. The Coastguard service would rather have an early, less urgent call than a real emergency where the call is too late. This is particularly true at night or when the rescue will be at night.

30   PERSONALITIES

The yacht skipper must be something of a psychologist. He or she needs to like people. The skipper needs to be able to encourage rather than force them to do things. Make it clear that you are the boss but try to do it with a degree of subtlety. It is often better to ask for something to be done than to order it. It is usually better not to use an imperative. 'Grab that rope!' or 'Duck!', will cause no problem but too many orders will offend quickly. It is always better to lead than to push.

Incompatibility

However carefully you select your crews you will be bound to get it wrong occasionally. With two crew members who don't get on, it is often fairly easy to make sure that they are in different watches. When you, as skipper, cannot get on with someone you have a bigger problem.

Reducing contact
It should not be an insurmountable problem, though it may well seem like it at the time. Try to minimise your contact by putting the problem individual with another watch. If it seems to be only you that finds them a problem this can work. If you all find it a problem then you will all have to share it.

Humour
When a particular individual presents a general problem, the difficulty will usually be apparent to all but the offender. It can then be treated with good humour by the rest of the crew. Take care that neither you nor anyone else is unkind though. He or she may not be as thick skinned as you think and it is a poor skipper who encourages disharmony.

You, and your crew, must remember that you are literally all in the same boat. You will be together until the end of the voyage. The situation must be treated lightly if the voyage is not to be spoilt for everyone. You, as skipper, must give the lead. Fortunately this kind of problem is fairly rare in my experience.

After many years of teaching sailing to literally hundreds of people of all ages, I have met very few whom I could not get on with. The exceptions are notable, memorable ones. With hindsight they can be hilarious so keep your sense of humour. Few of mine were aware of my antipathy, I hope. Never have I reached a stage where I have had to order someone off my boat, nor even come near it.

The non-sailor

I was discussing a past candidate for Yachtmaster with an RYA examiner recently. We both had vivid memories of this individual. My friend was philosophical. 'Ah well!', he said, 'He was the sort of chap we should have advised to take up gardening.' I mean no disrespect to gardeners but I know what he meant.

This sort of person is more problem than annoyance, especially if he is an otherwise likeable friendly sort of chap. He can be a danger to himself and to others. The skipper must prevent this without giving offence. Next time he asks to come you will need to find a plausible excuse.

Novices

Those who know nothing and are aware of this are no problem. They will be anxious to learn and will be willing to do what they are asked. Make sure they understand what you are asking. Don't blind them with technicalities. The skipper who treats novices with consideration and does not overstretch them will gain converts to the sport and useful, loyal crew for the future. The skipper who patronises or deliberately baffles with technicalities will not.

Know-alls

These types will upset everyone if given a chance. They can be a real danger. The skipper will need to assert himself early even if it means giving offence. Heavy weather, bad visibility or any other adverse conditions will often sort them out one way or another, but the process can worry less experienced crew. Whatever you do you must not let them take over your role and duty.

PART 8

Keeping a boat in good order

Boat maintenance is a subject which produces a great diversity of responses in sailors. For some it is the most important aspect of owning a yacht. For others is is simply a chore that takes away some of the enjoyment and prevents them from actually sailing.

Whichever end of that spectrum your particular view lies, there is little doubt that regular and effective maintenance is an integral part of yacht management.

31 MAINTENANCE ORGANISATION

Defects book

Repairs to and renewals of various parts of the yacht and its equipment are part of an ongoing process. To avoid being overwhelmed by them, organisation is important. A defects book should be kept on board so that jobs which need to be done can be noted as soon as they are spotted. Relying on one's memory at the end, or worse, at the beginning of a trip is no good.

The book should be organised into columns showing the date discovered, nature of defect, degree of urgency and date dealt with. Classifying things that need doing into levels of urgency helps a lot in planning action. The column indicating when a job has been cleared helps keep control and aids future checking.

'Routine'

All the regular recurring jobs such as winch cleaning and oil changes are not strictly defects unless they are neglected. These are best listed in the front of the book. Several columns should be ruled so that they can be marked off on more than one occasion. I prefer to deal with a winch a week rather than have the lot to do at once.

You may like to split the routine group by frequency, ie daily, weekly or monthly things, and seasonal things.

'Immediate'

The most important group of defects are those which affect the safe running of the vessel and need to be dealt with at once. They should still be entered in the record under the 'immediate' heading since it is useful to be able to see how effective a repair has been. Repeated failure of an item can indicate a further weakness – perhaps one of design, arrangement or effectiveness of the component, which might otherwise go undetected. It can also indicate inadequate repair work.

'Soon'

Call this group what you will. I use it to indicate defects which are not a hazard in themselves but which have an effect on comfort or convenience and those which will eventually cause serious problems if left. The kind of things I would include here would be a small leak above the water line, a fitting which rattles, worn whipping on a rope's end and the like. Important jobs in this section are those which are causing chafe or wear in something else. They need to be dealt with fairly quickly because they can otherwise reduce safety margins and/or increase maintenance costs.

Some of these jobs will be dealt with when they occur if the opportunity is there. None should be left more than a few days.

'When I can'

These are the kind of jobs that I tend to do in odd moments. Perhaps a minor modification, rearranging a stowage area, an odd spot of varnishing or painting. They are jobs which can easily get left too long if you are not careful. If you are adding lots of entries in the book it can be advisable to move isolated jobs forward if not able to deal with them. That way they move into the area of the book where you are likely to be looking.

'Next season'

As the name suggests, these are the things which can safely be left until the winter overhaul is done. A word of warning here. I find that it is far better to do as many of these jobs as possible soon after the end of the season rather than wait until just before relaunching. If you don't you may well find they get left until the next year.

There will be no point in doing some of them too soon of course. Anti-fouling for example must be left until you are ready to launch. Shot-blasting a cast keel, however, could easily be done in the autumn. The metal can then be treated with rust inhibiting paint then primed. It will save time later and reduce further degradation during the lay up period.

Some jobs such as minor gelcoat repairs are best done in autumn. The temperature and humidity are both more favourable then, rather than in spring when the air is likely to be colder and wetter. The resin will cure less well under such conditions and will have less time before being put to the test.

32 PLANNED SERVICING

Planned servicing includes regular checks on things that deteriorate in use, are subject to wear or are subject to rapid failure the onset of which can be observed. Examples of each could be winches, halyards and standing rigging.

In the first example, regular maintenance is required. With the second, a programme of staged replacement is needed. This is difficult to achieve but is best in the long run, both from reliability aspects and from the point of view of spreading the cost.

Rapid failure can never be totally avoided but regular checking can reduce the chances. What to look for is covered in Chapters 11 to 13 on rigging and fittings.

Engines

Engines form an important area in planned servicing for which correct procedures are laid down. Manufacturer's recommendations are worth observing. Daily, weekly and periodic routines are to be found in the handbooks and servicing manuals. These, if followed, will save money as well as protect you from problems associated with failure.

Winches

Amongst the routine maintenance jobs I mentioned winches. On a yacht of any size you may well have eight or more of these and they need regular checking if they are to give good service and not wear out. Winches can and do take a great deal of load. They will, given good care, last a very long time. This is just as well since they are expensive items. Sadly, many owners neglect winch care until damage occurs, and costly repairs or replacement may be necessary.

Figure 32.1 shows a Lewmar two speed winch stripped to its essentials. The springs, pawls and circlips (top right) are all easily replaced. Pawls tend to chip and should be replaced as soon as this happens since a damaged pawl can cause the winch to fail and can cause serious damage to more expensive parts. Reliability depends on smooth running of bearing surfaces but also on the rapid and reliable action of ratchet pawls.

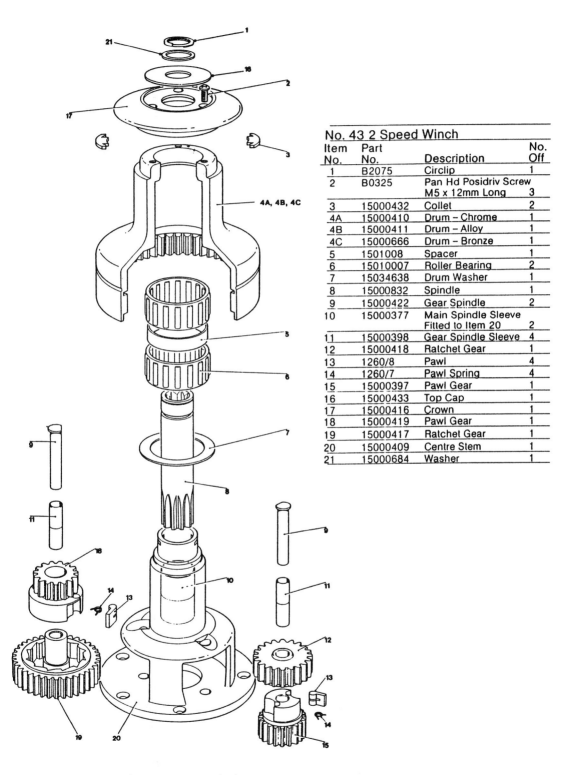

No. 43 2 Speed Winch		
Item No.	Part No.	Description	No. Off
1	B2075	Circlip	1
2	B0325	Pan Hd Posidriv Screw M5 x 12mm Long	3
3	15000432	Collet	2
4A	15000410	Drum – Chrome	1
4B	15000411	Drum – Alloy	1
4C	15000666	Drum – Bronze	1
5	1501008	Spacer	1
6	15010007	Roller Bearing	2
7	15034638	Drum Washer	1
8	15000832	Spindle	1
9	15000422	Gear Spindle	2
10	15000377	Main Spindle Sleeve Fitted to Item 20	2
11	15000398	Gear Spindle Sleeve	4
12	15000418	Ratchet Gear	1
13	1260/8	Pawl	4
14	1260/7	Pawl Spring	4
15	15000397	Pawl Gear	1
16	15000433	Top Cap	1
17	15000416	Crown	1
18	15000419	Pawl Gear	1
19	15000417	Ratchet Gear	1
20	15000409	Centre Stem	1
21	15000684	Washer	1

Fig 32.1 Lewmar winch

Stripping and assembly

If you have never stripped a winch before, the sight of so many small pieces can be alarming but it need not be. Work slowly when you dismantle the thing and see how it goes together. Winches are designed so that it is not possible to fit things the wrong way. If it won't go don't force it. Just try to rethink it.

The most common problem is an accumulation of salt deposits which can turn winch grease into a kind of thick cheesy substance. This will cause pawls to stick. If they stick they will not fully engage the ratchet and can chip or cause the whole drum to slip. I have known pawls to shatter completely.

When stripping and cleaning winches, put all the parts into a bucket as you go. Hold the drum in a bucket to remove the pawls and springs. You will lose far fewer this way. Check carefully for chipped or pitted pawls and replace any that are suspect.

Hot soapy water will remove both grease and salt. If the condition is particularly bad try Jeyes Fluid. An old toothbrush is useful for getting into the more intricate bits. Aluminium barrels are commonly used and need regular cleaning for prolonged life.

Use grease sparingly when reassembling and do not lubricate bronze or plastic bearing surfaces. Only recommended lubricants should be used on winches so, if in doubt, always check the makers instructions. Lewmar recommend light oil for pawls and springs. Certainly the first time you do the job you should either have the makers handbook with you or have the advice of someone who has done it before. Get him to show you on his winch rather than yours! There are a lot of self-styled 'experts' about.

Sheaves and pulleys

Sheaves must run freely under load and not just when you turn them by hand. Look for signs of wear or corrosion in the shafts, the sheave boxes and in the running surfaces. With multiple sheave boxes separators are often used to prevent lines from running off. These can become very worn. They can be sharpened by the rubbing action of cordage so that they are able to do considerable damage quite rapidly. Watch out for this problem and replace any that are doubtful.

Replacement

When replacing separators resist the temptation to 'make do' with any thin material to hand. The material used originally will have been the best for the job and it must be replaced with the same or similar. Beware particularly of using plastics which are apparently strong yet which have low melting points. Considerable heat can be generated when a rope rubs rapidly over a static surface. The material used must be able to withstand this.

Cleaning

Both blocks and sheave boxes can become clogged with salty residues. A jammed pulley can quickly wear a rope to nothing. In most cases these deposits are best removed with fresh water. The use of hot water with some detergent added can speed the process.

Knots and splices

In most instances the end of a permanently fixed line should be spliced rather than knotted. If a knot is necessary, it should at least be moused so that it can not work itself undone. It is often a good idea to mouse a knot used to make a temporary repair. This will make the repair more secure but don't let it tempt you into leaving the temporary to become permanent. Remember that a knot, even at best, is a point of weakness, whereas a properly done splice is as strong as the line itself.

Whipping

A splice can be strengthened as well as protected by whipping. This is particularly true of splices in braided lines such as those used for the sheets and halyards.

In the same way the ends of all cordage should be protected with whipping. Burning the ends makes a tidy finish. It should be considered in this light however and not as a substitute for whipping. Burning the ends of man-made fibre ropes will not only bond the fibres together; it will also produce a brittle lump which can separate.

Whipping not only keeps the end from fraying; in braided ropes it ensures that the core and sheath share the load evenly. Failure to do this can reduce the effective strength of the braided line to the point where failure will occur.

When Kevlar cored ropes are used, whipping is particularly important. Kevlar does not melt and so will not become bonded. Common whipping is satisfactory for the purpose and is easy to do. A sewn whipping will be stronger however. Make sure to keep whipping turns close together and the tension even. Extend the whipping to at least one and a half times the rope diameter. Use waxed whipping twine which goes on more tightly and evenly and lasts longer.

Cordage lengths

If you have made sure that every length of cordage used is a little over length, any wear noticed early should be no problem. Either end-for-end the line or cut off a short section at the working end and resplice. This will move the worn area away from the point of contact and prevent it getting worse.

It is essential that you find and remedy the cause of any wear unless purely due to age. If not the benefit will be short lived and the damage will simply start on a different part of the rope.

Check lists

As mentioned earlier, engine manufacturers provide check lists for engine maintenance. This idea can easily be extended to cover all the regular checks on any yacht. Make your own, they provide an invaluable way of making sure that things are not overlooked.

The common argument put forward against such lists is that you have to make up your own and so could easily miss things but this argument is not valid. I suggest you make up each list in note form at home to start with. When you next go aboard look about you and compare your notes with what you see needs doing. You will find you add many more items. Even if you have missed something your list is bound to cover more than you could without it.

The next stage is to keep a notebook handy and add things as they occur to you. This will often be whilst you are sailing so have it handy on board. You will probably get prompts from reading books or sailing magazines. All these should be added to the lists.

The final stage in the process is to refine the lists and to decide on the frequency needed. The order of doing things as well as the frequency will be much easier than you might think. Your completed check lists should be stored in some permanent form on board. The plastic folders that hold sheets of paper in transparent sleeves are best.

Don't confine lists to maintenance problems only. Have lists of all the loose items you need on board in order to sail, for bedding and wet weather gear, for spares and their locations, where the sea cocks are, what safety gear is carried and where, engine and gas routines, etc. In fact for anything which calls for an established procedure.

Portfolio

A carefully established portfolio built up in this way can be invaluable, not only to you but also to those who sail with you from time to time. It can be used to let them know where to find things and also to encourage them to put things away.

33 LOOKING AFTER ENGINES

The engine in a sailing yacht is only an auxiliary source of power and thus often under used and often neglected. Today most yachts have reliable diesel engines tending to give little trouble. Owners often cause problems because they do not understand potential difficulties and fail to carry out regular preventative maintenance.

Engine failure

Strictly, at least when at sea in a sailing boat, engine failure is no problem. If you have wind you sail. If you have none you wait. When approaching harbour the extent of the problem will depend on your advance practice. You should have learned early in your sailing how to pick up a mooring and to put down an anchor under sail. You should have enough confidence in your sailing ability to be able to enter a harbour under sail and to bring your vessel to a safe stop.

You have been neglecting a major part of your duty as a yacht skipper if you cannot do these things and should put the situation right as soon as possible!

Ability to sail

You ought to be able to sail your vessel out of trouble on any point of sailing. There should be only two situations where sailing alone cannot get you out of trouble; when there is no wind or when you are in a place that you should not be. When sailing you should always avoid putting the boat into a position which cannot be sailed out of. From this I exclude entry to or departure from a marina berth but very little else.

If your engine fails in a berthing situation you will have to work your vessel alongside others with minimal damage. The ease or difficulty of this manoeuvre will depend on wind and tide and on your skill.

Practice

All manoeuvres must be learned under sail. At first you can have the engine running. When confidence grows the engine can be warm but stopped. There is some argument about this but I feel that not having the engine running improves concentration a lot! Before long you will find that you hardly think to start it. By this time your general boat handling will have improved considerably. You will be well on the way to yachtmastery.

Learn to regard your engine as it is meant to be, an auxiliary means of propulsion and not a primary source. If you do this you will find that engine failure is little more than a nuisance in almost any situation.

Engine operation

Diesel engines are used in boats because the fuel does not burn too readily and because they do not need electricity to keep them going. In fact, if you have enough muscle power to get one started, you need have no electrics on board. Instead of a spark the fuel is ignited purely by the pressure in the cylinders. To do this a high compression is needed. Usually it is about three times as high as in a petrol engine. Several things follow from this.

Fuel injection

To withstand the high pressures, diesel engines tend to be bigger and heavier than their petrol equivalents. They take longer to get up to operating temperature as a consequence. The fuel has to be injected into the cylinder in exactly the right minute quantity and at precisely the right time to make it work. This means that a very high pressure is needed in the injector. It follows that the hole through which it is injected must be very small.

Injectors are pieces of precision machinery. Dirty fuel will block or damage them. Even a minute amount of water in the fuel will stop them working. Condensation that forms in the cylinder can cause rust which will damage the injector, either by enlarging the hole or by preventing it from closing properly.

Loading

Diesels like to be worked hard. Long periods of running under load are good for them. Short periods during which they cannot reach full operating temperature or running them with no load, or too light a one, are bad for them, particularly when new.

Without going into too much detail, the effect is to cause polishing of the bores and coating of the rings so that the piston seal becomes inadequate. This reduces efficiency, makes starting more difficult and causes smoking. The modern trend of fitting higher powered engines in yachts has made this problem worse since the engine is seldom run under full load.

Whenever possible, choose a time when the engine can be run under load to charge your batteries; during harbour manoeuvres or when motor-sailing for example. The engine should always be run for long enough time to reach full operating temperature, this means about half an hour to an hour minimum, to prevent moisture formed when the fuel burns from producing condensation in the cylinders.

Oil

Oil changes are important and must be regularly carried out for three reasons. Because of the higher pressures and temperatures involved the oil tends to break down more quickly, more waste deposits collect in it and thirdly, because the marine engine will not be run in a level position, lubrication may not be quite so efficient.

The level indicated by the engine manufacturer is particularly crucial in marine engines. Too much and you risk engine damage due to the crankshaft hitting the oil surface. Too little and one or more bearings can be starved of oil when heeled. The maximum angle of heel at which the engine can be safely run is usually specified. Make sure that you are aware of this and do not exceed it.

Cooling systems

Marine engines are normally water cooled for obvious reasons. Two systems are used. The open system uses sea water which is pumped in and round the engine before being ejected. The closed system has a sealed coolant, normally fresh water, which is cooled in a heat exchanger using sea water. The sea water is normally ejected through the exhaust system in both methods since it reduces the temperature of the exhaust and also helps to reduce noise.

The closed system has the advantage that the coolant is less corrosive to the engine but it is somewhat less efficient and requires two pumps.

Water filter

Both systems depend on a through flow of sea water. The water is often passed through a filter before going into the engine to avoid solid matter clogging the system. This filter needs to be checked regularly so as to make sure it does not become blocked. The filter will normally be found fitted directly to the water intake. Do not forget to close the sea cock before removing the filter and to open it again before restarting the engine.

If you close the engine sea cocks when the engine is not in use, a simple idea will remind you to open them again. Make up a small tag, a plastic label is best, marked 'sea cocks closed'. Hang the tag on the inlet sea cock when this is opened and hang it on the engine start control when the sea cock is closed. It could save you trouble.

Checking the flow

Every time the engine is started and from time to time when it is running, the cooling water outlet should be checked. Should the flow stop, the cause must be found and corrected. It is not sufficient to rely on the temperature warning device which often does not come in until the engine is badly overheated.

Strum box filter

Some boats have a mesh filter fitted on to the hull over the inlet hose. If this gets blocked it is difficult to get at. One solution is to carry a length of flexible tube to fit over the sea cock outlet Figure 33.1. When a blockage occurs, close the sea cock then remove the pipe connected to the engine and substitute your hose. Keeping the open end above the waterline, connect it to your dinghy pump. Reopen the sea cock and pump. This should work since the debris will be blown back the way it came. Close the sea cock again before removing the pipe and restoring the system.

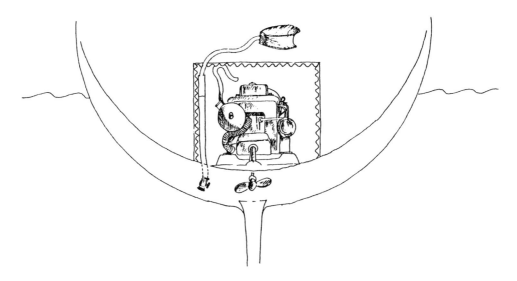

Fig 33.1 Clearing a blocked water intake

Fuel

Care over the quality and cleanliness of fuel put in the tank of any engine, regular cleaning of filters and/or changing elements together with periodic cleaning of the tank will go a long way towards improving reliability.

Fuel injection

If a diesel engine starts to smoke suspect the injectors and have them checked and reset. It is often possible to get an exchange set which saves time out of use. If you allow your engine to run out of fuel, air will reach the injector pump which will prevent the engine firing. A single drop of water reaching the injector pump can do the same thing. In either case the engine will need bleeding until all air or water has been cleared from both the high and low pressure sides of the system.

Clear the low pressure side first by opening the bleed nut on the fuel pump and pumping manually until clean fuel flows continuously from it. If the pump is provided with two nuts, slacken off the lower one first and retighten it before slackening the upper. Place a clean empty tin can under the pump to avoid fuel in the bilges because you may have to pump quite a lot through. You can put most of this fuel back into the fuel tank when you have finished the job. Next, using the makers instructions, bleed the high pressure side which usually involves opening and venting two or three bleed points in sequence whilst turning the engine over by hand.

If you do not have the correct instructions do not despair since it is sometimes possible to bleed successfully by slackening the nuts holding the injector feed pipes one at a time and turning the engine until bubble-free fuel runs out. You must continue to turn the engine when closing them again to maintain the pressure.

Compression

If a diesel engine fails it will almost certainly be due either to lack of fuel at the injector or to loss of compression. Long before failure due to the latter cause happens, starting problems and power loss will be noticed. If in doubt have the compression tested.

Outboard engines

The commonest failures of petrol/oil outboard engines are those concerning electrics; even more than dirty fuel. Salt water is not the ideal environment for electrical circuitry. Modern electronic ignition systems have considerably improved reliability but they still need looking after.

Keeping water out

Make sure that covers and cowlings fit properly and that the seals are intact. Use a water inhibiting spray from time to time on the wiring. Keep the plug insulators clean and the spark gaps set correctly. Use waterproof grease on all the nipples regularly and also on any exposed clamp screw threads.

Plugs

With two-stroke engines the spark plug gap enlarges comparatively rapidly in use whilst the contact point gap (if there is one) tends to close but more slowly. This will lead to difficulty in starting and in running at low speeds if the plug gap is not reset regularly; after about 25 hours running is sufficient.

Fuel problems

Fuel starvation produces similar symptoms but can also cause the engine to stop suddenly when the throttle is opened fully. Preventative maintenance should include cleaning the tank regularly together with the whole fuel system from tank to carburettor.

Stale fuel

Avoid leaving the fuel vent open when the engine is not in use because doing so will cause faster evaporation of the petrol. Oil does not evaporate so the mixture then gets too oily leading to plug troubles. If the engine has been left for any length of time unused, the mixture will degrade and it may not be possible to fire it. The remedy is to avoid leaving the tank full for long periods and always use fresh fuel when running the engine after a lay-up period.

Salt removal

Before laying up and every time the outboard engine is to be left unused for a while, run it through in fresh water to which a little water soluble oil has been added to remove salt from the system. A bucket will do but a test tank is better. If using a bucket be sure to clamp the engine firmly first and remember you cannot run the engine in gear. Never, even briefly, start an outboard engine without cooling water. Long before it overheats damage will be done to the pump which is not designed to run dry.

34 LOOKING AFTER THE HULL

Any structural damage which threatens the integrity of the hull must be an urgent repair on any boat. Whilst major repairs to the hull are outside the scope of this book there are many excellent works on the subject. In what follows I have limited my suggestions to GRP and wood being the two most commonly used materials found in modern boats.

Wooden boats will need even minor hull damage put right quickly to prevent rot. Ferro-concrete and steel boats are easiest to repair without leaving any signs. Minor damage to concrete can be repaired with a cement mortar although penetration damage may require the damaged area to be cut out and for the repair to include linking new metal reinforcing material to the old. Steel is even easier to repair since damaged or corroded areas can be cut out and new plate welded in place.

Two general points are worth making; if any hull damage is extensive a survey may be necessary and, thorough cleaning and preparation are worthwhile in every case before effecting the repair.

GRP repairs

GRP is more tolerant than wood but should not be left too long since water can be absorbed into the fabric through cracks and scrapes. If the gelcoat has not been penetrated, the job is best left until the boat can be taken out of the water. Before starting to fill holes, all traces of salt must be removed with fresh water and the damaged area left to dry out completely. Skimping on this is a waste of time since the repair will not hold and will need repeating.

Any repair to GRP will not be invisible so try to minimise the area worked on to that actually damaged. It is next to impossible for the amateur to repair gelcoat so that it does not show. Colour match even with white is very difficult. Small grazes that have not penetrated the gel are best left alone or treated with a gelcoat cleaner and then smoothed very carefully with extra fine wet and dry abrasive paper. Fibreglass polish can then be used to seal the surface. If you have to fill small holes be sure to wipe off any surplus filling material from surrounding areas before it sets.

Looking after woodwork

Varnish should be kept for below decks as far as I am concerned. I am talking here about boats with wood trim rather than wooden boats. I envy the owners of boats with beautifully varnished hulls and topsides. The appearance of their vessels is a delight, but I do not envy them the labour that goes to producing and preserving that appearance. Wood on boats needs protection. It needs protection from water, salt, abrasion and from the sun. Also, its appearance needs looking after. If these basic premises are accepted the rest follows.

Any damage needs early attention since if water is allowed to penetrate the wood, rot or swelling or both will quickly follow. Damage only happens when the quantity of water in the wood is wrong. Wood needs some moisture to maintain its maximum strength. Both rot and swelling can be limited or prevented, either by coating the surface with a waterproof layer, or by impregnating it with one. Paint or varnish provide the former and oil the latter. I prefer oil for several reasons which will become apparent.

Salt in wood

Salt-impregnated wood is much less susceptible to rot but tends to go from one extreme to the other with regard to its water content. Abrasion spoils the appearance of the wood and can, if it is excessive, affect its strength.

Sun

Too much sun causes several problems. It can bleach the surface thus spoiling the appearance. It can remove too much moisture causing the wood to become brittle and to crack. It can also overheat coated wood causing water vapour to push the coating off. This is a point to consider if you have wooden spreaders. They may look fine from below where the sun has not been, yet be bare and rotting on the top surface. A spreader failure can mean a mast failure.

Teak oil

Oil can prevent most of these problems. Teak, often used for deck fittings and trim, is very resistant to rot anyway but does not take varnish well. Cleaned and oiled, the wood will maintain its appearance. It will breathe rather than suffer sun damage whilst resisting the entry of excess water. Most of all, oiled wood provides a non-slip surface even when wet. This must make better sense for things like hand rails and for cockpit soles. It also resists abrasion better than varnish so works better for rubbing strakes and the like.

Wood to be oiled should first be treated with a cleaner such as Teakbrite, which improves the appearance of the wood before teak oil is applied. The teak oil should be put on by the application of several thin coats. Apply to dry wood only. Choose a day that is dry but fairly cool so that the oil penetrates the wood rather than drying on the surface. The wood must be touch dry between coats.

Varnish

Below decks, varnish will last well and give a good appearance provided the surfaces have been well prepared. If the original is chipped or peeling it is best removed first. If it is sound it can be keyed and smoothed with glass paper before applying two thin coats on top of the old.

New wood will need five coats for good results. The first coat should be thinned with turps and allowed to dry thoroughly before the next coat is applied. Subsequent coats need to be done at 24 hour intervals.

There is a great mythology about varnishing. I have found little evidence to justify the mystique with modern yacht varnish. As long as a good quality, clean brush is used and there is no dust, or undue moisture, in the atmosphere a good result can be obtained. In misty conditions varnish can bloom to produce a cloudy surface. A further application in dry conditions will normally remedy this however.

Upholstery and headlinings

I have frequently found yacht upholstery to have 'dry clean only' labels. This is ridiculous. I can understand a fabric manufacturer not knowing the conditions on a yacht, but not a boat builder who chooses such a material. Anything that will shrink if it gets wet is no good on a boat.

Cushion covers

Cloth is more comfortable to sleep on than plastic coverings, but needs more care to keep the bunks dry if you are the sort of sailor who goes out in a blow. Once fabric and or foam get wet with salt water it is very difficult to keep them dry. The salt attracts moisture and, as soon as the weather becomes humid, things start to get very damp. The only solution is to wash (or dry clean!) out the salt.

Use of a car vacuum cleaner regularly on your upholstery will keep its appearance up quite well. Remove any food spillages when they happen rather than wait until other dirt has added to the problem. The spray type carpet cleaner is good for removing grease spots but test on an inconspicuous area first.

Fastenings

Zips on cushions are frequently made from 'pot metal'. This dissolves in salt water at an alarming rate. The practice is inexcusable and I advise anyone buying a new boat to insist on all plastic or at least brass zips. Plastic zip sliders are available. I have been told they are not but have them on my boat so don't be fobbed off.

Headlinings

Headlinings can be kept smart with regular washing using detergent in warm water. If you do much frying your headlinings can collect a surprising amount of grease. This will produce mould quite fast if not removed. Mould stains are often difficult to remove. Oxalic acid works quite well but, again, check the effect on colour in an inconspicuous area first. It may do more than you think. Bleach in the correct concentration is fine on plastics. Some of the patent cleaners do an excellent job.

Bilges and pumps

Regular cleaning of bilges prevents the build up of nasty smells and strange growths. Proprietary bilge cleaners are available but will not make up for failure to do the job regularly. Lots of water sluiced round gives a good chance to check the pumps. Take the opportunity to check all of them, including any emergency ones. You should have at least two pumps anyway. This is particularly important if you have an electric pump. If you spring a leak and fill up fast, covering the battery, the pump may not work.

At least once a season take the manual pumps apart and clean them carefully according to the maker's instructions. Don't wait until you are sinking to find out that a pump does not work too well.

35 DRYING OUT FOR INSPECTIONS

Even if you leave your boat on the water from one year to the next it is important to dry out at least once a season to check on what is happening below. You will have to clean and antifoul the bottom anyway.

If you have a suitable place alongside a wall or quay, with strong fixing points on top and hard standing alongside free from obstructions this will do. It is a lot cheaper and easier to dry out there than to pay for a lift out. The first time you do this it is fraught. Relax; do the job properly and you will have no problems.

Choose a day with little wind and settled weather, preferably with a spring tide to give you more time. Festoon the side that is to rest against the wall with all the fenders you can lay hands on. Approach your chosen position just before top of tide. Have two good warps at each end and a further one amidships. Do not let her touch bottom before stopping. Once alongside, the bow and stern lines should be attached to the strong points on the wall with all the spare on board so that any adjustment can be made there.

You will need to have some water under you when you stop to give you time to tie up and get ready. You are aiming to touch bottom with the keel just far enough out from the wall to give the boat a lean of a few degrees towards the wall. You are going to continue to settle down after you have tied up so don't make the lines too tight in the first instance.

It helps but is not essential to have help here. Laying the anchor chain along the deck on the side next to the wall is sometimes recommended to provide the necessary heel. It is not essential and on a light displacement craft just standing there will usually be enough.

You will not know, if this is the first time that you have dried out this boat, whether it is liable to settle level, by the bow or by the stern. Your shore lines will prevent any serious problem whichever way she goes. Figure 35.1 shows all the lines you will need.

Getting the heel

Remove the main halyard from its stowage and attach it to a strong point ashore and in line with the mast, preferably several feet in from the edge of the wall. Now take your midships warp. Pass it round the mast above the boom fitting inside any lines running there so that it can slide up and down. Figure 35.2.

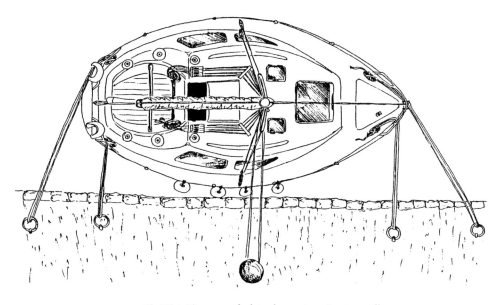

Fig 35.1 Lines needed to dry out against a wall

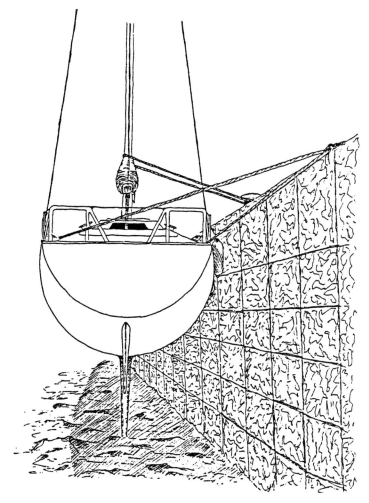

Fig 35.2 Drying alongside

Have one person on each bow and stern line standing on the near side. Take control of the main halyard yourself. As the yacht goes down with the tide take up slack on the main halyard to maintain the required angle of heel. It is not critical so long as it is about 5 degrees from vertical. The tension should be maintained on the bow and stern lines until she touches. At this point they are made fast. Once these are secured the crew should double up on each with the spare lines. If possible they should be connected to different strongpoints on both wall and boat from the first set. The first pair are the belt, these are the braces.

Next, have the line round the mast taken up tight and secured. With the main halyard cleated off all that remains is to wait for the water to go. Any small settlement will be taken up with the stretch of the ropes and if she tries to tip fore and aft the pairs of lines at bow and stern should hold her level.

What to look for

When you are dried out and cleaned off have a look at the packing round the keel to hull joint if it bolts on. With GRP boats a good deal of movement can take place here. Loss of the packing is common. It can allow corrosion of the keel bolts to start long before any problem is apparent from inside the hull.

Shaft support

The 'P' or 'A' bracket is a further source of problems. Try a vigorous pull and see if it will move. If so, it will have to go in your defects book. A slight movement need not be serious but it will leak and is not going to get better. If the movement is more than slight it will cause shaft movement. This in turn will produce wear in the cutless bearings and the stern gland as well as unwelcome vibration. In severe cases it can lead to structural failure.

Shaft

Next look at your shaft. Does it have an anode or should it have? Shaft anodes may not seem cheap but they are a great deal cheaper than propellers. Always assume that your propeller will waste away if it is not protected, as will the keel and skin fittings.

Skin fittings

Skin fittings should be checked carefully for cracks and for corrosion. This corrosion is often more common at, or along, the hull join than on the surface. Look for signs of discolouration of the gel. Good earth bonding internally plus a sacrificial anode provides protection.

Whilst on the subject of anodes don't forget that their effectiveness depends on contact both with the metal fittings and with the water. Don't paint them with antifouling. I once pointed this out to someone who was busy antifouling his. He told me that he knew they should not be painted but that he found that they lasted a lot longer if they were. Ah well!

Rudder gear

The last thing to look at whilst you are down there is the rudder. Check it and the mountings for movement. Spade rudders on GRP boats are often foam filled. Any cracks can let in water which may cause the foam to break down and reduce the rudder's strength. If it has any damage showing, carry out repairs so that it does not get worse.

Refloating

Do not remove any skin fitting unless you have a spare of the right size ready and waiting to replace it. If you have a hole in the hull which you are unable to fill when the tide starts coming in, that sinking feeling you will get is likely to be fully justified.

As the water returns, you should be checking that all the sea cocks that need closing have been closed. Once the hull is supported by the returning tide the main halyard should be slackened off to avoid putting undue strain on the mast. If the wall is at or below deck level the mooring lines will need adjusting too.

Before casting off make sure that the engine is started and working properly. If you have done work on it make sure it will go into gear. I have seen the results of omission in this area. The unfortunate owner had drained the oil from his hydraulic clutch and forgotten to refill it. Despite a calm day considerable damage was done to his gelcoat before the situation was retrieved.

36 LAYING UP

Unless you intend to use your yacht all the year round, you will have to lay it up in the winter. Laying up ashore is preferable to laying up afloat since it gives several advantages. The hull will get a chance to dry out. You will be able to carry out any repairs below the waterline more easily. It will be safer from winter gales. Getting the boat ready in the spring for the new season will be easier. When laying up ashore, the hull should be cleaned off immediately the boat comes out. This is much easier then and also allows a full inspection to be made for damage or osmosis. If possible the mast and rigging should be removed and stored separately.

Boatyard

Having made the decision to lay up ashore you will need to decide where. The most convenient, but also the most expensive, will undoubtedly be a boatyard. Most yards are able to provide water and electric power which will make cleaning and repairing so much easier. You will also have better security. Do remember however, that insurance of your boat in the yard is normally your responsibility and make sure that you check on this. Leave the yard staff to do the propping. They will be used to it and will have the responsibility if it falls.

Backyard

The next possibility, if your boat is not too big and you have room, is to have her brought to your own, or nearby, premises. This can make working on her more convenient but you will not have the yard facilities when it comes to chandlery and spares, nor will you have the expert advice that a yard provides. A cradle built for, or adjusted to, your boat is the best support system. If the ground is at all soft, use boards under it to spread the load.

Props, when used, must always be on load spreaders unless the ground is very hard in all weathers. Join pairs of props both across and along the boat with lathes nailed on and nail the props to the support boards. This bracing is important because strong winds can cause vibrations that may otherwise work the props free. Use wedges between hull and props to spread the load and to even it up. Keep the load on the crane until secure, then have it let off very slowly. Watch carefully for any movement.

Regulations

Some local councils take a dim view of boats in front, or even back, gardens so check on this. You won't want an injunction to move her served on you just as you have stripped out the engine.

Mud berth

The third possibility is a compromise. This is to have a mud berth, a drying one or to beach her on a high spring tide so that she is seldom afloat. Security is less good in this situation and you must be sure that she is safe from weather coming from any direction.

The bow should be driven on to the beach gently. Legs, if used, must be set up first. Shore lines should then be set to prevent any sideways movement. The stern can be held with kedge anchors or by a line taken back to a permanent mooring. This method is best used for boats with bilge or lifting keels since props are difficult to set satisfactorily.

Afloat

You can lay up on a mooring or a pontoon berth. Fore and aft mooring is preferable since it is kinder to the boat and gives two chances against dragging. Make sure that she will lie with her bows to the prevailing wind in good shelter. Fore and aft mooring can put great strains on gear.

The bow should be on chain but it helps to use a nylon bridle in addition. The bridle should be attached low down on the chain so that it is just taking the strain. This will reduce the effects of snatch loads. The aft bridle should be rope and must be slack enough so that the boat can swing a little at high water.

Chafe must be considered carefully. All points of entry of chain and ropes should be parcelled with rags. An alternative to rags where the entry is through a fairlead is to use a length of soft plastic hose fed over the rope. Make a small hole in the hose at the inboard end and tie the hose to the rope with a length of cordage fed through the hole (Figure 36.1).

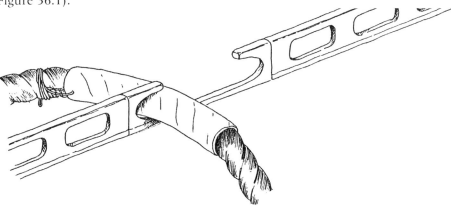

Fig 36.1 Reducing chafe through a fairlead

Stern lines will often rub on the transom. If this happens, do not use hose. It will remove the gelcoat over a winter. Instead, use old towels. These will wear away and will need checking but are much kinder to the gel.

If you must use a pontoon berth, guarding against chafe during winter gales is even more important. Fenders can do considerable damage to the topsides in a blow and a wildly girating pontoon puts enormous strains on the warps and deck fittings. Some of this strain can be reduced by springing with old tyres, secured by chain to the pontoon cleats and by well protected ropes to the boat. To protect the topsides it is a good idea to have mats made up using closed cell foam covered with old sail cloth. The mats will have little movement relative to the hull but will need to be kept clean over the winter.

Whichever way your boat is laid up she must never be left in winter without frequent inspections. If you can not do these yourself find someone reliable who will do them for you.

Stripping out

However the laying up is to be done, certain things are common. The biggest problem when the boat is out of use is dampness. This will be avoided to some extent if the boat is ashore but condensation will still occur with low temperatures. The suggestions that follow assume the boat to be laid up ashore.

For reasons of damp, if for no other, all the items of bedding, sails, cushions and spare cordage should be removed and taken home for dry storage. Sails have been discussed in Chapter 14. They should be washed free of salt, any stains removed and any necessary repairs carried out. If possible, the sails are best hung in a dry loft where air can circulate. Failing this they should be thoroughly dried then folded loosely and stored in a warm dry place. Berth cushions should have their covers removed, cleaned and repaired. Be sure to store any buttons in a safe place.

All instruments should be removed and taken ashore where possible and any needing servicing should be dealt with straightaway. All dry batteries must be removed from instruments and torches etc. Don't leave any spare batteries on board either since they will not survive the winter.

Mast removal

If it is intended that the mast is to be taken down, this should be done at the lift out when the crane is still available. All the rigging should be disconnected, inspected and cleaned. Each shroud is best labelled so that re-rigging is made easier next season. Store all bottlescrews, shackles, swivels, clevis pins and so on in a strong container so that none get lost. Old icecream containers are ideal. Spray the parts with light oil before storing so that the threads will be free.

Running rigging

Running rigging should be removed. This should be done whether or not the mast is to be left up. As each item is drawn out, make sure that a length of thin cord is substituted. Each should be labelled for ease of replacement. Inspect each item for wear and either renew or repair any damaged ones. If you order new parts now it saves a rush at the start of the new season. Any pieces that are being kept should be washed and dried before storage.

Spars

The mast and boom will need to be stored. If this is to be done on board some simple precautions are necessary. Even modern aluminium masts should be supported along their length. If they are not, a permanent bend can be established which is very difficult to remove. They should be chocked up at intervals of not less than six feet on wooden supports. If they are left touching any metal items, electrolysis will take place. Separate individual spars from each other with pieces of plastic foam.

Clean thoroughly all castings, channels for slides, luff grooves and so on. Include all sheave boxes and sheaves replacing any damaged items. Check all fittings for corrosion and tightness of rivets. Clean and service any mast winches.

Vulnerable fittings

Masthead and steaming or deck lights should be removed as soon as the mast is down and stored separately after cleaning. Now is the time to check the condition of the wiring and replace it or remake connections. Any masthead sensors and aerials should also be removed for storage. Free plugs and sockets can be sprayed with light oil, special electrical lubricant sprays are available, then covered with plastic bags tightly taped on to keep out moisture.

Engine

The engine should be winterised unless it is to be on a boat left afloat. In this case the engine should be run at least weekly and for at least half an hour.

Winterising
Winterising is concerned with reducing risks of corrosion. The cooling system and the cylinders are the most vulnerable areas. When the boat is to be laid up ashore, the cooling system should be flushed through with fresh water to which a rust inhibiting agent has been added and then drained.

Oil
All oils and oil filters should be changed whilst the engine is still warm. Cylinders can be protected by putting in engine oil. This can be done through the injectors. First

remove each injector and squirt in a small amount of oil. Turn the engine over by hand gently and then add a little more oil to each cylinder. Replace the injectors. Do not overtighten them.

I also spray the outside of my engine with aerosol oil after touching up the paintwork.

At the start of the new season the engine should be turned whilst decompressed at first to remove this oil. If this is not done the connecting rods and bearings could be damaged.

The foregoing is a limited description only. Full details of recommended winterising procedures can be obtained from marine engine main agents or the manufacturers.

Batteries

By far the best way to prolong the life of your batteries is to take them ashore and to keep them fully charged. Failing this, make sure that they are topped up with distilled water and are fully charged before the boat is lifted out. Flat batteries if left for a long period will seldom give satisfactory service again.

Below decks

Gas bottles should be removed from the boat. Drain all fresh water from the tanks if there is any risk of frost. If it is to be left then add purification tablets. Remove any bunk boards, leave all cupboards open and lift the cabin sole. This will aid air circulation. Try to remove all traces of water from the bilge by sponging out any you can not pump. Clean and grease all sea cocks and leave them open. Use of the crystal type dehumidifiers is quite effective. They will need to have the collected water drained out weekly and the crystals replaced when used up.

Heads
The heads system should be flushed through with clean water then disinfectant. Remove all traces of water from the system via the drain hole provided.

Galley
Remove all foodstuffs including cans as well as pots, pans and utensils. These are best stored at home. Clean all surfaces of storage areas inside and out and finish with a mould inhibitor. This should also be used to clean and protect headlinings. Baby's bottle sterilising fluid works well and costs only a fraction of the price of proprietary brands.

Cover

If the boat is to be in covered storage consider which vents can be left open without affecting security. Hatches often have a position in which they can be locked ajar. If it is to be stored in the open consider rigging a cover but be sure that air can circulate under it. Do not use the mast as a ridge pole unless it has very generous and frequent supports. It is better to make a couple of cross-leg supports with a length of 'four by two' as a ridge pole.

Don't leave your boat untended for six months or so and expect it to survive unscathed. Make regular visits and open her up to the air when weather allows. If you have followed all of these suggestions the start of the next season should cause you few problems.

PART 9

When things go wrong

When things go wrong, in any circumstances, you need to keep calm if you are to sort the problems out. On a boat a cool head is essential. At sea you are more truly on your own than in any other situation. What you do will depend on your personal resources. The last thing you need is the panic that so often takes over in stress situations.

Since panic comes from not knowing what to do, by far the best method of avoiding it is forward planning. Having advance plans for as many eventualities as you can think of reduces the risk. More importantly, it means that you can deal more quickly and effectively with the problems that do arise.

37 EMERGENCY EQUIPMENT

Every cruising yacht should have certain so-called 'safety equipment' as standard. I say 'so-called' because I feel it is wrongly named. When you need any of these things you are not safe. The essential items which I prefer to call emergency equipment, are given in the table below. The following paragraphs discuss some of the items in greater detail.

EMERGENCY EQUIPMENT
(minimum requirement)

Flares
4 Red parachute   4 White pin-point
6 Red pin-point   2 Orange smoke

Lifebelts 2 horseshoe c/w strobe light and drogue

Heaving line 20 m of floating line c/w monkeys fist or ball

Torches minimum two waterproof

Danbuoy c/w flag 2 m above water (plus light if not joined to lifebelt)

Fire extinguishers 2 Dry powder (13A/113B total capacity) fitted near exits
                    1 BCF or Halon for engine

Fireblanket fitted close to galley

Buckets 2 c/w lanyards on strong handles

Boarding ladder either fitted or quick mounting

In addition there must be a harness and a lifejacket for each crew member (including children's sizes if young children are aboard).

Flares

Flares should be in date and in sufficient quantity. The quantities included in the ready made up packs are minimum quantities. Although flares are expensive it is worth having a few extra, particularly the red distress flares. People who have had to use them often report afterwards that they were not noticed. I always carry the 'offshore' standard which are sufficiently high powered and fire to a sufficient height to be seen over a good distance. For safety, only the best is good enough.

Old flares

Out dated flares should not be thrown away. Keep those least out of date so that you have a double supply. I once passed on to the Coastguard a batch of about 100 old flares that had been given to me. They were later used for practice and I was told that none of them failed to work, although some were more than five years out of date. Never dispose of old flares by firing them off yourself. It is not just an offence, it is also very inconsiderate since it may give a false alarm, putting lives at risk and causing needless expense. Never throw them away ashore either. Your nearest Coastguard or police station will gladly take them for practice or disposal. Contrary to popular belief, it is not permitted to fire old distress flares on Guy Fawkes night.

38 DAMAGE

Minor damage

Minor damage to things that will not affect the safety of the vessel but will make life difficult must be separated from the kind that is potentially serious. Consider for example something like a broken split pin. If it secures a halyard shackle it could cause the loss of the shackle or possibly even the sail to fall down whilst one broken on a shroud bottlescrew could bring the mast down.

Whenever you notice any fitting that is faulty, or becoming so, it is necessary to consider the consequence of its complete failure. Any minor damage you sustain to your vessel should always be possible to repair from your own resources. Which spares you should carry depends on your particular boat. Start by thinking of things that may break and how you would repair them. Minor damage can become a major problem if you lack the basic items to remedy the trouble early. A supply of several sizes of cordage, filler, shackles, screws, nuts and bolts, split pins and insulating tape together with spares kits for the engine, dinghy, heads and any pumps, plus a good tool kit will solve most problems.

Tools

Your tool kit will need to contain several types of screwdrivers, spanners to fit the engine, particularly the bleed screws, and an adjustable spanner. It should also include pliers, a rubber mallet, a hammer and a general purpose saw as the basic items. A cordless drill, a 12v soldering iron and a couple of clamps are useful additions. If you know you need special tools for particular jobs include these also.

Major damage

This is something which will, or could, affect the safety of the boat. A shroud parting, a serious leak or steering damage would be the kind of thing.

Broken shrouds or stays

If a stay or shroud parts you can lose the mast. If it happens due to severe weather you almost certainly will do so, but quick reactions can sometimes save the day. I have had on occasion a shroud, the forestay and the backstay break. Each at separate times I hasten to add. On none of these occasions did I lose the mast.

Should the mast come down, the choice is between cutting it away or attempting to lash it to the hull. Bolt croppers should always be carried in case rigging needs to be cut. The decision to cut will depend mainly on the wind and sea conditions at the time.

It is never worth risking hull damage from flogging spars but it may be possible to salvage a part or all of the broken gear to use for jury rigging. It is often cheaper too, for the damaged spar to be repaired, than to replace it. This will depend on circumstances. Never risk the vessel to save the spar. For the most part, if you have sufficient fuel, it will be better to lash everything fast and make for port under power. If risk of further damage is high, cut free and do the same.

When a stay or shroud parts you will hear a loud bang. It sounds not unlike a rifle shot. You will see the broken item swinging free but all the others will be loose and flapping a little. Immediate reaction must be to get the broken one downwind fast. Provided the mast has been saved, you can now take a spare halyard and sweat it down temporarily to replace the broken item. Next reduce sail and set about making a more reliable repair.

If a shroud parts it will always be the windward one. A fast tack and easing of the sheets can give you valuable time. If the break is low enough down to reach the broken end you can make a temporary repair with bulldog clips. The free end will hang well outboard but can be caught with a boat hook, or by using a rope's end.

The two ends will seldom meet so you will need a spare length of wire of the same or similar dimensions as the original to bridge the gap. Use two clips on each side of the break and tighten the nuts fully only on the two closest to the break. Slack off the bottlescrew before you tighten up so that you can get some tension on to the repaired shroud once the clips are tight.

When the wire breaks, as it usually does, where it enters a fitting it will not be possible to bridge unless you carry a spare length with a fitting on it. You will need to make a tail loop or else turn the end into an eye to get some purchase on it. Putting eyes in nineteen strand wire is not easy, even in very thin sections.

One alternative is to fit two bulldog clips in opposite directions, close to the end of the wire, then use a short length of 7 × 7 with a thimble to form a loop. Clamp the thimble in with a bulldog clip and use two more to secure the tail to the nineteen strand above the clamping clips. Figure 38.1 illustrates this method. An advantage in this method is that it allows you to get the length exactly right by adjusting the position of the clamps.

A broken bottlescrew, shackle or clevis pin should be replaced with a spare. If the break in a shroud or stay is high up, any spare jib and/or the spinnaker halyard can be sweated down to the toe rail or to the chain plate as a temporary replacement. After this is done it is wisest to take down the sails and make port under engine since halyards are nowhere near strong enough to take even small sailing loads in this position.

Broken forestay
The headsail luff and halyard will usually hold. Thus this failure need not bring the mast down provided you are quick to ease off the main sheet and turn down wind to reduce the strain. The trouble is that the mast will not be fully tensioned and will sway

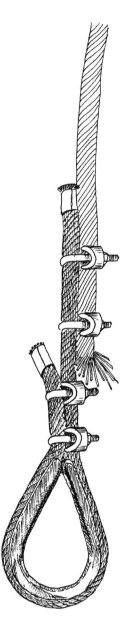

Fig 38.1 Repairing a broken shroud

alarmingly. Take any spare fore halyards down to the stemhead fitting and sweat them up tight. Do not attempt to remove the headsail until this has been done since it is now holding up the mast.

Once the spare halyards are in place, the main should be lowered and either deep reefed or left off. A small headsail can still be carried with a loose luff or can be hanked on to the spare halyard. A repair can be effected as described earlier but it will not be possible to set the jib on it. The sensible follow-up action is to try to make port with engine assistance avoiding a course which requires the vessel to be close-hauled. Greater strain on the forestay is generated when the main is sheeted in tight so avoid this.

Broken backstay

If the backstay breaks on a down wind leg, which is the most likely point of sailing, you will probably lose the mast unless you are lucky and also react fast. If you have swept back shrouds you will have a second or two for action so use it well. Head straight up into wind, without gybing. Free off the headsail and sheet in the main as fast as you can. The mainsail and sheet will now hold the mast up.

Get the engine going so that you can motor head to wind. Drop the headsail as soon as possible. If you have a good strong topping lift it will be invaluable now. Sweat it down tight to the transom, either to the remains of the original fitting, a spinnaker block or to the toe rail. Don't use the pulpit it will not be strong enough.

It will then be possible to drop the mainsail. Do not forget that as soon as you ease the halyard the boom will come down if the topping lift is not in place. Once the sail is down, take the main halyard back also and secure it. This will keep the mast up whilst you effect a repair.

Any repair you do to a shroud or stay should be treated with extreme caution and should be used only to make the easiest port for a proper repair or replacement. Once the initial excitement is over, give the nearest Coastguard a call and tell them what has happened. You do not need help now but at least they are alerted if things get worse.

Holed

'Am holed and sinking', invariably forms part of the MAYDAY message in RYA Shorebased Examinations. It has a chilling effect on candidates. Being holed however does not automatically mean that the yacht will sink. It will only sink if water is coming in faster than you can remove it. The need, if you are holed therefore, is to reduce the rate at which water comes in and to start removing what is already in.

Holing can result from structural failure, usually due to stress of weather, or from a collision. Structural failure can happen along seams, at skin fittings or along the keel joints. Fortunately it is rare in a well maintained yacht.

Collision with some floating debris such as timber or a container is most common. Such damage that results will be at, or just below, the water line. It will however usually be on the lee side. A tack in this situation may well bring the hole up to, or above, the water level. At all events it will bring the hole towards the surface and thus reduce the water pressure and therefore the rate of entry.

Once the instant action has been taken it is important to start pumping and to assess the damage. In many modern boats it may be necessary to remove fittings in order to get to the hole from inside. One needs to be quick and not hesitate to do damage to the interior. Any insurer worth using would rather replace torn out cupboards than replace the boat so get to it. Having found the hole, plug it with anything that will fit and stay in place. Clothing can be jammed in and held in place with bunk boards, locker lids or anything else suitable.

Some people carry pieces of marine ply for this purpose, ready drilled with screw holes. If you have a wooden boat it is a good idea to have some short, fat, wood screws for fixing these. Ones that can be screwed into the hull without drilling if possible.

GRP hulls will need to be drilled and the panels fitted using self-tapping screws. Use thick screws that will hold well and make sure that you have several drill bits of the right size. Underwater filler is useful and can be used either as a gasket with a backing pad or forced directly into the hole if it is a fairly small one.

A large hole can be covered from the outside by drawing a small sail over the damage and lashing it in place. Water pressure will hold it against the hull and reduce the flow dramatically but the actual fitting is easier said than done and attempts to block it from inside should be made at the same time.

Skin fittings

A skin fitting can be knocked off or can corrode so that it breaks away. It is important to know where all your skin fittings are and to inspect them regularly for damage. A lost skin fitting normally leaves a neat round hole. This is most easily blocked by knocking in a soft wood plug and suitable sizes should be in your repair kit. Better still, have a bung of suitable size attached with light line to each sea cock. I have never needed mine but it saves valuable time should one do so. Hoses attached to skin fittings can split and it is important to make sure the sea cocks can be closed easily if this happens. Sea cocks that do not need to be closed often should be checked regularly so that they remain free.

Engine failure

Strictly, at least when out at sea, engine failure is not a problem, if you have wind you sail. If you have none you wait. This is something of an over simplification but is true in most instances. What you do on approaching harbour will depend on your practice.

You should have learned how to pick up a mooring or to put down an anchor under sail very early in your sailing. You should have enough confidence in your sailing ability to be able to enter a harbour under sail and to bring your vessel to a safe stop.

You ought to be able to sail your vessel out of trouble on any point of sailing. If conditions are such that sailing alone can not get you out of trouble, you are in a place that you should not be. For this I would exclude entry to, or departure from, a marina berth or tight harbour but very little else. If your engine fails in such a situation you should try to work your vessel into the nearest vacant berth or alongside another boat without it; you will have to sail or possibly warp yourself in with assistance from other boats, or you must drop anchor.

Learn to treat your engine as it is meant to be; as an auxiliary means of propulsion and not as a primary source. If you do this you will find that engine failure is little more than a nuisance in any situation. The confidence this gives is well worth the effort.

All manoeuvres must be learned under sail. At first you can have the engine running. When confidence grows you can have it warm but stopped. Before long you will find that you hardly think to start it. By this time your general boat handling will have improved considerably and you will be well on the way to yachtmastery.

39 FIRE AND INJURIES

Fire

Fire is a major hazard on yachts and ways of avoiding the risks are given in Chapter 5. If you have a fire on board you will need to fight it. In any such case you must consider the possibility that you will not be able to control the fire and may need to abandon ship. For all but very small fires, the liferaft should be made ready for launching immediately. If the fire is serious, the raft should be launched and towed astern so that it does not itself become a victim of the fire.

Fires on yachts may be caused by the electrics, fuel, faulty engines, cooking or negligence. They will almost invariably start below decks. Always get out first before fighting such a fire since the oxygen available below is strictly limited and will soon be used up. In addition, many fire extinguishers produce toxic vapours in confined spaces.

Electrical fires

A fire in the wiring can be difficult to isolate. The first action should be to separate the batteries from the system. Once insulation breaks down, heat will still be produced until the supply stops. Heavy duty battery cables are rarely fused so the circuit will have to be broken. Switch off the master switch and isolator switch if you have one to isolate the battery supply and use a dry powder or BCF extinguisher. Remember that the whole wiring loom may be affected and the smoke and flames will not always appear at the source of the fire.

Once the fire is out, check all the wiring for signs of damage. Disconnect any that look doubtful and rig new wires for emergency lighting and essentials. Don't risk restarting the blaze by making the old wiring live again.

Fuel

Fuel fires can only be fought with gas or dry powder extinguishers or by smothering them. Avoidance is most important here.

Petroil mixtures for the outboard will tend to explode rather than burn so should be carried in small quantities, in well sealed metal containers, well away from heat or electrics and preferably where they will vent overboard.

If the fire is from a damaged fuel pipe try to turn off the supply but do not risk getting overcome by fumes if you need to go below or deep into a locker. Engine compartments are the most common seat of fuel fires. A BCF gas extinguisher is best here. It can be automatic or manual but you must be able to use it without opening the compartment to the air. A small fuel fire with a restricted oxygen supply can become an inferno in seconds if air is able to reach it.

A hole large enough to take the extinguisher nozzle can be drilled into a suitable entry point and closed with a bung. In the event of fire the bung is removed and the nozzle directed through the hole. The entire contents of the extinguisher should be enough to smother the fire and give you time to close off the supply.

Gas fire

Gas fires usually start with an explosion which may cause structural damage. A gas bottle is a potential bomb in any fire. Avoid storing them near batteries or the engine and consider throwing them overboard in the event of a serious fire. Tie a piece of line on so that you can recover them later if you like.

Such fires can be prevented more often than not. Remember that bottled gas is heavier than air. Try to avoid spillage when you light the stove. Fit an automatic gas alarm and test it frequently. Make regular checks for leaks at all joints and hoses. Use liquid detergent solution and you will get bubbles from even the tiniest of leaks. Above all, pump the bilges regularly. Continue for a few minutes after all water is removed to get rid of any gas.

Fighting a gas fire often involves secondary action. Usually in furnishings or fabrics that have been set alight in the explosion. Any extinguisher or water will do for this but you will need to act fast and not wait for the shock from the explosion to wear off. The first action in any gas fire must be to turn off the supply at source.

Cooking fires

Cooking fires are commonly the result of either negligence or of ignorance. On many yachts the galley is dangerously close to flammable material. In most cases this is actually due to faulty design. Constant vigilance is thus necessary. A pan left to boil dry or an unwatched frying pan can start a fire. Such fires must be smothered quickly, preferably using a fire blanket kept close to the stove, before they set fire to headlinings etc. The gas should be turned off at the bottle and the whole left to cool for a while before attempting to remove the blanket.

Injuries and first aid

The most common problem here is that of personal injury. Anyone who has spent a while at sea will know that a leaping boat is an easy place in which to get anything from a minor bruise to a broken bone. A good first aid kit is a must and its presence should go without saying. In my experience, many people have only a vague idea what to do when someone is actually hurt. A first aid kit is only as good as the use to which it is put. Make sure that you have the right contents in yours and that you know how and when to use the things you have got.

Get a good book on first aid, then pose yourself a few problems. Do I know how to stop bleeding? Could I recognise the symptoms of an internal injury? What *are* the first signs of hypothermia? What *would* I do if someone had a heart attack? These are just examples but they should give you the right idea.

The best idea is to take a first aid course. Your local St John Ambulance office will tell you where and when courses are being held. They, or the RYA booklet, will advise you on what you should have in your first aid kit also.

MAYDAY

In life-threatening situations, the distress signal MAYDAY, MAYDAY, MAYDAY, should be transmitted on 156.8 MHz (VHF Channel 16): giving the boat's name, position, type of assistance needed and number of crew.

If you need help but are in no immediate danger you should transmit the signal PAN PAN, PAN PAN, PAN PAN with the same information as for MAYDAY. If you use the term PAN PAN MEDICO in your initial call, it alerts the rescue service as to the kind of help you need. You can also use the Morse code signal V which is dot dot dot dash and display the international flag signal V. Other distress signals include slowly raising and lowering the arms, flag signal NC, a square shape displayed over a round shape, continuous sounding of fog horn, siren or whistle.

Pyrotechnics

Red hand flares and orange smoke signals should be used up to three miles offshore. When out of sight of land use two red star flares or red parachute rockets; the first two signals should be fired within two minutes. Hold flares away from the body down wind when firing and do not look directly at them.

Casualty evacuation

You will always have to face the possibility that an injury on board is so serious and so immediate that a return to port is not enough. In such cases it will be necessary for the casualty to be lifted from the yacht or from the water by experts. This will usually mean a helicopter rescue.

Full details of how this is done are summarised only here. The first action will have been either a MAYDAY or a PAN PAN call. You can help the helicopter crew if you know what to do. Once you know a helicopter is coming the following actions should be carried out:

1   Keep the casualty as still as possible but make sure he is warm.
2   Lower all sails and run under engine (to protect from downdraft).
3   Have a VHF listening watch as directed by the Coastguard.
4   Have ready at least one *hand held* flare (orange smoke by day, red flare by night)
5   By day have your sail number painted on deck or a bright orange cloth (a towel will do) spread on deck.

6 When called by the helicopter, follow instructions. You will be given a course and speed to steer.
7 When the winch cable is lowered do not touch it until it has been dipped in the sea (to remove the static charge).
8 Do not attach the cable to the boat. Just hold the tail on board.
9 Do not use the VHF when the helicopter is overhead. (The crew will be too busy to answer.)
10 Wait for instructions from the winchman and follow them.

Unless the vessel is in imminent danger the helicopter will take only the casualty ashore. The crew will not have facilities for more. Any argument will simply delay treatment. Explaining this to a worried spouse or parent in advance is better for everyone.

The above is in outline only. The RYA video *Life on the Line* shows the sequence excellently and also covers several other safety topics very well.

40 STEERING DAMAGE AND TOWS

Steering failure

Failure of the steering is a major hazard because it will affect the control of the boat and, in extreme situations, prevent you making port.

Spare tiller

Failure can be the result of heavy weather but it can also happen when a part of the control linkage breaks, the rudder becomes jammed or broken or the tiller breaks. Some items can be carried which will solve the problem. A spare tiller should always be carried and, particularly on a wheel-steered boat, provision should be made for using it. Make sure that the spare actually fits before you need it and that it is at least as strong as the original. Carry a spare cable for the wheel drum and be sure you know how to fit it.

Rudder failure

Rudder damage is more of a problem. It is actually easier to deal with if the rudder drops off than it is to have an immovable rudder jammed on one side. Should this happen you will probably be obliged to call for help. If the rudder drops off, some alternative will need to be found.

One often reads of suggestions for lashing boards to the spinnaker pole or a large oar. In practice, unless you have planned for this in advance with bolt-on fittings, it will be unlikely to succeed. The rudder takes a great deal of strain and it is almost impossible to lash anything to a round pole with sufficient rigidity to do the job. Even if you did manage it, in relation to the boat the angle of the spar which will be needed to get the blade in the water will make it very difficult to use.

A properly balanced boat needs little rudder. If you can ride out the worst of the weather you can help a lot by balancing the sails so that only a little force is required to steer. Some kind of brake that can be moved from one side of the boat to the other will work. Figure 40.1 shows a way of doing this using a cockpit grating. I have tried it and it does work, though slowly.

The control lines were led through the stern fairleads using short lengths of plastic hose to reduce chafe and then on to the spinnaker winches to make adjustments easier. The bridle was originally made with two fixing points on each side of the grating. This produced too much drag causing it to bounce. Both it and the yacht then

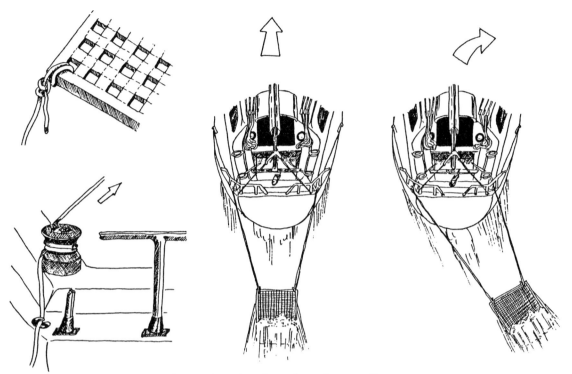

Fig 40.1 Jury-rigged steering using a grating

veered crazily from side to side. A single line to each side stopped this and the drag was still ample to make steering effective.

With a working jib and reefed main I was able to sail the boat on all points of sailing other than dead down wind. Removing the main made down wind sailing possible also. I found that the bridle needed to be at least eight feet long on the unpulled side for it to work. In use, you must take care to let out one side as the other is pulled in. An endless bridle would probably be best taken round both winches. It could then be left tight and just wound from one side to the other.

I did however, use the idea with the tiller lashed, not having the courage to remove the rudder first! I still believe it would have worked with no rudder on my Sigma. The main point I am making is that I have worked out a plan and tried something.

Asking for help

When major damage occurs one should try to be self sufficient but not be afraid to ask for help from a passing vessel or from the Coastguard (see MAYDAY page 188).

Help from ships
Experience of others indicates that help should not be sought from large ships without considering the possibility of further damage. The difficulty of getting alongside is horrendous and a tow is virtually impossible.

If you have done all you can and are still in danger or unable to shape a course you will have to ask for help. Do not use the MAYDAY call unless the vessel is 'in grave and imminent danger' or a life is at risk. Either use PAN PAN or direct your request specifically to a Coastguard or nearby vessel. Every year the emergency services are called to many situations that could have been solved on the spot. Abuse of the system puts others' lives at risk.

Towing

If help comes to you when disabled you may be able to take a tow. Remember that a lifeboat's function is the saving of life and the crew is under no obligation to save your vessel. They may do so and will probably try but are not obliged to.

By the time a tow is needed, all the crew should be wearing lifejackets which must be kept on during the entire operation.

A vessel taking you under tow can claim salvage. The negotiating of agreements first is all very well in theory but not in practice. If you are worried, make it clear that you are accepting a tow under Lloyd's terms on a 'no cure no pay' basis. Pass your own line, or at least offer to. Argue the details later.

Preparing for a tow

As soon as you think you may be towed get the gear ready. You will need your strongest and longest warp, at least 30 metres of it, preferably twice that or more. If you have a samson post, and are sure of it, the tow can be secured there. On a modern yacht, it is as well to run a bridle round the whole boat secured to all your cleats to spread the stress loads. In practice it is difficult, if not impossible, to spread the load over more than two cleats but it could help. Under tow from even a small coaster, the loads on the line will be immense and can pull out ordinary deck cleats on the average GRP boat. Some folk advocate taking the line round the mast but if it is deck-stepped this will bring it down.

In a heavy sea the tow line will need to be long enough to allow your boat to ride the waves independently of the towing vessel. If you cannot achieve this, snatch loads will be put on the line. These will transfer to your gear which will strain everything. With a towing vessel of a similar size to your own the problem is reduced. As the relative size difference increases so the problem increases.

Parcelling the tow

Have ready something to wrap round the cable where it leaves the vessel so as to reduce chafe. Towels are good for this job. Do this even if you are taking the tow. Be careful to avoid trapping fingers as you parcel.

Speed

When towed by a ship, it will probably pay you to take his line since it will be both stronger and longer. You can take some of the shock load off by hanging a heavy weight (the kedge anchor would do) on the tow line some way in front of your boat. You will need to plead with the ship to go as slowly as he can but understand that even his slowest speed is likely to be greatly in excess of your hull design speed.

41 CAUGHT IN HEAVY WEATHER

It would be easy to say that no one should be caught out in heavy weather. Modern weather forecasting is good, quite reliable and readily available from a variety of sources (see Chapter 19). Sooner or later though, if you do enough sailing, you will be caught out. How well you cope with the conditions will depend largely on how much you are prepared. Planning is better than wishing it had not happened, so this chapter is concerned with things you can do to ease the situation.

Making secure

Before it starts, and you usually have warning by forecast or other signs, the whole vessel should be checked. Make sure that everything that could move has been stowed so that any movement is at least very restricted.

Start on deck from the anchor back to the stern. If your anchor is stowed on the stemhead make sure it can not break free. Do not rely only on a captive pin but use lashings also. Imagine the problems you would have if the anchor ran out unexpectedly in a heavy sea; or just dropped so that it hung from the bow.

Where it is stored in a well: does the well lock? Can you tie the anchor to a fixed point so that in the event of a knock-down it won't fall out? How can you stop the chain running out in the event of a knock-down? Some of these questions would be best dealt with before putting to sea.

The next item is probably the spinnaker pole. You won't need it during the storm so make sure it is lashed down well. It must be out of the way if you need to go forward, and safe from harm. Whilst up front make sure that any spare halyards and guys are secure and tight.

It should have been done before, but check again that the jack stays for your safety lines are secure. Lives are literally going to depend on them.

Storm jib

Now is the time to set up the storm jib. All that time 'wasted' in practising this when you could have been sailing is going to pay off. You may not want to hoist it just yet but it is as well to have it hanked on and well secured to the guard rail so as to save time when you do need it. Make sure that the hanks work smoothly and that any lashings are ready.

Back in the cockpit clear away anything that is not actually needed. Make sure that all items that will remain, winch handles, torch, flares, are attached to the boat so that they will not go overboard. Lifebelts, and buoy and the like should be attached but in such a way that they can be quickly released if needed.

Are all lockers secured so that they will stay closed in a knock-down? Snap fasteners are best for lockers but if, as is common, you have only hasps and staples, put the padlocks on but do not close them. You do not want to be searching for keys if you need something in a hurry. The washboards may need to be in place during the worst conditions and they must have some means of securing so that they can not be lost in the event of a knock-down.

It should go without saying that all cockpit crew will be wearing harness now and will be keeping attached to the boat. I think that lifejackets also are sensible in very rough conditions; safety lines and harnesses can fail.

Down below

The best fix possible should be made and recorded, both on the chart and in the log. Only the chart in use should be on the chart table. I have had good charts ruined in very little time in heavy weather. The new plastic type charts are useful in these conditions. Clear away all plotting instruments into their proper stowage even if this is not, as it should be, your normal habit.

Hatches
Check the hatches are secured and that all sea cocks not needed are closed. Start in the forepeak and make sure that no gear can be thrown about. Any delicate item on a shelf should be relocated in a cupboard or locker. Will your books stay put if the boat is knocked down? The galley is best kept locked rather than on gimballs unless in use. It is far less likely to break free if fixed.

Heavy items
Batteries and other heavy items will have been fitted with restraints long before this. They should be checked however for tightness. Try to think of anything that could either cause or suffer damage and make it fast.

Lee cloths
Fit the lee cloths to the bunks that will be used by the watch off duty. Insist that all crew rest when not actually needed. If you have time, fill flasks with hot drinks or boiling water and stow them securely. Cooking may be impossible or extremely difficult for some time. Your stocks of chocolate, biscuits, nuts, dried and fresh fruit and so on will need to be available now.

On deck again

Start reducing sail early rather than late. Try to keep the rig balanced but don't go through the whole wardrobe in order to maintain performance, or you will only tire the crew – they will need their strength. The idea should be to have just enough sail to keep going at each change. If you think you will have to set a trysail it is best to do it as soon as the wind is strong enough rather than wait until it is a necessity.

Remember that your crew will be nervous – so will you. Anxiety tends to induce seasickness so anyone prone should start taking tablets now. Make sure that everyone has food inside them before the going gets too bad.

Plan of action

What has gone before is preparation. Now you have to outwit the sea. Think in terms of the easiest, safest course rather than the most desirable. Assuming that you are not going to be able to make port before the gale reaches you, you must anticipate the direction from which the weather will come and decide either to stop, gain sea room or to run for shelter. The word run here has the nautical meaning. It is much easier and more comfortable to sail off the wind in heavy weather.

Which way

In the open sea, with deep water, you will undoubtedly be better off staying out. Running off is the term. Going with or across the weather will be tiring and uncomfortable but safer than trying to make for what will be a lee shore and shallower water. Here you will have a choice: of keeping sailing with as little sail as possible, of going with it under bare poles or of lying to the sea hove-to or with a sea anchor.

Distance

You must assume that the gale may last for 24 hours if you intend to run. Then calculate the distance you could travel at your fastest speed. If you have not got room on this basis that choice is not open to you. Running under bare poles with warps streamed (see page 198) you will still drift quite fast. The surface drift created by the wind will be added to your wind generated movement. This is also a pretty uncomfortable way to perform.

When hove-to, most of the movement will be to leeward, although you will have some forward motion as well, even under bare poles. Some boats will actually claw to windward hove-to with a little bit of main only; it is worth considering.

Sea anchor

A sea anchor will reduce your movement over the ground almost to the rate of the surface drift. You will move the least distance so that the gale will pass over you relatively quickly. The advantages are that everyone can go below and keep out of the weather with the minimum of lookout while your position will change less than when following any other action. The disadvantages are that you will be unable to manoeuvre if close to another vessel and the boat takes more punishment. The boat will probably not mind but you will. Once streamed it is very difficult to recover either a sea anchor or warps.

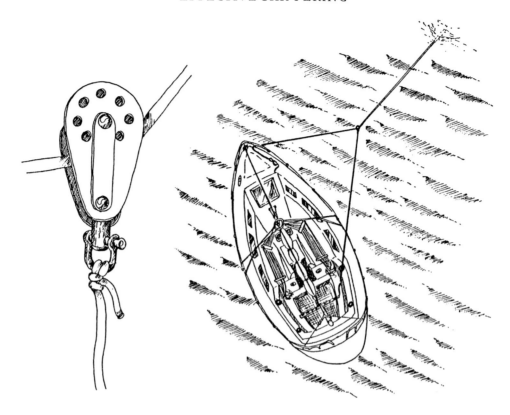

Fig 41.1 Heading control with a sea anchor

Figure 41.1 shows a way of setting a sea anchor so that some adjustment can be made to the angle at which the vessel lies to the wind and sea. This has obvious advantages but I have not tried it in anything like storm conditions. The stern line must be taken to a winch or adjustment will be impossible in strong conditions.

Keeping going

All of the last section makes the assumption that you are in such bad conditions that to go on is impossible. In my experience this is not often the case. More common is the situation where it is unpleasant but not impossible. Your ability and that of the crew is a major factor but you can often do more than you think.

The 1979 Fastnet Inquiry Report Recommendations, para 00.6, sub-section (b) relating to 'Tactics During The Storm' states:

'Insufficient evidence has emerged to indicate the best tactics. . . . There is however a general inference that active rather than passive were successful and those who were able to maintain some speed and directional control fared better.'

That particular storm was exceptional. Winds were up to force 11 and wave heights possibly as much as 90 feet with near vertical sides. The vast majority of the 303 yachts that started that race survived to make port under their own power. Of the 24 abandoned only 5 were not recovered with one of these sinking under tow. It says a great deal for the strength of modern yachts that keeping going was possible.

I have been able to keep going in winds of force 9 with gusts in excess of this. On one occasion off Ushant with several ships in difficulties, in a 36 foot yacht we were wet and very uncomfortable but safe. The waves were excessive; some broke over us whilst we clawed our way into deeper water. But we were making progress to windward, albeit with over 15 degrees of leeway, heading about 60 degrees to a wind with a mean velocity of 37 knots. At times it was exhilarating and at no time did I feel that the yacht could not cope.

The maximum steady wind experienced on that occasion was 44 knots so it was actually force 9. The only damage sustained was when a shelf in the forepeak ripped away as we came off a wave. One rogue wave washed the helmsman across the cockpit but his safety harness held. The wind was from WNW so we had to sail, either into the Channel or back into Biscay. All the other options were closed to us but I do not think it would have made any difference to my decision.

We all felt we had achieved something as, some 14 hours later, we motored the last couple of hours to harbour through lack of wind!

Exaggerating conditions

It is easy to exaggerate both wind and sea. Your first gale is always your worst by a very long way. The danger in exaggerating is that you can come to believe you have experienced worse than you have. This can give you illusions about the problems involved.

I have heard an experienced instructor telling of happy experiences beating into a force 9 with a novice crew. The actual Met. Office figures for the day in question gave force 5–6 and many other yachts sailing in the same area, including mine, found no wind over force 5. The point is that those novices will now *think* they have experienced force 9 and that *that* sailing was easy. It could make them less than prudent at some later time.

Let no one fool you. Beating into a real gale is hard and exhausting work. It is not something to look for, but it is something you can do if you have to.

Streaming warps

The reason for streaming warps is to slow you down. What you are trying to do is to avoid going so fast that you run off the top of a wave and pitchpole.

Pitchpoling is when the yacht does a cartwheel with the stern overtaking the bow. I have not experienced it but those who have, say it is not to be recommended. It is somewhat worse than being rolled from the beam and a great deal worse than a knock down when your mast dips in the water.

Streaming warps will tend to keep your stern to the wind so that the sea is following or, better still, quartering. This gives a safer and more comfortable ride. You may still be pooped by a breaking wave but it is surprising how seldom this actually happens in relation to the times you think it will happen if you look behind you with a big following sea.

In heavy weather conditions you will get the occasional 'rogue' wave. Such waves can come from any direction and can be generated extremely rapidly. In the 1979 Fastnet several skippers talked of such waves that appeared so quickly and unexpectedly that they were impossible to avoid. Only luck can be any use in such cases.

Lying ahull

There may come a time when you are unable to make progress. Provided you are in open water, the only thing to do then may be to lie ahull – that is to the wind with bare poles. This can only be done if no imminent danger exists and may well be the best solution until things improve. You will have to be reasonably sure that the boat will maintain its head in relation to the wind before you relinquish control.

Warps are probably streamed by now or perhaps a sea anchor is set and you are hove-to. The tiller will need to be lashed, either to lee or amidships. A very strong lashing will be needed but be sure you can release it quickly if the need arises. Once sure that the boat is steady (this is relative!), everyone should go below with the washboards and hatches secured and get into their bunks.

It may well be impossible to sleep but you must try to relax. The idea is to conserve strength and body heat so that you can act if required. At least one crew member should be kitted out ready to take action quickly but this duty should be rotated. An occasional lookout check for other vessels should be made if possible. The boat is stronger than you and will probably survive.

42 GROUNDINGS

Groundings come under two headings – the embarrassing and the serious. The former can turn into the latter however, if you do not take the right precautions.

Soft groundings

These are the sort that happen when you are negotiating a river channel, estuary or harbour entrance and have made a miscalculation. If you are being cautious and do not have too much speed you should come to no harm.

The mistake may be one of position or a tidal height error. The result is the same either way. What follows depends partly on the tide. If it is rising, or falling slowly, with quick reactions you can be off again with no harm done.

Under sail

Try to heel the boat. Sheet in the sails and get crew to hang on the boom and/or lean out to leeward. Get crew on to the foredeck since this will often lift the keel slightly. If you have grounded on the windward side of the channel you will probably blow off. Flatten the headsail, ease the main and get crew out on the boom to help.

If on the other side, you will need a quick tack or you will just go further on. Sheeting in the main but not the jib will help to force the boat round. Back the jib as you go through the wind to increase the tightness of the turn and to maintain the heel but take care not to run straight across on to the opposite bank. Neither do you want to spin round and be back aground on the other tack.

Under power

Get your crew to heel the boat in the direction of the shallows as for under sail. Now go astern with plenty of power, moving the rudder from side to side until she breaks free. The rudder movement will cause the boat to pivot about and will help to break the suction. Once she starts to go astern reduce power and try to back off on the same line as you came in.

If going astern does not seem to be working, try going ahead with the helm hard over in the direction of the shallowest water. Use only sufficient power to start you turning. Most yachts have more power ahead and it may be possible to pivot round until you are heading into deep water. Now you can drive hard ahead until out of the mud.

Stuck fast

If you are not fast enough to beat a falling tide you will be stuck and will have to wait until you can float off. There are several things you can do to ease the situation.

Which way to lie

The first thing is to ensure that, if and when she lies down, the yacht is lying with her mast towards the shallowest water. This way she will lie over less and will float earlier. Get the crew weight out on that side – along the boom if possible to get more leverage. If you have a dinghy ready, or can get one ready quickly, send someone ashore in it with a line from the mast top using the spinnaker halyard.

Once ashore the line should be pulled tight and attached to something solid as near a beam as possible so as to give a straight pull from the top of the mast.

As she starts to settle you will have to check that there are no obstructions under her that may hole the hull. If there are, they must either be removed or the hull must be protected. You will have to use anything you can for this: bunk cushions, bunk boards, the cabin sole or cockpit grating, sail bags. Any of these will do. You can not be squeamish. If she is holed, she may not come up again. Do not use the dinghy because you are going to need that.

Once the boat is settled get a kedge anchor out as far as you can into the stream. It is important to prevent the yacht from being driven further up the bank by the incoming tide or the wind. If you can also get the main anchor into use as well then so much the better. Now close all the sea cocks and put the kettle on (if you can!). Calculate when she is likely to float again. Go to the pub. Have a meal. You may have a long wait.

The wrong way

If, despite your efforts, the yacht has settled with her mast down hill you are going to have problems when the tide comes in again. Some of them you can start to prevent now. Take all your fenders; they should have stout lines attached, and tie each one tightly on as short a scope as possible to the top of the mast. When floating, they will help prevent the mast head staying down when the water returns.

Sealing the hull

Take the roll of waterproof duct tape that you keep on board and seal all the possible water entry points in the hull. This must include: vents for the engine, air, fuel and water; all lockers, even if they are supposed to be water tight; cockpit drains and bilge pump outlets if not fitted with sea cocks; windows and opening lights and hatches. The main hatch will need special attention. Fit the washboards and close the hatch. Tape over all joins and seams. Do not forget to seal the sliding section and any drain holes. The aim is to close the entire hull so that no water can get in. I have a roll of 5 cm plastic tape 50 metres long. I hope it will be enough if I need it.

When the water comes back it is going to be a long time before the yacht floats. The suction from the mud where she has settled can be incredibly strong. Some water will have got in as she settled but this should have been drained out again. A great deal more is going to get in if you do not stop it before she comes up again. If too much gets in she will not come up at all. It will probably pay you to lighten the yacht as much as possible. Take ashore all heavy items and drain out the fresh water. Both this and your fuel may be in the bilges anyway.

When the water starts to return, the dinghy can be positioned under the mast end to help lift it but it will be difficult to get it into a position where it will be effective. Only one person should be used for this to keep the load down. He or she should be wearing both harness and lifejacket and should be attached to the backstay so as to be able to return to the hull as soon as the dinghy is holding. The dinghy painter should be tied with a bowline to the backstay otherwise it will hang from the masthead when the yacht rights itself.

Floating off

Any yacht aground on anything but rock develops a suction force which tends to hold it down. Once the water starts to try to lift the hull it is often possible to break the suction by rocking the vessel. Be careful not to do this too soon if the hull is resting on some potential hazard however. You may actually cause it to puncture the hull. The water will rise a good way up before the yacht starts to come up and she can 'jump' as the suction is broken. Crew on board must be ready for this.

Now is the time to recover the dinghy and retrieve the fenders tied to the mast before they are too high to reach. The items used to protect the hull can also be recovered now. This is easier if they have been attached to the yacht with lines.

The methods so far illustrated assume that little or no sea is running. This will normally be true in the locations mentioned. I have however heard of a yacht which grounded in an estuary on a falling tide, fell into the stream, slid down as she began to take water and sank *before* the tide had actually reached Low Water.

Hard or rough-water groundings

Many of the ideas mentioned above can still be used and vessels can be saved. Grounding on rock need not result in the loss of the vessel if the hull is protected quickly, provided the sea is not rough. On the other hand, a vessel can be lost when grounding on soft sand in a choppy sea.

In such a situation getting the boat off before it is held fast is essential. If this fails it will probably be necessary to abandon the vessel. Fortunately most groundings are soft groundings and can be an interesting if sobering experience.

Checking for damage

All groundings unless the mearest touch, should be considered as potentially damaging. At the first opportunity the vessel should be craned, slipped or dried out and the hull and all fittings examined for possible damage. Rudders or engine shafts have been known to be bent even by moderately gentle groundings. Keels can start to leak and so on. One must bear in mind that the hull has been subjected to stresses for which it was not designed.

43 BAD VISIBILITY

I have heard it said, 'Fog is no problem now that anyone can have Decca or Satnav.' Not so. Useful as these aids are, they won't tell you *exactly* where you are. Neither will they tell you where the other chap is in his powerboat, ship or perhaps, yacht on a reciprocal course also using Decca. 'Radar can take care of that', I hear you say. Not true either I am afraid. Yacht radar is very limited in this respect. Of necessity, it is fairly complicated and slow to use. It needs lots of practice to interpret the display.

Treated purely as aids, electronics can be a great help. They can not as yet provide a complete answer to all navigation problems. When and if they ever do sailing will be a lot less fun.

The problems

Two problems are present in fog. One is the risk of running aground through not knowing precisely where you are. The other is of being hit by someone else who doesn't know you are there. The first is the lesser danger in most waters. The second is more of a problem.

Notice that I have said, someone who doesn't know *you* are there. This is important. You may well realise a big ship is close but can do nothing about it. You are not sure if it has detected your presence. You know it is there, but are uncertain of its precise location. Neither do you know its course or speed. Radar can not always help to find out this information *fast enough*.

Avoiding ships

The best way to avoid being hit by a ship in fog is to get into water too shallow for big ships to use. It is often sufficient to stay between the ten and five metre contour lines. Normally, no ship will be deliberately taken into water that shallow and it will be quite safe for you provided that there are no isolated rocks or shallow spots. If there are it is often possible to calculate a safe least depth to clear all dangers and to stay at that depth using your echo-sounder.

There is one exception to this rule however. At the entrance to a harbour it is quite possible that a depth of ten metres or even less is acceptable to the ship's navigator who knows precisely where he is. He may have to accept it in order to get in. Extra caution by small vessels is essential here.

Decca and Loran can actually increase the chances of collision in bad visibility when using waypoints. Accuracy of line is improved by these systems to the point where most vessels on a particular route are following the same track which can lead to concentration of vessels in a smaller area. When several vessels are on the same, or a reciprocal heading, between the same two points, risk of collision increases markedly. There is a good argument for aiming off in such circumstances.

Echo-sounder

Your echo-sounder is an important aid in bad visibility. It is also one which is not used often enough or it is used incorrectly. In shallow water particularly it is essential to make due allowance for the rise of tide if you are using the instrument to find your position. Used in conjunction with Decca it can give you much greater positional accuracy than either instrument alone.

Radio direction finder

The increased availability of Decca has reduced the use of RDF. Many people tell me they never bother with it now. I suggest that any aid you have, should be used when you are not sure of your position. It should also be practised when you are sure. The more information you can gather, the more likely you are to get things right.

Sound

One of the most important aids when sailing in fog are sound signals picked up by your ears and those of your crew.

Listening for fog signals

Fog can play tricks with direction, particularly if its density varies. I have found however that if you ask each crew member to point to the direction from which he hears a fog signal for example, a great deal of uniformity can be obtained. It is essential to point as soon as the signal is heard since disorientation is very rapid. I have used this technique successfully to find a buoy or a harbour entrance when visibility was less than 50 metres. It can also help to locate other vessels.

Other sounds

The low frequency sounds of surf carry well in fog. The sound is present even in calm conditions and can give adequate warning when approaching a shore. Voices carry well also. The presence of other yachts, fishing boats or motor boats can often be detected before their engines are heard. Cliffs and isolated larger rocks can be detected from the calls of sea birds. Vehicles ashore can be heard over long distances. It is as well not to neglect these useful indicators.

Making sound signals
The International Regulations for the Prevention of Collisions at Sea tell us that sound signals must be made. The advantage of hearing these is mentioned earlier. Making them effectively is another matter.

In practice, sounds you can make will be of little use in warning any but the smallest vessels of your presence. It is safer to assume that no one has seen you and take avoiding action yourself. That is not to say that you should not have lights on and a radar reflector in position. Sound signals should be made particularly when in close proximity to other small craft. These could all help but do not assume they will.

Sight

A good lookout even in very thick fog can give the helmsman valuable seconds in which to take avoiding action. Don't simply stare out in the hope of seeing something. Glance round every few moments. If you think you saw something don't stare straight at it. Instead try looking out of the corner of your eye. The human eye is much better at detecting movements and faint objects in what is called the peripheral vision areas – the outer edges of the eye.

Illusion
Constant looking with nothing to focus on causes the brain to take over. Your eyes will lose focus and you will then start to imagine things. These illusions can be very persuasive and can cause both alarm and confusion.

Density changes

There is a useful fact about fog conditions that is not often mentioned. It is the reduction in fog density that often occurs at the shore line. It is most noticeable in summer being caused by the temperature differences between land and water. You can make use of it when approaching the shore. The improvement in visibility that it gives, though not great, can be used to advantage.

Layer thickness
In lapse conditions the fog layer can be as thin as 12–15 metres. This is often less than the mast height of a yacht and it may be worth sending someone up the mast to find out. The masthead lookout will be able to see other masts, ships and the shore. A very useful facility. The greatest difficulty may be persuading the crew that you are not joking.

Positions

A good fix should be obtained as soon as fog is noticed. From then on it is important to keep working up regular EPs remembering to take tidal variations into account. There is no reason why Decca should not be used. In fact there is every reason why it should, but each Decca position should be properly recorded both on the chart and in the log so that, if the equipment fails, navigation can easily revert to traditional methods.

Coastguard

Remember that the Coastguard is in a position to give you an approximate fix if needed. You can ask for one and will be given one but please do not abuse this facility. Imagine what would happen to VHF Channels 16 and 67 in the Solent or the Dover Strait on a summer day if everyone was asking for fixes.

44 ABANDON SHIP

Fortunately these chilling words are seldom used in earnest on a yacht. Modern yachts are so strong that it is rare that they will fail to the point that leaving them becomes necessary. Returning to the 1979 Fastnet Report we read: 'Thus only two yachts were abandoned simply on the grounds that the liferaft was likely to provide more security than the virtually undamaged hull of the yacht.' This out of 303 yachts caught in one of the worst summer storms ever known in these waters.

It is not the boat that fails. Claud Worth in his book *Yacht Cruising* says: 'By far the most important factor in determining the seaworthiness of a yacht is the crew, next comes the gear and last of all the form of the yacht.' It would be churlish, unjust, even cruel to suggest that all those who abandoned their vessels in the Fastnet tragedy were wrong. I have neither the facts nor the right to judge. What I am saying is; because your yacht is intrinsically safer than the liferaft, it should not be abandoned until strictly necessary.

Liferaft safety

Lessons can be learned from the Fastnet disaster. Many of the lives lost were from, or in transferring to, liferafts. Considerable improvements have taken place in liferaft design since that fateful August. A yacht, until it actually sinks, is still a much safer haven than a liferaft. Abandoning your vessel must be truly a last resort.

The decision to leave

It is easy, sitting at home, to say that the truth is simple. That provided you can remove water from inside faster than, or at least as fast as, it enters, the vessel can be saved. In the real situation it will be extremely difficult to judge. The fact that the rate of entry will reduce as the level inside increases is true. Logic will confirm this. It is not so easy to accept when water is pouring in through a gaping hole.

Fire will be easier to judge than holing. Once your efforts fail to halt a blaze, there is little else you can do but leave. An early rather than a late decision in this case is also more vital since you will have to get the raft over and inflated sooner. The call for help also must not be delayed (see MAYDAY page 188). Delay could mean that you are unable to make it.

The only advice one can give is: wait as long as you dare but prepare for it. Take as much with you as you can on the assumption that rescue will be later rather than sooner. The decision, if it ever happens, will be yours at that time and with knowledge of the actual situation. It will be a hard decision, probably the hardest you will ever make.

I have often been asked, 'When should you abandon ship?' There is no real answer. I usually say something like, 'When I have to step off the top of the mast to get in the life raft!' It takes the edge out of the question and I know that I will leave it as long as I can if I ever have to do it.

Items to take

If the yacht appears to be sinking it will be necessary to get ready the things you are going to take with you *if you go*. This means that at least one person is going to have to stop the vital job of water removal, an action which itself may hasten the need to abandon.

The following table gives a list of things I would want to take with me in what is very roughly a descending order of priority. I suggest you think about it and I hope you will never have need of it.

Items to be taken when abandoning ship
This list assumes that the raft is equipped to RORC standard and that lifejackets are being worn.

Flares
Spare water
Clothing and waterproofs
Canned food and can opener
Hand held VHF and/or EPIRB
Signalling mirror
Torches
Bedding
First aid kit
Ship's papers and passports
Dinghy with paddles, pump and outboard
Chart – preferably waterproof
Sponges and bailer
Compass

PART 10
Seamanship

There is a truism at sea. If you get it right no one is watching, if you get it wrong everyone is watching. Most of us have been in a position where we wished that we had done things differently. Some people always seem to be in that position.

The best way to appreciate the seamanship skills of a skipper is to be a bystander when he or she brings a boat on to or away from a berth. You don't even have to watch. You can tell a lot just by listening, as I have said earlier. I have a theory that the ability of a skipper is inversely proportional to the square of the noise made when berthing.

You should hear few commands, no raised voices in either volume or pitch, no sudden bursts of engine, no crunching sounds, no crashing thuds of crew leaping frantically across an ever widening gap, no creaks or squeaks from overstrained gear.

Knowing the boat

Good seamanship depends on knowing what your vessel will do under a variety of situations. The sensible skipper will know within the first hour of using a boat a number of things about it.

He will know which way the propellor turns, and hence the way the stern kicks. This will affect the direction the boat will tend to turn under power. This direction will normally produce a tighter turn. He should also know what the turning circle is and what is the smallest that can be achieved; what the stopping distance is under engine at various speeds, both with and without the use of reverse; what happens to the steering in reverse.

As soon as possible he will find out how quickly and how much the bow pays off under the influence of a beam wind. He will also have an idea how fast the boat will drift sideways in a cross wind.

Some time spent manoeuvring under engine in order to find out these facts will be invaluable. All too often this important task is left until a tight manoeuvre is forced on to you. At this point it is often too late.

Exercises to test performance under sail should also be tried if conditions make this at all possible.

In this section some of the common manoeuvring situations are considered and some advice is given on how to avoid the worst problems.

45 MOORING TO BUOYS

At some time in your sailing you will have to pick up a mooring. It may be that you only ever use marina berths – if so you are missing a great deal. By far the most attractive places to visit involve either picking up a mooring or dropping anchor. If at any time you suffer an engine failure you will almost certainly have to do one of these two things.

Let us assume that you have come into a harbour and that you are directed to a visitor's mooring. The easy option is to drop the sails and motor up to the mooring. Even if you do this you will have to take certain actions and will have to assess the situation.

Under power

First you should get to a position where you can drop your sails without getting in anyone's way and where you can do the job with the least fuss. The first mistake is often made early on. This is to lower the sails too soon.

It will always be easier and safer to get the sails down and stowed in the shelter of harbour if there is space to do so, rather than out at sea. A look at the chart, if the place is unfamiliar to you, will quickly tell if there is room to do the job inside. If so then do it there.

It may be that dropping the headsail to give you more visibility and to take some power off is sensible. This has the advantage that the foredeck can be left clear for the pick up. Even if it is not prudent to enter without first dropping the main, this sail should never be stowed fully away until the vessel is secured.

Bring the mainsail down but secure it safely and tidily in a way that allows it to be hoisted again quickly if the engine fails. I know of at least one total loss that was due entirely to the fact that the main had been stowed and the cover put on before coming into harbour. This is the second common mistake. The ensuing engine failure on that particular occasion resulted in the yacht driving ashore on to rocks before the crew could rehoist the main or drop an anchor.

Approach

In order to stop easily the boat should approach the mooring slowly on a line which balances the effects of wind and tide. Look at Figure 45.1. If other vessels are already moored, your approach should be parallel to the lie of these boats. If not you will have

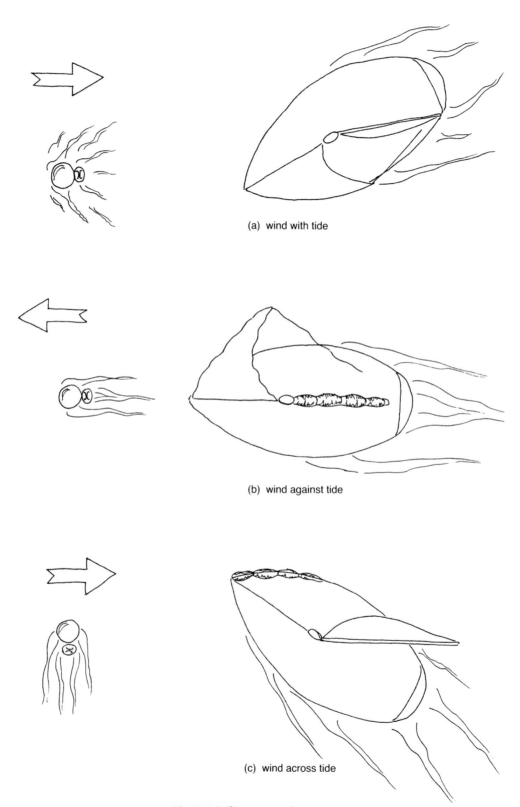

(a) wind with tide

(b) wind against tide

(c) wind across tide

Fig 45.1 Sailing on to a buoy

to assess the relative strengths of wind and tide and make your approach accordingly. To do this effectively may mean making a trial approach first before coming round again for the actual pick up.

Avoid an approach which is so fast that reverse becomes essential to stop you over-running. Make sure that you have a correct line so that you will not need to make constant adjustments on the helm in the last moments. The best approach is the one which needs no adjustment to speed or direction for at least two boats lengths so that the helmsman can leave the helm, as the mooring buoy begins to be hidden by the bow, and go forward to pick up or to lend a hand.

If you are not sure that you can do this, practice until you can. If the first attempt doesn't work the only thing damaged need be your pride. That is, provided you have worked out in advance where to go in this event. You can always turn away as soon as you realise it isn't going to work and make it look as if you are demonstrating technique to your crew!

The fatal mistake is to try to retrieve the situation too late. If you can't make it from a position where things are within your control, you are not likely to be able to retrieve from a difficult situation. The results of trying could be a lot worse than making a second or even third attempt.

Recently I watched a yachtsman trying to pick up his own mooring by approaching downwind and going hard astern on arrival. His reasoning was apparent. The upwind approach was a very tight one. After several attempts he managed to run over and capsize his own rigid dinghy which had been left on the mooring. He was lucky not to do more damage to his own or other yachts. An approach across the wind would have been easy, although it would have meant turning up to wind at the last minute.

The actual pick up
The mooring to be picked up should be under the bow, slightly to one (predetermined) side with the vessel stopped. Before the wind starts to take over, put the boathook under the pick-up buoy, if there is one, and lift the rope tail straight up. Forget the moulded handles fitted to many pick-up buoys, they are next to useless. Use a straight lift and avoid bending the boathook, it may break.

Securing
Once you can grasp the rope lay the hook behind you on the deck, or hand it to someone else, and pull in the pick-up rope over the bow roller until the chain or heavy rope comes aboard. If this job is done fairly smartly there is little strain involved. The cable end should now be secured to a deck cleat or samson post. Do not forget to replace the pin over the chain to prevent it jumping off the roller.

Unless the mooring is a particularly heavy one with a consequently extra thick pick-up rope the main mooring cable should be brought on board. If for some reason this is not practicable pass your own warp through the chain and secure with that. Never moor by passing a warp through the moulded handle on the pick-up buoy.

Completing the job

Report back to the helmsman once the job is done so that the engine may be stopped and the helm lashed. Now the temporary stowage of the mainsail can be made permanent and the boat tidied up. At night, do not forget to switch off the steaming and navigation lights. The boathook should be returned to its permanent stowage. No warps should be left on the foredeck unless actually in use.

Ring moorings

To secure to a ring type mooring the approach is as before. If two people are available on arrival, the boathook should be hooked into the ring by one of them and held. It is then necessary to pass a line through the ring and haul up tight.

Preparation

Preparation of the line is important. One end of a short mooring rope should be made fast to a deck cleat, on the port side if the pick-up man is right handed. The line should be lead out through the port fairlead or roller and several coils made up into the left hand. The pick-up crew member should lie down on the foredeck holding the coils in the left hand and the free end in the right. On arrival at the buoy the free end should be passed through the ring with the right hand. The coils should then be dropped to provide some slack until the rope can be pulled up. The mooring should be lifting from the water by the time it is secured.

Doubling up

For anything more than a very short stop a second line should be prepared. This line should first be secured to the opposite cleat to that of the first. The free end should then be passed through the ring twice to form a round turn before pulling in tight. This line forms the main mooring line. It is important that it is tight enough so that any movement of the yacht will not cause it to go slack. If this happens chafe can occur.

Once the second line is secured, the first line should be formed into a round turn also.

No pick-up buoy

Some moorings have neither ring nor pick-up. If you are obliged to take one of these make an initial approach to see if it has a strop attached. If so you will have to grope for it with the boathook. It may be that the pick-up line has been lost or cut. A secure mooring can still be made.

Prepare a warp with one end firmly secured and about 6 to 8 metres outboard. Secure the other end inboard through the same fairlead or roller temporarily. Next split the loop that is outboard into two handfuls coiling that for the left hand clockwise and that for the right anticlockwise. Lean over the pulpit with a half coil in each hand.

The approach to the mooring needs to be slow and accurate. When the mooring is just forward of the bow, throw both handfuls forward and outward. The warp should uncoil as it goes forward into a large loop which drops over the buoy. All way must now be taken off the boat. It helps if the boat falls back a little. The idea is to draw the loop closed to form a bight, round the chain under the buoy.

The temporarily secured end can now be pulled in until the buoy is drawn up to the bow. Don't leave it at that. Pass a second warp through the chain and make this fast as your actual mooring warp.

Leaving a mooring under engine
Have the mainsail uncovered and prepared so that it can be hoisted instantly if needed. Start the engine and check that it will go into gear. Release the tiller lashing. If two mooring lines were used on a ring or chain link remove the round turn from one of them and rig it as a simple slip line. Now remove the second line altogether. This preparation is worth the effort since the simple slip line will hold until ready and will not snag when let go.

If a chain mooring was used, the deck crew should prepare to slip by transferring to the pick-up line.

The helmsman should give the word to slip. The foredeck crew must not release until told to and must report back when free. The boat should be allowed to fall back on wind and/or tide until clear of the mooring before the engine is engaged. If there is insufficient movement the engine should be run astern just enough to get clear of the mooring.

The helmsman and the crew should watch out for other, possibly submerged, moorings both when approaching and leaving any mooring.

Mooring under sail

If conditions allow, mooring under sail is best done under main alone. The absence of a headsail leaves the foredeck clear for working and ensures good all round vision for the helmsman at a time when this is most useful. The lack of headsail does reduce the manoeuvrability of most yachts however and you must know how yours behaves under main alone.

It is particularly important to make certain that an escape route is available and practicable before starting the approach.

Stow the headsail
The headsail can be stowed on the guard rail before the manoeuvre is started and then cleared later, but it is important to make sure that the tack is removed from the stemhead fitting and secured up to the pulpit. If this is not done there is a danger of fouling the sail as the chain is brought in, with disastrous results.

The approach
Various combinations of wind and tide are possible. For each a different approach is needed. The aim in each case is to use the two forces rather than to fight them. You should finish with the head of the yacht lying to the combination of wind and tide. It is for this reason that a headsail has to be used in a wind against tide situation, especially if the tide is appreciable. It will not be possible to stop whilst going downwind if the mainsail is still up.

46 PONTOONS, WALLS AND JETTIES

Coming alongside a pontoon under power

When wind and tide are running parallel to the pontoon the technique is much the same as that for mooring to a buoy. Decide which side will be against the pontoon by assessing the net balance between wind and tide. Under power it will almost always be the tide that has the greater effect. Remember that the natural forces should be used to help the manoeuvre.

Fenders and lines

Set fenders to suit the level of the pontoon. With most pontoons this will mean that the lower end is just touching or just above the water. Attach breast ropes to bow and stern remembering to lead them in from the outside so that they do not foul anything. They must run from fairleads direct to the pontoon when taken ashore. It is often a good idea to secure the bow breast rope to the offside cleat so as to leave the one closest to the pontoon for the bow spring.

Stern spring

Have a stern spring with a loop or bowline prepared ready to attach to the pontoon near the bow. This will be taken back on to a sheet winch to prevent the yacht falling back once the way is taken off.

Crew responsibilities

The crew should be clear as to who is handling which rope and should be told to wait for instructions before making fast. Each rope should be coiled and brought back or forward to the shrouds. Crew should be standing on the toe rail, outside the guard rails, holding on to the shrouds for the last few boat lengths approaching the pontoon. This makes it easier to step ashore. Avoid crew leaping over guard rails at the last moment. This is a dangerous practice that can lead to serious injury.

Final approach

Approach the pontoon at an angle of about thirty degrees until the bow is a metre or so off. The boat should have just enough way on to maintain steerage. Turn alongside the pontoon so that the shrouds are the closest point. Both crew should be able to step comfortably ashore with their lines. Each takes a half turn round the appropriate cleat. Just aft and just forward of the yacht are best. The half turn is important since the momentum of even a slow-moving yacht is much too great for a strong man to stop unaided.

Securing

Once the yacht has stopped, the shore crew should make a complete round turn on the cleat and bring the spare line aboard to secure it. The line already prepared as the stern spring can be dropped over the same cleat forward of the bow and the slack taken in on a sheet winch.

Single handed

When doing this job single-handed, a mid-ship cleat is a godsend. A temporary strop can be used around the chain plates instead of a cleat but avoid putting sheer strains on these fittings. Chain plates are usually too far forward from the ideal position and can cause the bow to swing in so an extra fender well forward is needed for this job. The cleat ought to be correctly positioned but the extra fender is still a good idea. Once the boat is stopped, the breast ropes should be set as before.

Tidying up

Any adjustment to fenders can now be made and the bow spring can be attached. All spare length in the warps should be on board the yacht. This makes a safer, tidier job and avoids cluttering the pontoon. It also allows any adjustments to be made from on board.

Wind/tide off the pontoon

The technique is the same but the angle of approach must be somewhat greater to prevent the bow paying off. It is important that the breast ropes are taken on to the pontoon cleats whilst the yacht is still moving forwards. If this is not done the yacht will drift away fast and considerable effort will be needed to pull it in. The helmsman can assist by going astern as soon as the lines are round the cleats in order to take the way off but this must be a short burst of power only.

Working in

If the shore party have been slow, resulting in the yacht drifting out so as to be lying someway off the pontoon, they should be told to make fast temporarily. The stern spring should be heaved ashore and secured. This can then be winched in to bring the yacht closer to the pontoon. If a spring can not be passed, the shore party should make fast both lines as they are. They can now work together to shorten each in turn. Working on one line at a time is both easier and safer (see Figure 46.1).

Care must be taken not to lose one line whilst the other is still secured since this will put the boat out of control. A turn should be made round the cleat and the rope grasped as far from the pontoon as possible and lifted. This is much easier than a straight pull. As the boat starts to move the lift should be lowered and the slack taken up on the cleat. This will need to be repeated several times.

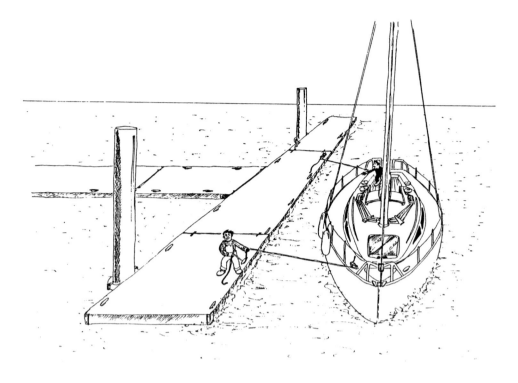

Fig 46.1 Working in to a jetty

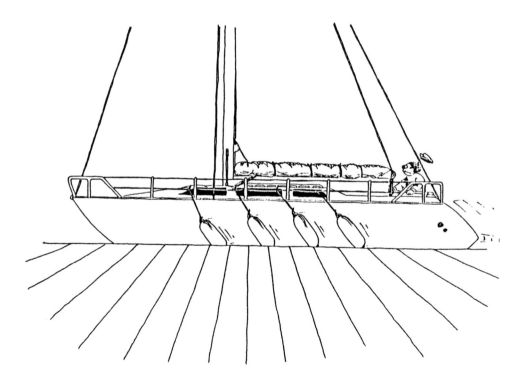

Fig 46.2 Scrubbing out fenders

Wind/tide on to the pontoon

The approach is the same as for wind along the pontoon but aim to turn up a little earlier so as to stop a couple of feet from the pontoon with the bow slightly into wind. The yacht will then blow down on to the pontoon and stop more gently. If the arrival is too close whilst way is still on the pressure of the wind combined with the forward motion can scrub out the fenders as the boat stops. This will result in damage to the hull (see Figure 46.2).

Walls and jetties

The actual approach to a wall or jetty is the same as for a pontoon. The first difference is that the fenders will need to be extending a little above the deck level to protect the hull.

Fender boards

If the jetty or wall is not solid, fender boards will be needed. In British waters it is common for these to be provided. If so they will be hung from the jetty or wall by chains and will need to be brought up to deck level and secured to the top guard rail. Fenders should be used between the board and the hull. When the boards are attached to the wall, remember to release your own ties before leaving!

In some harbours they are not available and, if you have room and are likely to need them, it is a good idea to carry your own. In some areas you are *expected* to provide your own boards and if you have none, you will not be able to use the facility.

A short aluminium or even wooden, ladder is an effective solution, where weight is a problem, and can have other uses. Alternatively, a 30 cm × 2.5 cm plank can have 15 cm holes drilled at intervals without spoiling its use.

Allowing for tide

The next thing to remember is that, unlike the pontoon, the wall will not go up and down with the tide. Since the yacht will rise and fall the lines will have to be sufficiently long to allow for this. In such situations it is best to set the breast lines fairly slack and to attach them to strong points well forward of the bow and aft of the stern. Springs should be of the same order. Where space does not allow this, frequent adjustment may be the only answer. If the lines are not long enough they will need to be tended constantly.

Getting ashore

When the wall is a high one you will need to know how your shore party are going to get up before you start the approach. It is best to aim to bring the boat in, if possible, so that the fixed scaling ladder is amidships; then pass a temporary line round the frame or a rung whilst the shore party climb and make fast. If the ladder protrudes from the wall make sure that it can not damage the hull whilst making fast.

Final position

Once the shore lines are secured, the yacht should be worked back or forward so that the ladder position does not coincide with the widest part of the vessel.

Beware of going alongside a wall on to which you can step at high tide. You could be marooned, either on board or ashore, as the tide goes down. If no convenient ladder is available then inflate the dinghy and use that to reach a point where you can get up and down.

Alongside another vessel

Breast ropes and springs should be set as for a pontoon. In addition, shore lines should always be added. It is both dangerous and unfair to rely on the other yacht's shore lines to hold you. This is particularly so when three or more vessels have to be rafted together. Remember that although the springs and breast ropes will not need adjusting with the tide, the shore lines will. Failure to appreciate this can cause problems for all concerned (see Figure 46.3).

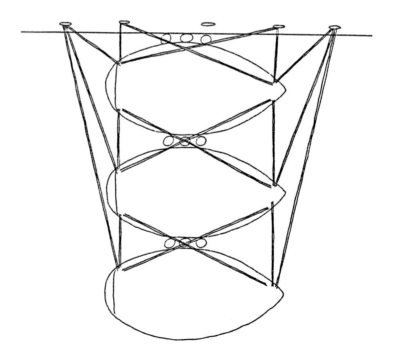

Fig 46.3 Lines needed for rafting up

47 SLIPPING MOORINGS

Just as in mooring, it is best to use the wind and tide to assist the departure from a fixed mooring. Where the net result of wind and tide is from ahead or offshore it is often possible to leave the position without even putting the engine in gear.

Wind/tide from ahead

Remove the springs first with the breast ropes still attached. Rig a slip line from the aft deck cleat (see Figure 47.1) outside everything to a cleat or ring ashore. Use only as much rope as is necessary to go from boat to shore and back, with a short end on board. The stern line can now be let go and recovered. A spare fender should be held in readiness to protect the after end of the yacht as it turns. This fender should not be secured but should be held by its lanyard in the hand so that its position can quickly be moved as required.

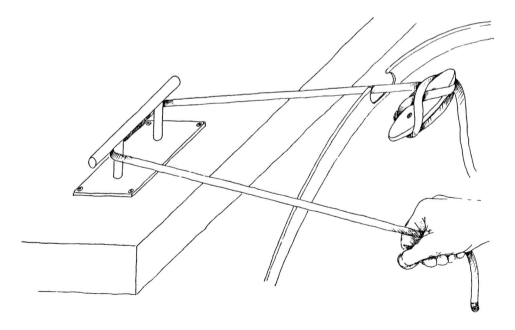

Fig 47.1 Preparing a slip line

If the bow breast rope is now recovered, the yacht will fall back on the slip spring and the bow will begin to move out. The engine can be used with low revs and the helm central to reduce the load on the stern fender. Once the bow has moved out far enough to drive clear, the engine revs can be increased and the spring slipped as the boat pulls away. The spring line must be recovered quickly but smoothly so that it neither snags nor runs under the yacht.

Wind offshore

The operation is the same as above but the engine will probably not be needed to get clear.

Wind/tide onshore

This is the most tricky manoeuvre but can still be achieved with little trouble. The lines are rigged as before but the spring may need to be rather longer. The bow line should be released first and the stern line retained to start pulling the stern in. The roving stern fender will be particularly important.

Springing off

Once the bow line is let go, the engine should be run astern fairly smartly. As the slack in the spring is taken up the bow will start to swing out against the natural forces. The engine power should be kept on until the outward swing starts to slow as the spring reaches the limit of its elasticity. The engine is now returned to neutral with the helm over towards the shore. The spring in the rope will pull the stern forward again accelerating the turn. Once the boat is at about 30 to 40 degrees to the shore the engine should be put ahead and the boat motored away (see Figure 47.2).

The spring should not be released until the boat starts to move away from the shore. This precaution allows for a second attempt if the first is unsuccessful.

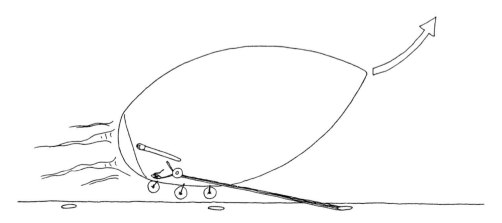

Fig 47.2 Springing off a pontoon

Factors for success

The key factors for successfully completing this manoeuvre are to do with timing. Both engine control and steering must be confident. Since the elasticity of the spring line plays a crucial role, it is important that only nylon warp is used. This has the required elasticity. The use of second-hand prestretched halyards or sheets as mooring warps is to be deplored anyway. Please note that this manoeuvre is almost impossible with such cordage.

Wind/tide from astern

The foregoing method may be successfully used if the wind/tide combination is light. If not, it is probably easier to reverse the procedure and spring from the bow to pull the stern out by going forward before moving away in reverse. The steering limitations of the vessel when going astern must be borne in mind during such a manoeuvre. The natural forces however, will tend to push the bow away from the pontoon as the boat goes astern.

Pile moorings

Although pile moorings are becoming less common they are still encountered in some areas. They will usually be found in tidal rivers where it is essential for boats to be moored fore and aft. These moorings can cause problems. If you are to take an unoccupied space it is possible to do the whole job from on board but can be made much easier with the use of a dinghy.

Tide only conditions

If the wind is in the same direction as the tide and the line of the piles or is very light, the following method can be used.

Start by preparing two long warps, bow and stern. Motor up to the gap between the piles and stop with the bow into the tide at arms length from the forward pile. A metal bar is normally found on the pile to which a rope is attached. Pull up this rope and a ring will be found which slides on the bar. Pass the bow warp through the ring in a round turn and bring the end back on board.

Picking up astern

The next job is to pick up the stern moor. Allow the bow warp to pay out and the boat to fall back so as to bring the stern close to the second pile. It will seldom be possible to reach the pile without hitting the stern if it is directly behind so manoeuvre to come alongside. With a tide running this is usually possible on helm alone without engine.

Pass the stern warp through the ring in the same way as before. The boat should now be motored slowly back towards the forward pile until central between the two. The two warps should then be adjusted to suit with most, but not quite all, of the slack taken up.

Rise and fall

The rings on the piles are to allow the boat to ride up and down with the tide without chafe on the mooring warps. If the tide is very strong it will be easier to pass the bow line round the bar only, at first, as a slip line. Once the stern warp is secured the boat can be brought back to the forward pile and a bow line correctly set before the slip line is released. The stern line can be dealt with in the same way if necessary.

Passing it round the pile

It is not a good idea to try to pass a line right round the pile. If this must be done it is best done from a dinghy.

A vivid memory is still with me, after many years, of a willing and eager crewman who tried this. He was standing in the stern trying to pass a line round the after pile as the boat moved up to the forward one. This is a manoeuvre which, if successful, can be very slick.

As the pile came close he found that it had no bar. He therefore attempted to pass the line right round the pile. He was able to get an arm round, but, in order to catch hold of the free end, needed to relinquish his hold on the boat. Losing his balance as he caught the end, he decided to hang on to the pile.

I still have a vision of that lad, gripping hard to a green and slimy pole, slowly descending into the water as gravity took over. The boat continued slowly up to the forward pile.

'Don't let go of the rope!' yelled the skipper on noticing what had happened. I shall never know if his concern was for the lad's safety or the need to complete the mooring.

Pick-up lines

Sometimes the piles are connected by a pick-up line which is supported on small floats. This makes the job easier since one only has to come alongside this line and follow it to the slide rings at each end.

Fore and aft moorings

In some places, where space is limited, mooring between two buoys may be the rule. These may be linked by pick-up lines or they may not. In the first case mooring is easy. The only danger being the risk of running over and fouling a pick-up line.

When they are not linked it can be more difficult than pile mooring. This is because they are not always aligned with the stream and also they can become well separated due to drift and to the way they were last dropped. For these reasons it is usually easier to use the dinghy.

If possible, come alongside a boat that is already moored first. Raft to this and then use the dinghy to put lines to the buoys.

Stern line first

If you are the first to arrive and have no dinghy ready it is best to pick up the stern mooring first with a long slip line. It is always easier to keep steering control whilst motoring ahead than astern and it is easier to reach a buoy over the bow than one over the stern. Care must be taken not to run over the stern line if the first attempt at the bow mooring fails and you have to try again (see Figure 47.3).

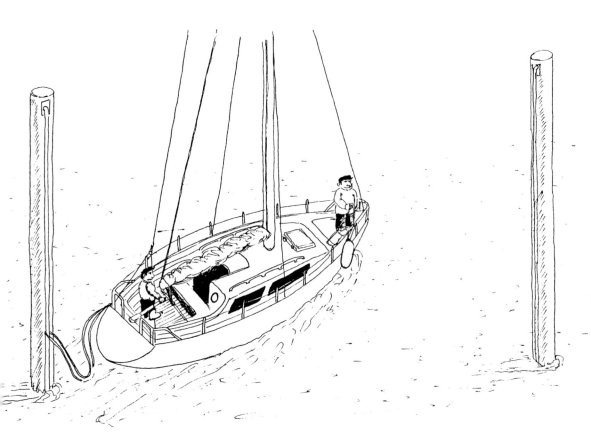

Fig 47.3 Pile mooring across wind or tide

48 MARINA BERTHS

The problems of marina berthing and unberthing worry many people. Often there is little turning space. The slot you are to enter is closed at one end and is often substantially shorter than your boat. The space may be only just sufficient to take you with little room for error. You may have no choice as to the slot you use. These manoeuvres should always be done under engine unless you are a professional.

Some finger pontoons, particularly those used in continental marinas, are flimsy unstable platforms on which to jump.

Conditions

In light winds and when little tide is present all these difficulties can be overcome by using a slow approach and lining the yacht up perfectly before attempting to enter the slot. Many marinas are so designed and positioned that this situation is more common than one might expect. Sometimes however it is not.

Strong wind or tide conditions can oblige you to go in much faster than you would like, leaving little room for error. The mistake that is most common is to try to use the light wind technique regardless of conditions.

Choice of berth

The first thing to do is to decide on the berth you are going for before getting into a tight spot. To attempt to go up and down each lane looking for a vacant berth is courting disaster, especially if you are going to have to turn round in order to get out again. Instead put someone ashore on the first convenient pontoon and get them to find a suitable berth. Keep the yacht outside until this decision is made.

Once you know where you are going you can plan. Having someone ashore to receive you is a great boon. Make full use of this.

The plan

Three major possibilities exist. The natural forces will be acting out of, into or across the berth. Each situation will need some variation in method. The easiest berth to take will be one which can be entered bow first with head to wind. This will also be the most comfortable since it will allow you to leave the washboards out even in heavy rain. It will permit through ventilation when you want it and minimise drafts when you don't. Your scout should look for such a berth therefore, if you can't spot one yourself.

Fenders

Prepare the yacht with fenders on both sides. Those on the side that will be against the finger pontoon should be low down. On the other side the height will depend on the size of boat occupying the adjoining berth. If both are vacant set all the fenders low and raise those on the outside to toe rail level once mooring is completed. If you have a 'V' shaped bow fender set it low enough to protect the stem should you overrun.

Warps

Use fairly short warps for breast ropes. The bow warp should be prepared and secured then brought back over the pulpit and the spare coiled on deck. This line will be passed to your crew member ashore. The stern warp will be needed in the same way as for pontoon mooring. Have a bow spring ready prepared to check your forward movement.

The manoeuvre

Once ready, start motoring down between the pontoons. The pace will depend on the wind. Have just sufficient speed to keep drift to a minimum. When the bow is across the gap you intend to enter, the yacht should be about a boatlength downwind of the space. In any case it must be no closer than 2 metres, preferably more, from the downwind moored boats. Start the turn as the bow starts to cross the gap. Take the power off now but keep the turn tight. This will get the head round fast and at the same time slow the boat down.

A line ashore

As soon as the boat is heading straight into the gap, reduce speed, by going astern if necessary. As soon as practicable, the bow line should be passed to the person ashore who takes a turn round a cleat, directly ahead if possible, but does not pull in. The stern line, together with the bow spring, is taken ashore at this time. The stern line should be passed round the cleat and the loop in the spring slipped over it.

Checking the movement

The bow crew can now check the forward movement of the yacht with the spring. The stern crew must prevent the stern from swinging out. The stern line can be passed back on board to the helmsman at this stage who can adjust and secure it.

Once the way is off the boat it will start to fall back on the wind. The bow line can be used to control this. A second spring can now be set. When this has been done the bow line can be transferred to the cleat on the finger pontoon, passed back on board and secured. The yacht is now moored and final adjustments can be made.

Short handed

In the method described above, four crew are needed. If fewer crew are available, the shore man will have to be dispensed with. The bow man will now have to go ashore first and do that job. With only two people available, the helmsman will have to tend the stern line. It helps to have it prepared as a loop. One end is cleated on board and a bight of about two to three metres long is formed. The loop is closed with, and secured on, the same cleat.

As the pontoon cleat comes within range, the helm should be relinquished and the bight held open with both hands until it can be dropped over the cleat. A good judge of speed and position is essential.

With both breast ropes secure, the boat will be drawn into the finger pontoon as it falls back on the wind. Final adjustments can then be made with the springs.

Stern first

If the wind is blowing into the open end of the berth consider going in stern first. It will be more comfortable and a lot easier to get out again. Rather more space between the pontoons will be needed to make the turn successfully, or the shore man this time will need to be on the upwind pontoon opposite the berth (see Figure 48.1).

Preparation

Breast ropes should be prepared as before but the spring this time should be from the stern. An additional, long bow line will be needed for the man on the windward pontoon. The crew tending the shore lines will need to get off as early as possible. The bow breast rope man should also take the stern spring.

The approach

Make the approach as before in the same position relative to the wind. As soon as the turn is started the extra bow line should be passed to the shore man who takes a bight on to a cleat. This line acts as a check line whilst the boat is moved back into the berth. As soon as this line is on, the way should be taken off the boat so that the stern comes round with the wind. The boat can now be manoeuvred back into the berth with the shore man and helm working together. The crew member handling the stern line will need to be ready to go on to the pontoon as soon as it comes within reach.

Berthing

The stern line crew must get ashore as soon as possible to guide the stern into the berth. The bow line and spring can be taken ashore next. The spring eye should be dropped over the cleat and the breast rope used to prevent the bow swinging away as the spring takes up.

Once the breast ropes are secured the extra bow line can be recovered and the remaining spring set.

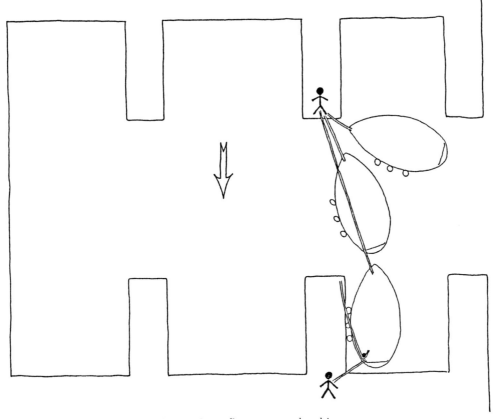

Fig 48.1 Stern first pontoon berthing

Wind across the berth

The problem here is to get in without being set across so fast that the bow pays off and spoils the manoeuvre or causes damage. A faster than usual entry to the berth is necessary so the crew must be quick to get breast ropes ashore both to control lateral movement and to take the way off if necessary.

The helmsman must use reverse to take way off as soon as the breast ropes are ashore. He should assume that the bow will pay off as the yacht comes across the wind and adjust the angle of entry accordingly.

Two shore lines will be used so if a third crew member is available he should be stationed on the downwind side with a spare, unattached fender ready for use as required.

Leaving a marina berth

If you have the wind on your bow, when moored with bows in, you can simply motor out with no difficulty. Let the lines go and the boat will fall back. Put the helm over so that the bow pays off on the wind in the direction that you want to go. You probably won't need to engage the engine until out of the berth and heading along the pontoons.

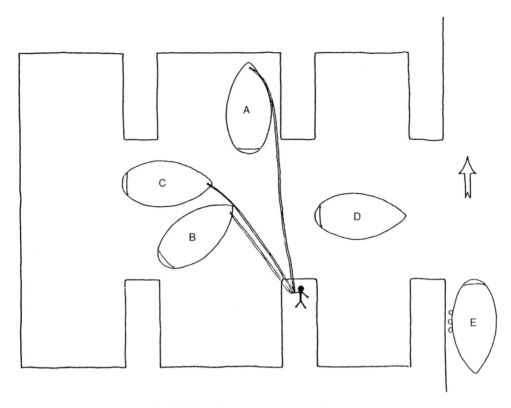

Fig 48.2 Warping out against wind or tide

Wind astern

The situation that causes most problems is the one where you have gone in head to wind but the wind has shifted so that it is now astern blowing you into the berth. If you attempt to motor out astern you will have difficulty getting the head round against the wind and could finish up being blown down against the sterns of more than one boat. Even if you succeed in getting the head round you may find that the same thing happens. You slip sideways during the time you are losing stern way and gathering forward way. The solution is to have a man ashore again. With one or more crew ashore you can warp the boat out of its berth and motor off in perfect safety (see Figure 48.2 shows the sequence of operations).

Warping out

Position your man ashore on the upwind pontoon or on a moored boat on that side and pass him a long line. Secure this line to your bow cleat passing it outside everything on the side of the boat leading to open water. Don't use a loop on the cleat because you will have to let the inboard end go later.

Letting go

Once ready, remove the springs and let the mooring lines go whilst motoring backwards. Use just enough power to move you slowly out of the berth. Once clear of the berth take the engine out of gear and put the helm over to let the stern fall off down wind in the right direction. Your shore crew should be taking in all the slack on his line as you go. This holds the head against the wind.

Slipping the safety line

Once the boat is parallel to the pontoons, the bow safety line can be slipped from on board, the engine put ahead and the boat motored out. If the wind is very strong it may help to have a second safety line, from the stern to the windward position, slipping this at the same time as the bow line.

It is essential that the bow line is slipped from onboard or it will run back under the boat as you go ahead and foul the propeller. Your shore crew can now coil up the rope and move to the end of the pontoon. Do not attempt to pick him up from his initial position. It can be done but is risky. It is better for him to move to the end of the pontoon where he can be picked up safely with the boat head to wind.

49 UNRAFTING FROM MULTIPLE MOORINGS

Multiple berths are of several kinds. They may be rafts on a pontoon or wall. They can also be rafts on swinging or fore and aft moorings or piles. The techniques are similar but not identical. Berthing to them is no different from going alongside any other boat because you will be the outside one anyway. The difference comes when you want to move away and someone else has come in outside you.

Any boat joining a raft should always have lines attached to the shore or other fixed mooring. This is not only safe and considerate to others, it is the key to getting away again.

Leaving a pontoon or piles

If you are part of a raft and wish to leave from any position other than the outside one, it will be necessary for you to release another boat or boats temporarily. It will be your responsibility to do this in a way that ensures the safety of the other boat unless it has a crew on board who take part in the manoeuvre.

Choice of direction

The first thing the skipper must do is decide what effect removing any lines will have. This will depend on wind and tide and also on the direction in which his boat is to depart. It will usually be best to move out down wind or tide depending on which is the stronger, though this may not always be possible.

In any event, the boat outside your own must not be detached totally from the main raft. Its upwind/uptide shoreline will be in tension. This may need to be adjusted but should always remain joined.

Preparation

Once the engine is running, the springs holding you on both sides should be removed. Recover those that belong to you. Those belonging to the outer boat should be left attached to it. They will need to be transferred to the inner boat once you have got clear. Make sure that fenders on the adjoining boats will be effective when they come together. Next detach the shore lines of all boats outside your own from the shore at the down wind/tide end only. Recover them on to the boats concerned leaving them ready for replacement. Figure 49.1a–e shows the sequence of operations.

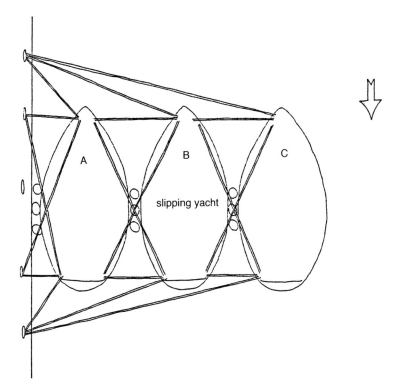

Fig 49.1a The complete raft

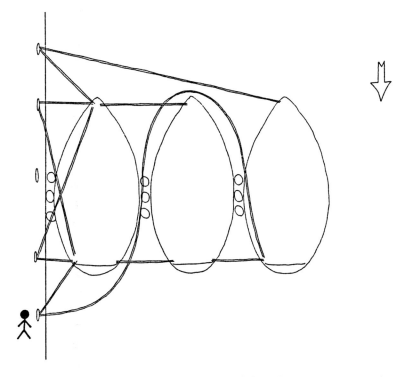

Fig 49.1b Springs removed and shore line set

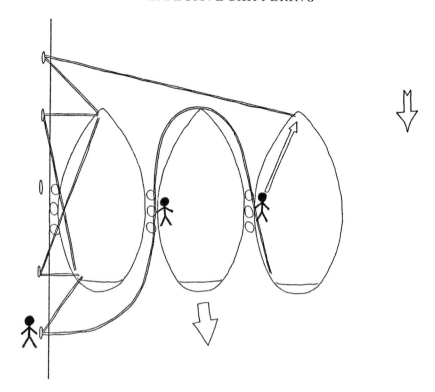

Fig 49.1c Breast ropes removed, the yacht starts to move out

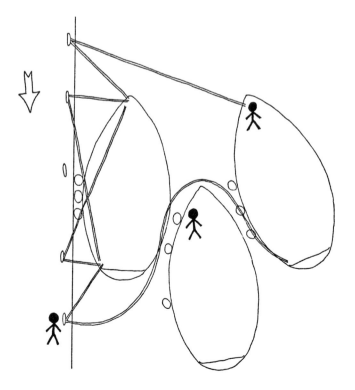

Fig 49.1d Bringing in the outside yacht

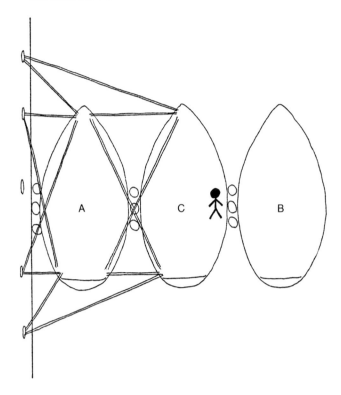

Fig 49.1e All secure again, the yacht collects the crew

Safety line

Take the free end of the shore line of the boat immediately outside your own, still connected to his nearside cleat, forward, or back as appropriate, outside everything. Pass it round your own bow and back to the nearside downtide/downwind cleat of the boat inside yours. It may be necessary to extend this line to pass it round your boat. If so use the same boat's stern spring.

Slipping

Detach and recover both your own shore lines; that in tension last. Rig your own breast ropes as slip lines to the inner boat, if this has not been done when mooring. Remove the breast ropes of the outside boat from your own boat. Have a crew member positioned near the downtide end to hold that breast rope and prevent the boats drifting apart. You are now ready to depart.

Restoration crew

Leave one of your crew on the inside boat. His job will be to take in the line you have taken round your boat, when you move out. He will need to replace the springs between the boats now touching. He will also need to replace all the removed shore lines and to shorten those left attached. Since he will be restoring a number of lines, this will take some time.

Getting clear

Move out slowly downtide. Your crew should work to keep the two boats beside you as close together as possible. Once your own boat is clear you can remove and stow your own shore lines and springs. Do not remove the fenders yet. Depending on the location; you can now either move out of the way until your man left behind is ready, or you can come alongside on the outside of the raft with temporary slip lines until he is ready.

Checking

Before you depart finally make sure that all lines have been replaced correctly and that the springs have been set so that the spreaders can not clash. This is the restoration crew's job but skipper's responsibility.

Double mooring buoy rafts

Most of the actions will be the same as for a pontoon or piles. The safety line taken round your own bow should however be taken directly to the downtide mooring. If the tide or tide/wind combination is across the raft this is particularly important since otherwise the raft can quickly open up. It is difficult for one person to close it again without such a line should this happen.

Single buoy rafts

Where several boats are rafted on a single buoy departure is easy, as long as all boats have lines to the mooring. Remove all lines connecting your boat to the others. Next release your line to the mooring and back out. As you back out, the raft will close and all that is needed is for the crew left behind to reset the springs.

50 ANCHORING ESSENTIALS

I was surprised, when I first started running Yachtmaster courses, that few of the candidates had spent any appreciable time at anchor. I am used to it now. To anchor for lunch or to go for a swim seems all right. To actually stay overnight or to leave a yacht at anchor and go ashore is just not on with many otherwise very experienced sailors.

I suppose the proliferation of marinas with all their attractive facilities is partly to blame. It is a great pity, because anyone who has not spent a night or two in a quiet anchorage has missed one of the most pleasant aspects of sailing. Not being able to anchor would, as far as I am concerned, put an unacceptable constraint on my choice of locations.

Why the concern?

I suspect that for many it is simply anxiety. Will an anchor really hold me? Have I got it right? These are the questions in the back of many a mind. Yet those same people will quite happily pick up a mooring without any knowledge of how good it is and treat it as though it was 100% safe.

An anchor is much the same as a mooring after all. The essential difference is that, whilst both connect your vessel to the bottom, you detach the boat from the chain on a mooring, whereas with an anchor, you detach the chain from the bottom.

Properly chosen, and correctly used, your own ground tackle must be more reliable than some ancient chain about which you have no knowledge and of which you can only inspect the top few feet.

Basics

When choosing the spot to drop your hook you will need to have enough depth under you to stay afloat with a reasonable safety margin at low water. You will also need to calculate the greatest depth to expect. Check and recheck the tides to be sure of these.

There is no need to make a meal of it. The information required is the rise of tide and actual depth on arrival, the range that day and the boat's draft. Estimate the minimum clearance you want under your keel. In calm weather a metre is sufficient but in a swell it is safer to double that figure. Adding the rise, plus the draft of your boat, to this figure will give you the least depth you must read on your echo-sounder as you drop the hook for a twelve hour stay.

To find the maximum depth you will have at high water, subtract the rise from the range and add this answer to the echo-sounder reading of actual depth.

To find the scope required multiply the maximum depth by three (five if using rope). This will tell you the minimum you can get away with for a twelve hour stay. Remember this minimum starts from where the scope comes out of the water, not where it is attached to the boat. More is said on this later.

Shelter from the existing, forecast and possible winds is important as is the quality of the holding. Pilot books will tell you about both the shelter and nature of bottom to be expected.

Holding checks

Once settled make a careful check of your position and recheck at least three times at about five minute intervals to be sure you are holding. The best marks to use for this are natural transits. They are easier to check than bearings and more reliable. Remember that the greater the horizontal separation between marks the more sensitive the transit is to position changes.

Try to choose things which can still be used after dark. A lone tree on the sky line will be more use than a bush halfway up the cliff. If the marks will not be visible after dark, take bearings on ones that will and make a note of them. The marks used do not need to be charted but do need to be permanent in relation to the time you intend to stay.

Choice of tackle

The relative properties of the types of anchor most commonly found on yachts are discussed in most basic books including *The Shorebased Sailor*. The point is that no single anchor is perfect for every purpose. This means that you will need to carry at least two in order to be properly equipped. It makes sense to have two anyway. You could lose one and you may need a kedge.

Main anchor

By far the majority of yachts carry either a CQR or a Bruce as main anchor. The main anchor should be as large as you can carry. It must, in any event, be of the size rated for the boat. If possible go up one size from the minimum recommended. As the second anchor I prefer to have a Bruce since it will most frequently be used as a kedge. Both should be of good quality. A cheap imitation is worse than useless for either purpose.

Kedge

The advantages of the Bruce are its single piece construction with no sharp points coupled to its good holding power in relation to its weight. This makes it much easier and safer to use from an inflatable dinghy which will be the most likely means of setting a kedge. The kedge should be at least of the minimum size recommended for the boat.

It is folly to have an undersized kedge anchor since it may have to take the place of the main anchor if you lose that. What chance have you of holding in conditions where the main anchor has failed with an undersized replacement?

Fisherman's
If you can find stowage for it, a good sized fisherman's is worth carrying as a third anchor. It is the only anchor that will give good holding in weed or on rock. Fishermen most frequently anchor in weed or rocks, hence the name. Make sure it is large enough to be of use though. The size can cause problems in stowage but this is better than having one that is too small.

Anchor cable
The anchor cable comprises all the flexible connection between anchor and boat. All anchors should be fitted with at least six metres of chain at the anchor end. This will need to be fairly substantial if the cable is to continue in rope. An anchor will only work so long as the pull on it is parallel to the sea bed. The chain used must be heavy enough to do this. As soon as the stock starts to lift the anchor will begin to break out.

A further consideration is chafe. If insufficient chain is used part of the rope will be on the sea bed. In some conditions this can result in chafe that could seriously weaken the rope or even part it. In practice, this factor dictates that the six metre minimum should only be used on the kedge anchor. This will only be in use for short periods and the practical problems of taking it out in a dinghy far outweigh any other considerations.

Chain or rope?
Some people advocate using all chain for the anchor cable. Personally I think that this view needs to be qualified. In some situations, such as anchoring in deep water or with large tidal ranges, it will be impractical due to weight considerations to have all chain on a yacht under 15 metres. I once delivered an 8.5 metre yacht that had 250 metres of chain. It sailed horribly. Provided a reasonable length of chain is fitted, say about 20 metres, rope for the remainder is perfectly acceptable.

Cable marking
Anchor cables used to be marked with pieces of leather, cloth and so on. This was to make it possible to know exactly how much scope was out. The practice has become less common lately. The abandonment of all forms of marking is unwise. Marking out a two metre length on the deck and flaking the chain out alongside this is an acceptable practice but is not a perfect substitute for marking the chain.

If the scope has to be changed for some reason or in bad conditions when it may not be possible or prudent to flake out the chain, only marks on the chain will solve the problem. Any system used must be unambiguous and easily understood by the foredeck crew.

A simple method is to use insulating tape in several colours. Red, yellow, green, blue, black and white tapes are easily obtained. Using one colour mark one link at two metres, two links at four and so on up to eight metres. At ten metres mark two links, one with the initial and the next the following colour, at twelve mark two with the primary colour and one with the second and so on. The order of the colours I have suggested is that of the rainbow which aids the memory. Orange has been left out since red tape quickly becomes orange in use.

I have found the survival rate of insulating tape to be pretty good if at least three thicknesses overlay each other. A check on condition is not difficult in any event. Paint can be used but does not last nearly so well.

The suggested system will mark up to sixty metres of cable. If you have more than this, precise length will become less critical as the scope increases. You could mark at ten metre intervals beyond 50 metres.

Scope and swinging circle

In a crowded anchorage subject to tidal changes you will need to consider the scope in relation to both your swinging circle and those of adjacent vessels.

In light conditions it is probably best to opt for the recommended minimum scope in order to restrict the swing. However, a boat lying to rope will have a much larger swinging circle than one on chain and here the size of chain in relation to boat size is also relevant. This is because, in practice, the chain lying on the bottom will move relatively little, whilst rope will tend to follow the boat. Scope for heavy weather is discussed in Chapter 51.

The amount of movement will depend on the weight of chain used. This means that, although you may well be able to estimate your own circle, you will have very little indication of the circle of any other vessel so must guess. The safest thing to do is to wait for the tide to turn and to see what happens. It may be necessary for you to move, to change your scope length or to suggest that someone else move.

It is an accepted tradition that the last to arrive is the first to move, but that tradition is not always observed these days. Don't argue the toss if the offender will not move; it is better to move yourself than to risk damage.

Sometimes you will find that you anchor at what you consider a safe distance from another vessel only to have a later arrival drop his hook between you both. If you cannot dissuade him, grit your teeth and move. It will be less expensive.

Cable length

The total length of anchor cable to carry must be related to the expected anchorages and to the required scope. If your cable is all chain, a minimum of three times the maximum water depth anticipated plus a little more to cope with the distance from the water surface to the securing point will just do. The prudent mariner will exceed this by a good safety margin however.

With rope the minimum length jumps to five times the anticipated depth. Most anchor cable lockers will accommodate more than this. As a rule of thumb I would suggest carrying 100 metres of cable with a quarter of this length in chain. Use chain one size above that recommended for your boat length. The extra weight should not cause a problem with the suggested arrangement and it improves peace of mind.

The best rope to use is a multiplait type. This consists of eight lays of interwoven nylon. Four are made up with a left-handed twist and four with a right-handed one. The result is a cable which has good stretch, is easy to handle and which does not tangle or kink in the locker.

Chain/rope joint

All ropes can be spliced on to chain and multiplait is no exception. I do not like rope/chain splices however since they can introduce a potential weakness. Grains of sand which inevitably get into anchor cables can remove the galvanising from the chain under the rope. At the same time, the sand will wear the inner strands of the rope. Once rusting starts the wear increases rapidly. Very little evidence is visible before quite considerable weakening has occurred.

The great advantage of the rope/chain splice is that it will pass over a roller fitting easily. Nevertheless I prefer to use an eye splice with a good sized thimble and to shackle this to the chain. Such a join, whilst bulky, is strong and will last. It is a truism that a chain is as strong as its weakest link. Lives will depend on that join. The shackles at each end of the chain should of course be secured with seizing wire. The whole should be regularly checked.

Laying the anchor

The risk of dragging can be reduced by using sensible procedure. If the anchor is to hold well it must dig in when the load comes on it and the chain must be straight, particularly where it comes immediately away from the anchor.

To achieve the ideal situation, the boat must be stopped at the time the anchor reaches the bottom and then fall back slowly as the cable is paid out. The cable should not be snubbed to dig the anchor in until at least half the scope is paid out. Once the scope is all out the vessel should be taken astern to straighten the cable and test the hold.

Dangers to watch for are:

1 Lowering the anchor whilst the boat is still moving forward. This can cause the pulling of a loop of chain under the anchor.

2 Continuing to lower cable after the anchor is on the bottom and before the boat has started to fall back. This can pile chain on top of the anchor. Both actions can cause the chain to wrap round the flukes of the anchor stopping it from penetrating.

3 Snubbing before sufficient chain is out to prevent the stock from lifting when the pull comes on. Particularly dangerous in weed conditions, this will cause the anchor to bounce along the bottom gathering debris as it goes. Once this happens, with anything but the fisherman's, the anchor will be virtually useless unless lifted again and cleared.

4 Paying out too slowly as the vessel falls back can result in premature snubbing. Close liaison between foredeck and helm is necessary.

5   Using the wrong anchor for the bottom or choosing an unsuitable bottom. Use the chart and pilot books to find out the type and quality of the holding as much as possible.

Anchor signals

Few if any of the boats I find in anchorages use the correct, black ball, day signal. Rather more show an all round white light at night. The failure to do both is wrong. In the event of a collision resulting in damage, insurers will check on signals. Failure to display them may result in the insurer absolving itself of liability.

In waters used by large vessels, the day signal is particularly important. The watch keeper on the larger vessel will be having difficulty seeing your chain. From his position there is little difference in apparent movement between a yacht at anchor and one that is moving slowly under engine. Such confusion could be dangerous. At night you could be run down.

51 ANCHOR PROBLEMS

At anchor in heavy weather

Some evidence exists that a mixture of rope and chain will provide better holding than will all chain in gale conditions. This is because the elasticity of rope prevents snatch loads being applied to the anchor.

In heavy seas the anchor cable will be jerked taut at the vessel end from time to time. This generates shock loads in the cable. Chain, having no elasticity, passes such shock loads to its ends. At the boat end this can produce instantaneous forces on the stemhead and deck fittings greatly in excess of their design loads. Such forces can induce failure of the fittings.

At the lower end, the instantaneous shock load on the anchor can be equated to a hammer blow. A succession of such shocks can cause the anchor to break out and drag. Once an anchor breaks out like this, it may reset itself, and often will in good holding; however, its holding power is very considerably reduced. In any case, it would be an unwelcome event when riding out a gale.

The use of nylon rope, which has good stretch properties, will tend to damp out these shock loads thus putting less strain on both deck fittings and ground tackle. In severe conditions, risk of chafe at the stemhead fitting can be reduced by passing the rope through a length of plastic hose which can be positioned over the roller or fairlead. Lashed to the cable with a leather bootlace, this will all but prevent chafe. A length of such hose can be permanently threaded on to the cable before the bitter end is made secure. This makes it a simple matter to slide the hose along to the correct position when needed.

Increasing scope

As mentioned in the last chapter, the scope is the length of cable between anchor and surface; not the length between anchor and cleat. This length must be increased from the minimum as the wind and sea conditions deteriorate so that the catenary, the curve in the scope, is maintained. In a crowded anchorage, this can present problems, especially when the crew of the boat immediately downwind of yours have gone ashore and don't come back. Increase the scope gradually and watch that you don't ride back on to their chain.

If you can not increase the scope you will have to consider changing your position, otherwise you must find an alternative way to improve your holdings. Taking the anchor up and resetting it can be a terrifying experience in a blow and one which you are loath to contemplate. Dragging your anchor in the same conditions can be even more terrifying. It may be necessary, if you have to move, to buoy the anchor cable and let it go to be recovered later. This is where your spare anchor becomes important.

Second anchors

One alternative is to lay a second anchor. This can be done either at an angle to the first on a separate cable or on the same cable as your main anchor.

I am not greatly in favour of the former method. It has two main drawbacks. The first is that the two anchors will not both work together. A modern light displacement hull does not ride steady to the wind in a blow. It tends to veer from side to side. This results in the pull on two anchor cables not being together but being switched alternately from one to the other. Whilst the presence of two cables will tend to reduce veering it will not appreciably improve the holding. This situation is aggravated by the second problem.

The yacht is unlikely to have sufficient chain to be able to set both anchors on the same type of scope. One will be mostly chain and the other, the kedge, mostly rope. The benefit from this is doubtful because of the stretch in the rope. Add the problem of laying the second anchor. Do you try to motor up to a point beside your main anchor or do you inflate the dinghy and try to row out the second?

An easier and more effective solution is to set a second anchor on the main cable. This will markedly improve the catenary and will improve the holding ability of the composite by a factor of about three.

The technique is to start the engine and motor up the line of the scope taking in as you go until about half the scope has been recovered or, at least, until the end of the chain is aboard. The second anchor is now shackled to the chain at least three metres from the end and the whole lowered again. Once the original scope has been paid out the boat will hold slightly forward of its starting position. If space allows, more scope should now be paid out to increase the total length by the maximum water depth.

Should you be setting both anchors at the same time in anticipation of a blow the two anchors can be closer together. They must always be separated by at least 1.2 times the maximum depth of water. If this is not done subsequent recovery can be extremely difficult.

An alternative to the technique just described can be used in rough conditions. This is to pass a second anchor down the original cable. The weight acts to improve the catenary shape.

Instead of raising the cable to attach the second anchor a loop of chain a foot or so across is shackled to the spare anchor with the main cable passing through it. A line attached to the anchor is then used to lower it down the cable on to the sea bed. The line is necessary to prevent the second anchor from working its way right along to the first and perhaps tripping it.

When a heavy load is placed on the cable it will be found that the second anchor barely lifts from the sea bed and thus the pull on the main anchor is kept parallel to the bottom. The holding power of such a combination, whilst not as good as the earlier method, is still a considerable improvement on a single anchor. It will remove most of the shock loads.

It has the advantage that very little of the original scope need be recovered so reducing the risk of breaking out the main anchor you have already set. It is important that the chain loop is run down far enough to be on to the main chain and not on rope since a considerable degree of chafe damage will otherwise occur in rough conditions. In practice it is not difficult to feel when this has happened.

A further use for this chain loop will be discussed later in this chapter.

Reducing veer

Mentioned above was the problem of veer in light displacement boats. This can be reduced in several ways. On a ketch, simply hoist all or part of the mizzen sail. This acts in the same way as the small mizzen sail often seen on fishing boats. Veering is more of a problem on a sloop-rigged boat but can still be reduced.

A special steadying sail can be carried or the storm jib can be used. This can be hoisted on the backstay using the main halyard or the topping lift. It should be sheeted tight. The kicking strap fitting makes a suitable point of attachment. It will do a great deal to reduce veering but will also increase wind resistance and thus, the tension on the anchor cable. The change to a steady pull, rather than snatch loads, on the anchor cable should be of overall benefit, however, and the increase in comfort is great.

You will need to watch that other boats, which are still veering, do not drive into yours. In such weather conditions however, an anchor watch should be maintained so that this risk should not go unnoticed.

Fouled anchors

The sea is a perverse thing. When you don't want it to, your anchor will drag for no apparent reason. On another occasion in the same place it will hold so fast that you are unable to lift it.

Both situations can result from fouling the anchor. In the former case this is usually due to the way you have anchored. In the latter case it is probably the location.

Snagged anchor
The problem of an anchor that holds too well is different. This can happen if the bottom is rocky or foul with old chain etc. I once brought up, with considerable difficulty, an anchor from which hung a very ancient pram. How it got there intrigued us for a long time. I am sorry to say we were obliged to put it back where we found it.

Tripping lines
I am not a great believer in tripping lines. My experience has found them to be more trouble than they are worth. In my time I have had the float cut to ribbons by a propeller and the line picked up on someone else's propeller causing my anchor to break free and lift off the bottom. If you must use a tripping line it is best to bring the upper end of it back on board.

Recently a near disaster was directly caused by a French registered yacht which had set a tripping line by tying the lower end to the anchor crown and the upper, without a float, half way up his chain. When the tide turned, the loop formed by this line caught round my anchor, to which I had been lying quite safely in gale force winds for 24 hours, and tripped it. Both vessels dragged and the situation was only retrieved with considerable difficulty. In any event he had put down his anchor far too close to us and needlessly so.

Breaking out the stubborn anchor

The first thing to try, if you have no tripping line, is a change of angle. This will often cause the anchor to unhook itself from the obstruction. Take up all the slack in the chain and secure it. Then motor over the anchor to try to break it free.

Before using force, a less strenuous method can be tried. Remember the loop of chain used for weighting the anchor? This same loop can be used now. Close the loop round the anchor chain with a shackle and attach a strong line to this. If the loop is now run down the tight chain it can be induced to slip on to the shank of the anchor. It is fairly easy to feel when this has happened. Next the chain is slackened off and the line taken up taut. With a bit of luck this will cause the anchor to trip and it can be recovered. I have done this so I know it can work.

Applying force

If this does not work, motor round in a circle trying to screw the anchor out. Even if the anchor does not move at first, the links of the chain will gradually tighten on each other and effectively shorten the chain.

This effect puts an immense pressure on the chain which ought to break out the anchor. There is no point however in screwing round until the bows start to pull under! All you will then achieve is a broken anchor or chain. If it gets to this stage, take the strain off. Unshackle the chain and buoy it with a spare fender. You can then get a diver to retrieve it later. The cost of a diver will usually be less than the replacement cost of the tackle.

Debris

A further problem that I have experienced is the collection of debris, a mass of weed (or a pram?) making the anchor very heavy to raise. If you have no anchor winch this can be a problem.

My solution is slow but effective. A stout warp is run from a sheet winch down the side deck and over the spare roller. A fairlead would do if you have no spare roller. By lying down on the foredeck it is possible to tie a rolling hitch some way down the chain. With the other end of the warp on the winch the anchor can now be raised bit by bit. As the rolling hitch reaches the bow roller the chain is temporarily belayed on to a cleat. The warp can then be slacked off and the rolling hitch slid further down the chain.

Using this method took us about fourteen or fifteen minutes to haul in 10 metres of fouled anchor chain but no one broke their back in the process. Clearing the anchor actually proved more difficult than raising it. It had collected a tangled mess of old steel cables

Kedging

The kedge anchor has two main uses. Both are concerned with preventing swing but for different reasons.

In some small harbours or anchorages there may not be sufficient room to swing safely with the tide and still avoid obstructions. In a river or alongside a channel any swing may cause the yacht to obstruct the fairway or to ground on the bank.

Rivers and channels

In a river, the bow anchor should be set upstream of the strongest set. This will normally be the ebb but check the pilot book to be sure. In the absence of any strong wind it is usually best to set the upstream anchor first. Have plenty of scope so that the vessel can be allowed to fall back well beyond the required position. Now set the downstream anchor and recover some of the main anchor scope.

Both anchors will be more effective if they are far apart. At the very least they should be separated by a distance equal to three times the maximum water depth plus one boat length.

Once both anchors are set, let out some scope again so that the downstream cable has some slack. If the river has a tidal range, this scope will need to be adjusted with the tide. Both cables should not be tight at the same time unless in a cross-wind. Pressure can sometimes be reduced in a cross-wind by putting bias on the rudder thus using the stream to turn the boat into wind. Experiment will be necessary to find the best position.

If you are on a bow mooring and use a kedge from the stern, anchor signals are still required since your own tackle is down.

Kedging off

When the kedge is being used to haul off a grounding it will be taking more than its normal load. Use as much cable as you possibly can by extending with warps if possible. When taking the kedge out, the anchor should be laid in the stern of the dinghy with the cable coiled loosely beside it. The onboard end should be secured and the cable paid out from the dinghy as you row away. Any attempt to pay out the cable from on board the vessel will make the job of the rower very hard work indeed. It is equivalent to streaming a warp!

Sailing to an anchorage

There may be times when it becomes necessary to put the anchor down under sail. This is not so difficult as some demonstrations I have seen would suggest.

Choose your spot carefully and, if possible sail round it to check depth over the area. If your boat will do it (most will) and there is little or no counter tide, the operation is best done under main alone leaving the foredeck clear. Once sure of your spot, move away to a slightly down wind position.

In addition to the anchor crew you will need someone to tend the main halyard and topping lift. Have the kicker slackened and approach the chosen position on a fine reach. This will permit good control of both speed and direction but watch for tide set. Spill wind as you approach to keep the speed down and to stop when required.

As soon as the boat stops, have the anchor lowered to the bottom. Don't rely on the crew judging when this has occurred; use the echo-sounder and the chain markings as well. As the anchor is lowered, the boom should be topped up a little using the lift. This will spill wind and cause the boat to fall away as the cable is paid out.

It is sometimes difficult to prevent the head falling off the wind so that the boat begins to reach away. This problem can be reduced by scandalising the main. To do this, simply ease the main halyard about six inches, no more. Next raise the boom on the topping lift with the main sheet freed off. The result will be a series of wrinkles down the luff which should prevent the sail filling.

Careful paying out of the cable should now provide sufficient drag to allow the boat to fall back down wind without falling off much. Minor veers can be corrected at the helm, remembering that the helm will be reversed as the boat moves back.

In stronger winds, sufficient resistance will be created by the scandalised sail to set the anchor. In light winds, the boom can be held forward to back the main and thus help drive the boat backwards.

Sailing from an anchor

The problem here is that your yacht will be lying directly head to wind so that you cannot sail straight up to the anchor.

In light conditions it will often be sufficient to hoist sail and have the anchor crew start pulling in. The momentum created is often sufficient to make the job straightforward. Don't let the sails fill whilst this is being done.

If the above does not work you will have to apply strategy. First decide on which tack you want to be when the anchor breaks out. Start the manoeuvre by sailing off on the opposite tack with sufficient helm to maintain pull on the chain. Once the anchor is abeam you can then tack towards it and the crew can take in.

The approach to the anchor must be slow enough for the crew to recover the scope without riding over it so use as little sail as possible. Good foredeck work is essential for this manoeuvre. Once the anchor is weighed don't just sheet in. Sail free to keep the heel down, maintain good control and give the deck crew time to recover, stow and secure the anchor.

Finally I would suggest that you try these manoeuvres several times where there is plenty of room before you actually have to do it. Once you have mastered the techniques, these skills can give a great deal of satisfaction, both to the skipper and crew, as well as contributing to safety generally.

52 SAILING WITH CHILDREN

Skipper confidence

Sailing with children can be fun but it can also be stressful. The first, most common and least often recognised cause of this stress is skipper confidence, or rather lack of it.

The skipper-parent who is not confident of his or her own ability in handling the boat will worry about the children more. This unease will communicate to the children. It can make them nervous, fractious or downright awkward. The same effect is produced on children when the parent is not the skipper but lacks confidence in the skipper.

The solution has to lie with the skipper rather than with the child or parent in such instances. There are ways round the problem. When new to the activity, the family couple will be anxious to get the children fully involved. It is after all, going to be important that the children learn to share happily in the family activity. It may be that one parent is a reluctant sailor anyway. Lack of faith in the partner's ability will exacerbate the problem. This can cause problems for the parents' relationship quite apart from the children.

The best way to get round these problems is to break the whole family in gently. Start with a skippered charter. That way the ultimate responsibility for the vessel does not rest on the parents and so they can relax more. The whole family then benefits. If they like it, either or both parents can attend courses to improve both confidence and skill.

Skippered charter is not too expensive. It can cost little more than a bareboat. With a reputable company the skipper will be capable and inspire confidence. The contribution that this makes to family harmony can be priceless. After a little experience with a good skipper, the next stop can be a flotilla holiday. This time you will be skipper but help should be close at hand if needed.

RYA courses

Both parents should take RYA courses eventually so that they can learn the best ways to do things. Such courses should be without the children so that the adults can concentrate on learning. It is often a good idea for the two parents to go independently of each other. I will not dwell on the domestic benefits that this can bring but it does improve the learning performance of both adults. Next it is worth considering a family instruction course. Several RYA schools run these and they do go a long way towards getting the family together as a team. That, after all, is what they will hope to be once afloat in their own vessel.

Safety

Safety for children is only a little different from that for adults. Many parents worry more than they need to. Children on boats prove to be quite safety conscious. With very young children the unstable platform can pose problems. Under eight I feel, they should be wearing harness all the time that they are on deck. I also put young children into buoyancy aids even if they can swim. The reason is that a buoyancy aid, as well as keeping them afloat if they fall in, also provides a fair degree of protection from injury caused by falling within the boat. Children are particularly vulnerable in this respect.

Children's buoyancy
The best types of aids are the ones consisting of a series of air filled tubes sewn into a vest. These have a good cushioning effect against falls and also a high degree of permanent buoyancy. Whilst not a substitute for a lifejacket they are of more practical use in easy conditions. Hopefully, in conditions where rescue would be difficult, very young children will not be on deck.

Above all, do not put a small child into an adult aid. It may seem that it will be OK. If it supports an adult it will support a child. The trouble is that the support may well be in the wrong place and it will probably not be possible to adjust it to fit. This can be more dangerous than no aid at all.

Harnesses
Harnesses worn by small children must also be the correct size. It is no good putting a small child into an adult harness and tightening everything up. The support will again be in the wrong places and could cause inversion of the child in the water.

I prefer screw-type clip hooks on child harnesses since it is much more difficult for inquisitive little fingers to get them undone than it is with the snap types more commonly fitted on adult harness.

Setting an example
If you have jackstays running round the boat, which are best for adults also, the harness need not restrict mobility which is so important for children. A child is less likely to resist wearing a harness if the parents wear one also, even when it may not seem strictly necessary.

Netting
I am not a great lover of netting on guard rails since it always seems to get in the way. It does provide a good degree of protection for small children however, and is worth rigging all round if you sail frequently with under fives.

In the galley

Cooking is a hazard for anyone at sea but an adult body is usually above the galley level and legs can be protected by oilskin trousers and boots. Not so the small child. The galley must be a forbidden area at sea. If you do not have a system for locking the stove in a fixed position in harbour, fit one. A gimballed stove against which a child leans, or holds for support, can be a serious hazard.

Seasickness

Under fives are seldom seasick in my experience. Small children, who get used to sailing at an early age, rarely suffer as they grow up. If your child suffers, or is likely to, try dosing with preventative tablets the day before starting sailing. This works for adults too and is much better than waiting for the start of nausea. I prefer Stugeron or similar. Since they have no taste and can be crunched up they are easier to take. With children particularly, always check that the product you use is safe and that you are giving the correct dose.

Sunburn

Children are more prone to suffer from this than adults and are less likely to take precautions. The amount of harmful radiation is much greater at sea than on land because of the reflection off the water. It is thus particularly important to protect them from the start.

Protection

Floppy sunhats will protect the neck and face as well as reducing glare to the eyes. If children need sunglasses give them good quality ones. Cheap kiddie glasses generate problems in themselves. Tee shirts will protect their tops and will also keep off the wind even when wet. Trousers should be worn most of the time until a tan has built up. Small children like to play naked or nearly so but will burn very quickly so protect exposed skin with sunscreen creams.

Use a so-called total barrier to start with and reduce this only as they acquire a tan. Try to prevent children from sitting in the sun for prolonged periods: this is often a problem on a boat with little shade available. In light winds an awning can be rigged.

Injuries

Buoyancy aids can help to prevent serious knocks as mentioned earlier. The particular problems of children are not always apparent to adults, however. Grab handles are almost always out of reach until children get close to teenage size. Consider what other handholds they have available at their level. If there aren't any then provide some. Remember that a child will fall further than you will in a pitching boat even though it may not fall so hard.

Dinghies

It can not be too often said that the most dangerous trip at sea is one made in a dinghy. This is particularly so for a child. Children move quickly and are often unaware of the balance of a dinghy.

Risks can be reduced in several ways. Buoyancy should be routine at all times, for the adults also. Show the child what the effect of body movement is going to be so that awareness is present. Do not let children sit on the bow or transom of an inflatable or rigid dinghy when under power. This is great fun but is highly dangerous if the child should fall in. No one can react quickly enough to prevent the propeller causing appalling injuries.

Swimming and rowing

I like to teach children to swim early. Anyone who falls in and can swim, however little, is less likely to panic; it is panic that costs lives. They must also learn to row as soon as possible. The best way to do this takes courage on your part but is actually pretty safe with the right precautions. Shown the basic rudiments and then left to get on with it they will soon learn. First, however, start them safely. A good buoyancy aid is part of the drill; go with them to start with and wear yours too. Once they are happy, attach the dinghy securely to the boat with a strong floating line. Tie the paddles and a bailer to the dinghy and harness the child to the dinghy with a long enough line to prevent his becoming trapped in the event of a capsize. With this arrangement the child can row in a wide circle round the yacht. Neither child, nor dinghy, can lose anything vital and you can pull both back to recover them if anything should come amiss or if the child gets tired.

Inflatables are best for this exercise even though they are more difficult to row. They are less easy for a child to capsize and if this happens, the child is not so likely to be injured by the capsized boat. It goes without saying that you must watch the operation at all times.

Dinghy capsize

If the dinghy capsizes and the child does not appear, do not panic. The child will be under the boat held up by the buoyancy aid in a large pocket of air. He will not be able to get out of this space. You can pull in the line, but not too fast or you may force the child under water. You can then recover the situation with no harm done. Warn the child that this may happen beforehand and explain what to do so that he does not panic either.

Going it alone

Eventually the time will come when the child will want to row without the tether. This is the moment of truth for you. You will have to agree sooner or later. You are now faced with either letting him or her get on with it, or going yourself each time. This can become very tedious and is not good for the child's morale.

Try to choose the occasion yourself rather than have it foisted on you. Watch for improving skill. The other thing to watch for is suitable places with no significant tide stream or other dinghies about, particularly those with outboards. Onshore winds, fairly calm conditions and the probable destination, if drift is the only force left, are the other things to think about.

If asked without fuss, to take the dinghy and go ashore for milk, bread, a paper or whatever, any child will be keen to prove capable and responsible and will be thrilled by your show of confidence. If not totally confident himself this will prompt caution. The success of this venture will promote safe handling for the future.

Two or more children together increase the risks in a sort of square law progression, particularly if one or more is keen to impress the others. The worst combination is young teenagers of mixed sex. Beware of the new friend of your child who airily tells you he or she has been doing it for years. Check with the parents first.

Boredom

One of the greatest problems when sailing with young children is boredom. The mere act of sailing soon palls even if they take an active part. By the age of five a child can learn to manage the tiller and may steer quite well. What he or she will not do is keep it up for long. At that age, five or ten minutes is enough and the child will simply stop, probably without saying anything to you, as his attention wanders. Even at ten years old the span will not necessarily be much greater.

If you are ready to take over, this presents no problem. You will have to accept that one adult will probably have to entertain and occupy the solo child for most of the time. If you have two or more it helps but you will still need to separate them from time to time just as you have to at home. It is best to assume the need and to include it in your planning. Make sure you have plenty of familiar toys, games etc. Also books and pencils for the five and up range.

Play area

One useful idea for the very young is to turn a quarter berth into a safe play area by closing it off with either slip-in boards or with netting. I suggest a quarter berth rather than the forepeak since the children will still be in contact with you if kept aft. The child who is prone to seasickness may have to be settled in the cockpit. Keep him well covered, as children lose body heat more rapidly.

Helping to sail

Taking an active part in the sailing: at the helm, tacking, taking hand bearings, log readings and entries are great fun for some children but not for all. Don't worry yourself or them if they don't get it right at first, after all, did you? Make sure you know where you are so that it does not matter. If you have chosen your weather, route and journey length with the child in mind, precise accuracy should not matter too much at this stage.

Length of trip

Frequent stops, which means short passages, are important. Four hours is the maximum period for most children at first. Put the anchor down and get them to a beach for a swim or to make sandcastles. Start the rowing lessons or drop the sails and put out a line for mackerel. These are the fun bits for children, making the sailing part worth it.

Fishing

Fishing is always fun. They may not want to eat the catch but they will love the excitement. Mackerel will go for anything bright that moves in the water provided it does not move too fast. Two knots is about the best speed. Use enough weight (about 300–400 grams) to get the hooks at least to half the water depth. Choose an area from your chart with a broken bottom, rocks or wrecks are best. You should catch something most times. Have a bucket ready. Scales can make an awful mess. If you don't intend to eat the catch, use wet hands to take the fish off the hook carefully and return it to the sea at once.

Food

Food is best kept simple with little and often being the rule. Avoid rich foods and keep the intake of sweets and sticky cakes as low as you dare.

In warm conditions, a good liquid intake is important. Squash is more easy to take than milk when feeling a bit squeamish. Plain lemonade or water is best for those actually being seasick. This goes for adults too. It is essential that the liquid intake in children is kept up, even if they resist. Children can last quite well without food, making up for it when they feel like it, however seasickness is more common with an empty stomach.

Heads

Use of the heads poses a practical problem for small children at sea. Even ten-year-olds may need help with the mechanics. I have known children (and a few adults!) so afraid of sinking the boat that they avoid the heads altogether. A chamber pot or simple bucket is the easy solution. 'Bucket-and-chuck-it' was, and still is, the only solution on many yachts.

Privacy will probably not matter to younger children with the family crew but must be considered from quite an early age when non-family are aboard. Reluctance to ask for help can lead to needless discomfort, constipation, or even bladder problems so don't take it for granted that youngsters will go to the heads by themselves or ask you for help when they need to go.

Sleep

Children will often sleep more on a boat than ashore. A double berthed forepeak with a filler piece or the modified quarter berth mentioned earlier are probably best. Very small children will need lots of cushions or pillows in the play area for both comfort and safety. Over fives will certainly want to be able to get in and out of their sleeping area at will so this must be borne in mind.

Going ashore

Marinas provide facilities that are particularly useful for young sailors. Proper washing and showering facilities, launderettes and driers whilst useful to all of us, border on the essential with kids. This is quite apart from being able to avoid using the dinghy. Marinas do have pitfalls however.

Pontoons are dangerous places for children, with ropes and cleats to trip over, gaps through which they can fall into usually foul water, a very unsteady motion, anchors projecting over them often at head height and so on. I feel that small children should not be allowed on to pontoons unattended and even larger ones should wear their buoyancy aids. Running and or playing chase games must be forbidden at all times. Let them take the rubbish, bring the hose and fill the water tank. Given some small responsibility a child will be happier and will behave more sensibly.

In conclusion

The chapters that make up this book will, I hope, have given you some food for thought and will have taught you some new ideas that you can put into practice afloat. It is a truism that we don't stop learning until we are dead and this is never more so than in sailing.

We all have our own reasons for taking to the water but the great majority of us do it because we enjoy it, though the particular enjoyment may differ. For some it is an escape, for others a challenge, others still derive their pleasure from using the forces of nature in a more benign manner than our modern, energy-driven society usually allows. The specific motivation does not really matter so long as we get pleasure and satisfaction from the sport.

For me at least, doing things properly, sailing efficiently and getting the best performance I can from the boat under me is a large part of both the pleasure and the satisfaction.

In these pages I have put together some old and well tried systems and ideas, some new thinking on how and why things work the way they do, some ways of making your sailing safer and less stressful, some answers to problems that my students have raised over many years. I hope that this distillation of my experiences has made you think and has added to your knowledge.

Above all however, I hope that it has helped and will continue to help you to become more proficient and to enjoy your sailing more in the future. That after all is what sailing is all about.

Appendix

CREW DUTIES

It is often convenient to appoint an individual crew member to take responsibility for specific duties. A list of duties that need to be covered and their possible distribution follows.

Notes

1   The skipper always has overall responsibility for the running of the vessel.
2   Posts can normally be rotated to avoid one person having all the nasty jobs.
3   Titles are strictly honorary on a cruising boat. The idea of nominated individuals is to ensure each job gets done and not to impose authority.

Mate

Safety

Liferaft security, operation and condition
Flares location, operation and validity
Lifebelt condition including strobe lights
Harnesses condition and quantity
Lifejacket condition and quantity
Danbuoy condition and function
Heaving line location and condition
Firefighting apparatus location
   and operation
Man overboard procedure (MOB)
Operation of MOB recovery equipment
Abandon ship procedure
Damage control equipment and use
Security of hatches and washboards
Serviceability and use of bilge pumps
Damage checks above and below
   water line
Use of jackstays and strong points

Mooring and running

Stowage and condition of anchors
   (main and kedge)
Serviceability of anchor cables
Preparing the anchor for lowering
Serviceability of stemhead fittings
Condition and location of mooring
   warps in use
Positioning of fenders and mats
Security of fairleads and cleats
Anchor shape and motor-sailing
   cone hoisting
Correct use of lights
Watch keeping and lookouts

Sailing master (or bosun)

Sails and sailing
Location, condition and stowage of all sails
Folding and bagging of headsails
Stowing and covering the mainsail
Condition of all running rigging
Location, condition and stowage of sheets and lines
Condition of all running blocks and/or tracks
Serviceability of turnblocks, fairleads and jammers
Servicing of winches
Location and stowage of sail ties
Security and serviceability of all loose spars
Securing halyards and rigging when moored
Preparing spinnaker gear for hoisting
Packing spinnakers
Clearing spinnaker gear after use
National ensign, flags and courtesy ensigns

Engineer

Engines and electrics
Checking oil levels
Checking cooling water including filters
Checking sea cocks
Fuel state, including spare
Starting and stopping routines
Battery state
Outboard serviceability and stowage
Outboard fuel state and stowage
Serviceability of lights, pumps etc
Alternator function checks
Serviceability of earth bonds
Condition of fuses and switches
Torches including spare batteries
Spares, tools and repair kits
Serviceability of deck fittings
Dinghy including pumps and repairs
Emergency lighting

Purser

Operational
Securing for sea:
> hatches, washboards; loose equipment; lockers and contents; bunks and bedding; closing of sea cocks

Bilge pumps (routine pumping)
Gas detector operation
Galley area and general cleaning

Resources
Fresh water system (quantity and replenishment)
Gas (stowage, quantity and control, spare)
Food:
> ration state provisioning, location and stowage; menu for each day; storage and use of perishables; replenishment; location of emergency water/food; cooking and eating utensils

Wet weather gear (sufficient for each individual)
Bedding (sufficient for each individual plus spare)
Drying of wet gear

Navigator

Instrumentation
Pre-sailing checks on:
Log(s) including impellers
Echo-sounder
Wind speed/strength/direction indicators
VHF/MFSSB/Long Wave Rx
Decca/Loran/Satnav/RDF
Radar
Compasses (hand and fixed) including lights
Clock-barometer

Navigation
Charts (condition, area coverage and corrections)
Pilot books – as for charts
Navigators note book
Deck log
Weather maps and forecasts
Drawing instruments:- Protractors, dividers, etc, soft pencils and rubbers

BIBLIOGRAPHY

Reading The Weather, Alan Watts; Adlard Coles Nautical, 1987
Repairs at Sea, Nigel Calder; Adlard Coles Nautical, 1988
The Best of Sail Trim, edited by Charles Mason; Adlard Coles Nautical, 1975
The Shorebased Sailor, John Myatt; Heinemann Kingswood, 1988
Understanding Rigs & Rigging, Richard Henderson; Adlard Coles Nautical, 1986
Weather at Sea, David Houghton; Fernhurst books, 1991

INDEX